Boom, Bust & Echo

BOOM
BUST
&
ECHO

**Profiting from the Demographic
Shift in the 21st Century**

David K. Foot
with Daniel Stoffman
Drawings by Brian Gable

This edition published in 2000 by Stoddart Publishing Co. Limited
895 Don Mills Road, 400-2 Park Centre, Toronto, Canada M3C 1W3
180 Varick Street, 9th Floor, New York, New York 10014

Previously published as Boom, Bust & Echo 2000

Distributed in Canada by
General Distribution Services Ltd.
325 Humber College Boulevard, Toronto, Canada M9W 7C3
Tel. (416) 213-1919   Fax (416) 213-1917
Email cservice@genpub.com

Distributed in the United States by
General Distribution Services Inc.
PMB 128, 4500 Witmer Industrial Estates, Niagara Falls, New York 14305-1386
Toll-free Tel. 1-800-805-1083   Toll-free Fax 1-800-481-6207
Email gdsinc@genpub.com

04 03 02 01   2 3 4 5

First published in hardcover in 1996 by Macfarlane Walter & Ross
Updated, expanded edition published in paperback under the title
Boom, Bust & Echo 2000 in 1999 by MW&R, a subsidiary of
Stoddart Publishing Co. Limited, and in 2000 by Stoddart Publishing

Canadian Cataloguing in Publication Data available
from the National Library of Canada

U.S. Cataloguing in Publication Data available
from the Library of Congress

THE CANADA COUNCIL   LE CONSEIL DES ARTS
FOR THE ARTS   DU CANADA
SINCE 1957   DEPUIS 1957

*We acknowledge for their financial support of our
publishing program the Canada Council, the Ontario Arts Council, and the Government of Canada through the
Book Publishing Industry Development Program (BPIDP).*

Printed and bound in Canada

Contents

A new demographic shift has profound
implications for Canadian economic and
social life in the new millennium.

Demography, the study of human populations,
is the most powerful tool for understanding
the past and forecasting the future.

Why your year of birth is one of the
most important things about you.

Why the real estate boom happened,
why it ended, and what the future holds
for homeowners and investors.

For investors with a long-term perspective,
demographic analysis reveals which areas of the
economy will enjoy the most growth and which
investments will be most likely to succeed.

Contents

Contents

Acknowledgments

*B*oom, *Bust & Echo* got its start in 1990 when Margaret Wente, then editor of *Report on Business Magazine*, assigned Daniel Stoffman to write an article on the work of David Foot. The article was so popular, and so frequently reprinted, that it was obvious a need existed for a fuller explanation of the impact of demographics on Canadian life. The enthusiastic response of Canadian readers to *Boom, Bust & Echo* after it was published in 1996 convinced us to write this revised and enlarged paperback edition.

We are indebted to Richard Loreto and Tom McCormack, partners with David Foot in the Madison Avenue Demographics Group, for their support, both intellectual and practical; to Catherine Dowling for her efficient research assistance; and to Wendy Thomas for her vigilant editing of the revised manuscript. A new feature in this edition is the collaboration of Brian Gable, editorial page cartoonist of the *Globe and Mail*, who found many witty and ingenious ways of depicting demographic phenomena in visual form. We also are grateful to David Cork for sharing his knowledge and insight; to our publishers Jan Walter and Gary Ross for their enthusiasm and constructive ideas; and to Judy Stoffman for her encouragement and invaluable advice.

The Rise of the Echo

Just before Christmas 1997, *Titanic*, a movie based on the sinking of the largest ocean liner in the world, arrived in the world's theatres. Would it be a hit? Rule Number One in Hollywood, as screenwriter William Goldman once wrote, is that "nobody knows anything." That is, nobody knows before a movie opens whether it will be a hit or a flop. *Primary Colors*, a film released three months after *Titanic*, was a good example of the truth of this dictum. Everyone expected it to be a big success because not only was it a good movie with a popular cast, it also had perfect timing. The movie, about a Clintonesque presidential candidate whose sexual adventures get him into trouble, arrived in theatres just as allegations about President Bill Clinton's personal life were dominating the U.S. media. Yet despite garnering oceans of publicity and rave reviews, *Primary Colors* failed to attract much of an audience and soon slipped from view, much as the *Titanic* had vanished after colliding with an iceberg off the Grand Banks in 1912.

Before its release, the main thing *Titanic* seemed to have going for it was the track record of Canadian director James Cameron, who had shown his flair for cinematic spectacle in the *Terminator* movies. On the other hand, skeptics warned, the story had been dramatized many times before, both in movies and on television. And, for the predominantly youthful movie audience, the sinking of the *Titanic* was a legend from a distant past that had little current relevance. Moreover, disaster movies were a dime a dozen.

As it turned out, however, *Titanic* had better timing than

Primary Colors. Cameron's mastery of special effects was only part of the reason for the movie's great success. Even more important was his casting of two young actors, Leonardo DiCaprio and Kate Winslet, as the romantic leads. An important demographic shift was underway in North America at the end of the 1990s. Millions of members of the echo – the offspring of the boomers – were becoming teenagers. And some female members of this important population cohort were reportedly lining up to see *Titanic* 30 times or more, so smitten were they with DiCaprio's charms. Had *Titanic* been made a decade earlier, it would not have succeeded on the same scale as it did in 1997 and 1998 for the simple reason that a few years earlier there weren't as many teenage girls to line up for tickets. *Primary Colors* also had a popular star in John Travolta but his boomer fans, while numerous, are older. They don't have time to make 30 trips to see the same movie, and, even if they did, they are too grown up to do anything so silly. So while *Primary Colors* had good political timing, *Titanic* had good demographic timing. And demographics are more powerful than politics when it comes to filling theatre seats.

Eager to exploit a favourable demographic shift, the U.S. movie industry had 60 high school-related films in production as of May 1998. These movies were aimed at a domestic audience of 76 million American echo kids, the offspring of 79 million American boomers. Meanwhile, a Toronto newspaper also scented demographic change in the air. "13-year-old girls rule the world," it declared in huge type in a headline over a story about the popularity of the Spice Girls and other stars with strong youth appeal. As readers of the first edition of *Boom, Bust & Echo* know, it was perfectly predictable a decade ago that teen culture would be more prominent towards the end of the 1990s than it was in the early years of the decade. The reason is not that Leonardo DiCaprio or the Spice Girls are more talented than comparable artists of the 1980s or early 1990s. All that's changed is that a larger cohort, the echo, has replaced a smaller one, the baby bust, as the latest group to be in their teen years. And teenagers attend concerts and movies more often than older people and are the biggest buyers of recorded music.

2

The coming of age of the echo gives Canada a more complex demographic environment than the one described in the first edition of this book. The boom is still the dominant group because it is the largest – almost 10 million out of 30 million Canadians. But the boomers' offspring, the echo kids, total 6.5 million and are the second most important cohort group. As the millennium approaches, most of the echo is in its teen years with the eldest entering young adulthood. Because they are older, they have more money and more autonomy than they did in the mid-1990s. The predictable result is that, at the approach of the millennium, the echo is becoming a more important social and economic force than it was until just recently.

The complexity of this new demographic environment shows itself in many ways. In the spring of 1998, for example, *Rolling Stone* magazine produced a cover story on Vancouver's relatively tolerant attitude towards pot smoking. Yet this was an old story – the only new element was the recent growth in numbers of the pot-smoking segment of the population. That same segment was increasingly taking to the ski slopes – not on skis but on snowboards, which were overtaking skis in popularity because of their appeal to young people who already knew how to balance on skateboards.

Yet in the midst of this youthful exuberance, signs of aging were everywhere. Canadian book publishers, for example, were enlarging typefaces to accommodate the failing eyesight of aging boomers who make up the largest group of readers. When Margaret Atwood's first novel, *The Edible Woman*, was published in 1969, it was set in nine-point type. But back then Canada was a country dominated by young people and optometry was not yet a growth industry. By 1996, when Atwood published *Alias Grace*, the eldest boomers were on the verge of 50 and some of them were squinting at nine-point type. So *Alias Grace* came out in 12-point. The aging of boomer eyes also explains the 25% jump in 1997 of map publisher Perly's sales of its large-print street maps for Montreal and Toronto and the larger, more readable faces Timex has put on its newest watches.

At the millennium, Canada is a country with expanding populations of both 50-year-olds and 20-year-olds. Therefore, it's a country where both cheap beer and $20 bottles of wine can enjoy rising sales and where impecunious kids cram into basement suites while affluent 50-somethings lavish $100,000 renos on already luxurious empty nests.

Because it had the world's biggest baby boom followed by a sharp drop in births that resulted in a baby bust, Canada has an unusual population age structure. The differences in population among various age groups are more pronounced than in other countries, although the United States has a similar population profile. Canadians are increasingly aware of the importance of taking demographic phenomena into account when discussing such community issues as whether to build a new hockey arena or close a hospital.

In fact, the general population is often more sophisticated about demographics than elements of the media and others who should be knowledgeable. For example, newspaper writers and Statistics Canada researchers regularly confuse Generation X, the youngest boomers born in the first half of the 1960s, with the baby bust, the people born from the end of the 1960s through to 1980. When those born during the early 1960s were in their 20s, the term "Generation X" was invented to describe a group that was uniquely disadvantaged as a result of being the youngest members of a huge cohort. If Gen-Xers were Gen-Xers when they were in their 20s, they are still Gen-Xers now that they are in their 30s. The term is meaningless if it is applied to just anyone who happens to be twenty-something. The many Gen-X readers of *Boom, Bust & Echo* know this and write letters of protest when newspapers misuse the term.

Not only are Gen-Xers misidentified, the boom as a whole is often subject to excessive criticism and derision. Older Canadians sometimes view boomers as self-indulgent and self-absorbed while post-boomers are heard to complain that the boomers are greedy and power-hungry. Many younger Canadians seem to think all boomers are hypocrites because they abandoned youthful radicalism and idealism in quest of wealth and power.

A *Toronto Star* article in 1998 by a 23-year-old journalist expressed this view. The writer has it in for the boomers because she thinks they don't respect younger people. She would like to "force these ex-revolutionaries to sit in their expensive corner offices and look at what they used to be. We will show them pictures of the misguided youth with long hair, beads and baggy pants they once were. . . ."

This is colourful but wrong. As anyone who attended a Canadian university during the 1960s can attest, most students were oblivious to the protest movements of those times. Only a small minority of young boomers were involved in radical politics or in the hippie movement. Boomer big shots occupying "expensive corner offices" in the late 1990s haven't abandoned their youthful radicalism – most of them had none to abandon.

Why does the false impression linger that a majority of young people in the 1960s were involved in radical political and social movements? Because of demographics, of course. The massive size of the generation is the crucial element. The hippies were always a small percentage of the boomer population but a small percentage of a huge number is still a lot. And when thousands of bizarrely attired people from every corner of the country congregated on a few short blocks of West Fourth Avenue in Vancouver or Yorkville Avenue in Toronto, it made an impressive and, to some, frightening spectacle. Similarly, student militants on campus sometimes could summon large crowds for rallies and sit-ins but the "revolutionaries" of the newspaper writer's imagination were a minuscule percentage of the total enrolment.

The key fact about the boomers at the millennium, as it was in the 1960s, is their sheer numbers. Other Canadians will have to live with the prominence of the big generation until large numbers of its members start dying, a process that won't get underway for about another 25 years. In the meantime, the passage of the boomers into their 50s is having profound effects on the social and economic life of Canada. These effects, described in the first edition of *Boom, Bust & Echo*, are intensifying as the millennium approaches and increasing numbers of Canadians turn 50.

The challenges presented by the demographic shift are not insurmountable. We know this because European countries, such as Germany, France, Austria, and Belgium, that have much older populations than Canada are flourishing. Nevertheless, successful adaptation to the demographic shift requires a spirit of innovation. Changes are needed, for example, in the way health care is delivered, in the way workplaces are organized, and in our approach to retirement. And because institutions in both private and public sectors often seem to prefer inertia to change, it will take pressure from the grassroots to bring the necessary reforms about.

Readers of the first edition of *Boom, Bust & Echo* will be interested to know that several chapters in this new paperback edition have been extensively revised and augmented with new material. They are Chapter 2 (real estate), Chapter 3 (investment), Chapter 5 (retailing), Chapter 7 (cities), Chapter 9 (health care), and Chapter 11, which deals with the impact of demographics on important areas of public policy such as the Constitution, immigration, and pensions. The other chapters have been revised and updated wherever necessary.

Two-Thirds of Everything

I n 1985, tennis was booming in Canada. Tennis clubs had waiting lists, public courts were crowded even on weekdays, and sporting goods dealers had trouble keeping up with demand for the latest graphite racquets. The sport was gaining new adherents daily.

But as the 1990s progressed, something unexpected happened: the waiting lists evaporated at the tennis clubs. The managements of these clubs found themselves doing what would have been unthinkable a few years earlier – advertising for new members. By the mid-1990s, participation in tennis was down substantially. Those who oversee and promote the sport were bewildered.

They shouldn't have been surprised. What happened to tennis was not only predictable, it was inevitable. Because of the combination of a low fertility rate and increasing life expectancy, the Canadian population is aging, which means simply that the average age of Canadians is increasing. And older people don't play tennis as much as younger people.

The tennis boom started in the early 1970s when most of the boomers, who make up almost a third of the total Canadian population, were in their teens and 20s. Those are prime tennis-playing years. In 1998, the boomers were 32 to 51. That's a stage of life when tennis racquets are more likely to be left in basements and closets than taken to the courts. Of course, many middle-aged and older people still play tennis just as they always have. A former governor general of Canada, Roland Michener, for example, was still playing in his 90s. Nevertheless, the reality is that the average 90-year-old and the average 40-year-old are both less likely to pick up a tennis racquet than the average 20-year-old. The tennis boom was predictable in 1970 to anyone who understood demographics. And the decline in participation was just as predictable in 1970 as it was obvious by 1995. Equally predictable is that tennis participation will pick up over the next decade as the large "echo generation" – the offspring of the boomers – moves into its tennis-playing years.

Demography, the study of human populations, is the most powerful – and most underutilized – tool we have to understand the past and to foretell the future. Demographics affect every one of us as individuals, far more than most of us have ever imagined. They also play a pivotal role in the economic and social life of our country. Yet because demographic facts seem so obvious once they are pointed out, many people are inclined to resist them. Life, they say, can't possibly be that simple. By refusing to accept the obvious, they make life more complicated and unpredictable than it has to be.

Demographics explain about two-thirds of everything. They tell us a great deal about which products will be in demand in five years, and they accurately predict school enrolments many years in advance. They allow us to forecast which drugs will be in fashion ten years down the road, as well as what sorts of crimes will be on the increase. They help us to know when houses will go up in value, and when they will go down.

If more of our decision-makers understood demographics, Canada would be a better place to live because it would run more smoothly and more efficiently. Had Ontario Hydro's forecasters, for example, understood demographics, they would have been less likely to squander $8 billion in 1977 on the unnecessary Darlington nuclear power station. Similarly, private developers would have had fewer offices and condominium units standing empty during much of the 1990s. School boards, if they used demographics, would not open new elementary schools just when they should be expanding high schools instead. Yet school boards across Canada often do things like that, just as hospital managements close maternity wards and then have to reverse themselves when births pick up a couple of years later.

Demographics are about everyone, and that's why this book is for everyone. Demographics tell you, as an individual, a great deal about who you are, where you've been, and where you're going. If, for example, you were lucky enough to be born in 1937 and you've been successful, it wouldn't hurt to learn a little humility. You haven't had much competition, because few people were born in Canada in 1937. That demographic good fortune probably had as much to do with your success as you did.

On the other hand, perhaps you had the misfortune to enter the world in 1961, one of the worst years in this century to be born. You're one of a huge crowd of late boomers, also known as Generation X. The mass of older boomers who preceded you occupied most of the best jobs and pushed the price of real estate way up, possibly out of your reach until recently. Chances are that life has been a struggle for you. And your parents, the lucky people who were born in 1937 or thereabouts, probably don't understand how tough that struggle has been. For your own peace of mind, you need to understand that some of the setbacks you have experienced may relate more to demographics than to any personal failings. The more knowledge you have about those demographic realities, the better prepared you are to cope with them – and perhaps find a way to turn them to your own advantage.

Anyone involved in planning for the future needs to understand demographics. That's true whether you're planning your own personal future or that of a school system, a hospital, a chain of restaurants, or a multinational corporation. It is simply not possible to do any competent planning without a knowledge of demographics – not only demographics in general, but Canadian demographics in particular, because the Canadian population structure is unique.

Demographics are critically important for business. They probably won't alter a company's financial results from one financial quarter to the next. But the management of a business that fails to pay attention to demographics for five years may wake up to find itself in a different business than it thought it was in – or not in business at all.

In 1993, a major cosmetics company noticed some market

developments that senior management found puzzling. Demand for certain products, such as bright lipsticks, was falling dramatically while demand for others, especially skin care products, was rising. Even men were starting to buy skin creams. What, they wanted to know, was going on? Was this just a passing fad, or were new long-term trends emerging that they needed to know about? The company had already done plenty of research. It had a sophisticated grasp of certain demographic facts, such as how the ethnicity, geographic location, and income levels of its customers related to product preferences. But it had missed the aging trend.

Like its influence on tennis, the impact of aging on behaviour at the cosmetics counter is obvious – once it's been pointed out. What this company needed to understand was that the number of potential customers in their 30s and 40s was rising, while the number in their teens and 20s was falling and would not start increasing again until the late 1990s. In other words, this was not a temporary phenomenon but rather a long-term trend that would influence the company's sales figures for many years to come. It had to accept the reality that, try as it might through advertising or in-store promotion, it could not alter the fact that a 38-year-old is less likely to wear certain kinds of lipstick than an 18-year-old. The 38-year-old, on the other hand, is much more likely than the 18-year-old to buy an expensive skin cream.

Moreover, a huge number of males are now moving into middle age. Because this market is so large, it is worthwhile for cosmetics companies to launch new products designed for men. Not only are there more middle-aged men than before, but boomer males seem more willing than their predecessors to spend money on their appearance. This new development in the cosmetics marketplace is one of the effects of demographics: because the baby boom was so large, a cult of youth dominated North America when the boomers were young. The appeal of this youth culture was so strong that middle-aged boomers like to believe they are more youthful than previous generations were at the same age.

These demographically driven market shifts have important implications that require careful consideration for any company in the intensely competitive cosmetics industry. What happens to marketing strategy? Do you shift some dollars to men's magazines and to media that appeal to older women, and take dollars away from vehicles aimed at young women and teenagers? What about your sales force? Who has more credibility behind the counter: a gorgeous 22-year-old who has never had to worry about her perfect skin, or a gorgeous 52-year-old who still looks great because, she says, she knows how to apply the right products?

Fortunately for this company, it had a product mix that could be adjusted to fit these changes in the marketplace with comparative ease. In fact, population aging is a boon for the cosmetics business in general because, as people get older, they become susceptible to the lure of products that promise to perpetuate a youthful appearance and they are more likely to be able to afford them.

Other industries are not so fortunate. During the 1970s and 1980s, the beer industry aimed its advertising at sports-minded young men, who are consumers of large volumes of relatively inexpensive brands of beer. It stuck to this strategy even as its customers grew older, less fascinated with sports, and more inclined to sip a high-quality specialty beer than to guzzle a run-of-the-mill mass-market brand. Fortunately for consumers, the inertia of the large companies allowed the microbreweries to establish a foothold in a shrinking market by producing different products. The beer market was going to flatten regardless of what marketing strategy the brewers adopted, but the transition could have been much less painful had the big companies anticipated demographic change rather than reacting to it long after it had already occurred by creating specialty beers of their own.

That's what this book is all about: giving you, the reader, the power to anticipate demographic change. But it's important to understand that these are long-term trends. The farther ahead in the future you are looking, the more relevant demographics will be to you. If, for example, you are a businessperson whose chief preoccupation is this year's bottom line, the book won't be of much use to you. But if you are a strategic thinker interested in the well-being of your organization, including its bottom line, three years and more into the future, this book is for you.

If demographics explain about two-thirds of everything, what are some things they can't explain? Electoral politics is one. At first glance, this might seem surprising, because conventional wisdom is that people get more conservative as they get older. If that were true, population aging would be a convenient explanation for the success of right-of-centre political parties in recent years. The problem with that thesis is that political scientists can find no direct relationship between age and Canadian voting patterns. Moreover, the Canadian electorate in recent years has become increasingly volatile, with the result that it is harder than ever for governments of any political stripe to get re-elected. Yet demographic trends are predictable precisely because they are not volatile. That's why they won't help anyone place a winning bet on the next election.

However, while demographics won't predict electoral out-comes, they can be most useful in predicting electoral issues. For example, daycare was a big issue in federal elections during the 1980s when the large boom generation was busy producing children. By the 1990s, most of those children were past the need for daycare, with the predictable result that much less was heard about this issue in the 1993 and 1997 federal elections.

Demographic projections aren't always as straightforward as some of the examples cited so far. Sometimes several trends come into play at once, making forecasts difficult. For example, the fertility rate – the average number of children per woman – declined during the 1960s and 1970s. That might have prompted a prediction that families would be moving into smaller houses during the 1980s and 1990s because they would have fewer people to accommodate. That hasn't happened, because countervailing trends were operating at the same time. One was a gradual rise in family incomes, resulting in part from the entry of more women into the workforce. More people can now afford the individual privacy that a larger house offers. Moreover, an important demographic trend – the huge number of boomers compet-ing for the small number of senior management jobs – has meant that many people are finding themselves working harder than ever and having to take work home. Many others have left large organizations and established their own businesses operated out of home offices. As a result, yesterday's five-bedroom house has become today's three-bedroom, two-office house.

Demography makes use of a wide range of data, including the size of a given population, its birth and death rates, the number of immigrants it attracts and the number of emigrants it loses, the geographical dispersal of its members, and its ethnic composition. But when it comes to predicting behaviour, the most useful demographic variable is the age composition of the population. Who is more likely to join a gang that "swarms" people and steals their basketball jackets, a senior citizen or a teenager? Who is more likely to attend a chamber music concert, an 11-year-old or a 51-year-old? Because age is so powerful a predictor of human behaviour, the answers to these questions are obvious. If you know how many people of each age are around today, you can make a reliable forecast about how those same people will behave tomorrow.

This book does exactly that. What kinds of foods will people buy and what kinds of cars will they drive? Where will they choose to live? Which investments will they favour? These and many other things can be confidently predicted simply on the basis of readily available data on the age of Canadians.

The two keys to these forecasts are the number of people in each age group and the probability that each person will participate in a given behaviour. Express the number of people doing a certain thing as a percentage of the number of people in the population and you get the activity participation rate for the society as a whole. Probability and participation rate are the same thing, except that probability applies to an individual while participation rate applies to a whole society. Multiply the participation rate by the population, and you get the actual number of people who are bowling or buying houses or having heart attacks or whatever else you may want to measure. (See Appendices I and II for more on demographic forecasting.)

Participation rates are not 100% predictable because they are affected by such transient economic factors as recessions, income levels, and unemployment rates. They are also affected by such social factors as marital status and ethnicity. But the number of people who will participate in a given activity is two-thirds predictable because of the age factor. Age is the best forecasting tool because it is guaranteed to change. A person's ethnicity will remain the same ten years hence. Her employment status may or may not remain the same. The one thing that is certain is that she will be ten years older.

How stable are these participation rates? In other words, how likely is it that a 45-year-old in 2005 will behave the same as a 45-year-old in 1995? Very likely. Occasionally, behaviours do change: the decline in smoking when the public finally understood its lethal impact on health is a prime example. But in most cases, participation rates of the various age groups in different activities are quite stable over time. That is what allows us to use demographics to predict future trends in retailing, recreation, and a host of other human activities.

In fact, age is a proxy for many of the socioeconomic variables that differentiate human beings. A 30-year-old, for example, is more likely to be married than a 20-year-old. A 40-year-old probably has a higher income than a 30-year-old. For this reason, focussing on age captures many other factors and simplifies the analytical process.

Analyzing human behaviour according to age has the great advantage of allowing us to know what is actually going on instead of living in a fog of misconception. Most journalists look at the total participation in an activity – crime, for example – and then exclaim in print, "It's going up!" or "It's going down!" But these changes, if based on the population as a whole, may be misleading, reflecting only the changing age composition of society. In an aging society, the number of crimes goes down because older people don't commit as many crimes as younger ones. A drop in the overall crime rate, therefore, may have no connection to any change in behaviour, the economy, social attitudes, or law enforcement techniques. It may be unrelated to anything at all except a decline in the number of people in the crime-prone youth age groups. On the other hand, the appearance of a higher crime rate among a particular age group would signify genuine change.

The ability to forecast undesirable outcomes, such as a rise in certain kinds of crime or increased use of hard drugs, highlights another important use of demographics – making predictions in the hope that they will be wrong. If we know, through demographic analysis, that certain things are likely to occur, then we can take steps to prevent or at least mitigate those outcomes. When that happens, a demographer can only be delighted to have his forecast proven wrong.

Canada's population pyramid (see Figure 1) contains a massive bulge, representing the huge generation of baby-boomers born in the 20 years from 1947 to 1966. By comparison, the Depression and World War II generations that preceded the baby boom are small, as is the baby bust that followed it. But the most recently arrived group, the offspring of the boomers or the baby-boom echo, is comparatively large. That is why the words "boom, bust, and echo" are in the title of this book. The different behaviours of these different demographic groups, and the interplay among them, are what make Canadian demographics so useful as an analytical and forecasting tool.

Because of these wide variations in the size of the different age groups in Canadian society, changes in social and economic behaviour resulting from the aging process are more evident in Canada than in European countries that have not had such sharp fluctuations in birth rates. On the other hand, much of the thinking in this book can be applied to the United States, which has also experienced a boom, a bust, and an echo.

In popular discussion of demographic issues, much confusion results from the frequent misunderstanding of two key demographic terms: fertility rate and birth rate. The fertility rate is the average number of children born to women over their lifetimes. The birth rate is the total number of births divided by the size of the population. It's important to grasp this distinction. For example, many people know that Canada's fertility rate, which for most of the last decade has been 1.7 babies per woman, is below the 2.1 babies per woman needed to replace the population. (You need two children to replace yourself and your partner. The extra tenth of a baby is needed to compensate for women who don't have any children and for children who don't live

FIGURE 1: CANADA'S POPULATION PYRAMIDS, 1998

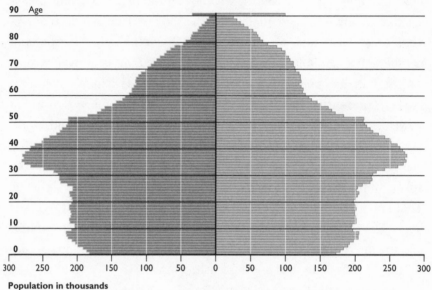

CANADA
MALE   FEMALE

Population in thousands

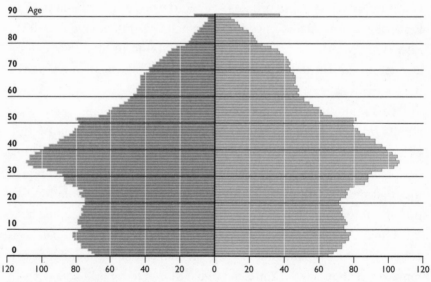

ONTARIO
MALE   FEMALE

Population in thousands

Source: Based on unpublished estimates from Statistics Canada.

into adulthood.) Knowing that the fertility rate is less than replacement, many people assume the Canadian population is in danger of precipitous decline. That's why low fertility is often offered as a rationale for maintaining high immigration levels.

But despite below-replacement fertility, the Canadian population would have been increasing even without any immigration because Canada has had one of the highest birth rates among industrialized countries. That's because Canada during the 1980s and 1990s had a higher percentage than other advanced countries of women in their prime childbearing years. We had, in other words, a high birth rate and a low fertility rate at the same time. China, which restricts the number of children its citizens can have and has a huge population in the childbearing years, is now in the same situation.

The analysis in this book is based, in large part, on statistical facts like these. In this way, it is different from the work of other authors who attempt to forecast economic and social trends. John Naisbitt, for example, analyzes the content of newspapers and other publications to find out where the world is headed. Faith Popcorn relies on focus groups. Allan Gregg, Angus Reid, and Michael Adams use public opinion surveys. These are all legitimate forecasting methods that often result in important insights. This book, however, is built on a different foundation: demographic facts. In this approach, an analysis of historical data is used as a jumping-off point into the future. Once you've read this book, you'll know enough to analyze demographic data yourself.

But before you can do that, you need to grasp the most basic demographic fact of all: every year each person gets a year older. Many sophisticated and educated people have great difficulty understanding the significance of this one simple fact. That's why phrases such as "population aging" are so often misunderstood. If, for example, you think population aging means that senior citizens are about to become the dominant group in society and if you start a business based on that assumption, you may go broke. If you had checked the birth figures for the 1930s, you would have known that the ranks of seniors have grown very slowly in the last half of the 1990s. In fact, the real era of "grey power" is 20 years away, and in the meantime, there are far more promising markets to tempt retailers and far more pressing social issues for all of us to worry about than a non-existent preponderance of seniors.

HOW TO READ THIS BOOK

This chapter and the next, which describes the various cohorts that compose the Canadian population, provide the basic knowledge of Canadian demographics necessary for an understanding of everything that follows. Once you have read these two introductory chapters, we encourage you to read the rest of the book in whatever order suits best. Because different readers have different interests, each chapter has been written as a self-contained whole. If you're not interested in real estate, for example, you can skip the chapter on that subject with no loss of understanding of the chapters that follow. But it's important to note that many ideas and themes recur throughout the book. For that reason, readers are encouraged to take advantage of the cross-chapter references, which are a guide to the places in the book where each idea is fully explained.

Chapter 1

Boomers and Other Cohorts

E ach of us is a member of a "cohort." The baby boom is a cohort
that includes everyone born during a 20-year span of sustained
high numbers of births in Canada. It also includes those born
elsewhere during those same years but now living in Canada. The
other cohorts in Canada span shorter periods of time.

Most of us think of ourselves as individuals and underestimate how much we have in common with fellow members of our
cohort. And of course each of us is an individual. The 70-year-old
who continues a lifelong pursuit of rock climbing while most in her
age group have switched to more sedate recreations is a unique individual. So is the 12-year-old who prefers opera to rock music. But the
chances are good that the young opera lover will rent his first apartment, buy his first car, and get married at about the same age as his
peers. The timing of those events in his life will be determined largely
by demographics. Before we can understand what demographics have
in store for him and for all of us, we need to know the various cohorts
that make up the Canadian population. Let's take a look at them now.

PRE-WORLD WAR I (BORN 1914 AND EARLIER)
Forget about the outmoded notion of "senior citizens" as one unified
group sharing many characteristics in common. It's no longer true,
if it ever was. An 85-year-old has no more in common with a 65-year-
old than a 45-year-old has with a 25-year-old. They are different people, from different generations, with different interests, different

financial circumstances, and different preoccupations and needs.

The most senior of seniors – those 84 and over as of 1998 – constitute the one segment of the over-65 population that is currently growing rapidly because they were born in the first decade and a half of this century, when a high birth rate accompanied a booming Canadian economy. During this period, Canada also welcomed the largest concentrated influx of immigration in its history as part of a policy to settle the prairie provinces. Although the over-80s have a higher death rate than people in younger age groups, they are a growing cohort in the sense that those turning 85 at the millennium are more numerous than their predecessors in the over-85 category. In 1998, 483,000 members of this cohort, born both in Canada and elsewhere, were living in Canada.

Because women, on average, live six years longer than men, there were twice as many women as men in this age group. In their productive years, few women had independent careers outside the household and so they had little income of their own. They were married to men who didn't have transferable pensions. Not surprisingly, therefore, most of them are poor. Their greatest needs are appropriate housing and good health care. And their tragedy is that not enough of us are paying attention to them. As a society, we should be searching for innovative ways to combine housing with health care and related support services so that these women can conclude their lives in dignity and comfort. But the public sector has been too preoccupied with deficit-cutting to think about imaginative solutions to social problems, and most of the senior seniors are too poor to interest the private sector.

The increase in the number of older widows in our society is having a major impact on a younger group of people – people in their 50s and early 60s who are finding themselves taking on the responsibility of caring for elderly, and increasingly ill, parents (see Chapter 9). Traditionally, this is a task that falls to daughters more than to sons. Some women will be shouldering this new obligation on top of major responsibilities at work.

Imagine a vice-president of a large corporation in Toronto, preparing for a crucial meeting. She's an ambitious and talented woman who doesn't plan on making vice-president her final stop on the corporate ladder. She has her eye on the CEO's job, and this meeting is an important step in that direction. Then she gets an urgent call from Saskatoon, saying her mother has just broken her hip. Forget the big meeting: Mom needs her now more than ever, and she's on the next plane to Saskatoon. For the next few years, a great deal of her time and energy will be devoted to her mother. Because of real-life scenarios like this, many women who have the ability to make it to the top in business and government are not going to get there.

WORLD WAR I (1915 TO 1919)

It's always an advantage to be part of a small cohort. That's why even a small difference in one's date of birth can make a big difference in life. If you were born in 1910, you were part of a big cohort. If you were born in 1917, you were part of a smaller group. That in itself was no guarantee of success, but it was an important advantage. It meant you were in a smaller class at school and therefore had more attention from the teacher. And when it was time to go out to work, there were fewer competitors for what jobs were available.

During World War I, many Canadian men went off to battle and, as a result, many Canadian women stopped having babies. That's why people born in the last half of the teens of this century have enjoyed the lifelong advantage of having little peer-group competition. On the other hand, they entered the workforce while Canada was still in the grip of the Great Depression and jobs were few. After that, their careers were disrupted by World War II. Even so, they were better off than those born a few years earlier, who were part of a larger group and had to establish careers during the Depression. In 1998, 524,000 members of this cohort were living in Canada. In general, people born in the second part of the teens have done better than those born just before.

THE ROARING TWENTIES (1920 TO 1929)

When the boys came home from the war, they quickly made up for lost time, with the result that lots of babies were produced during the

1920s. These offspring of the Roaring Twenties are young to mid-seniors at the millennium and, despite the lifelong disadvantage of being part of a large cohort, they've had a pretty good run. Some of them went overseas to fight in World War II, which had the result of reducing competition for jobs for those who remained in Canada.

Moreover, because of the war effort the economy was growing, and so the 1920s kids had a better chance to get established than those born in the 1910s. The Roaring Twenties generation also helped to produce the boom that began in 1947. The boomers proceeded to drive up the price of the real estate and other assets that the kids of both the 1910s and 1920s owned. So, in general, these people have done well but, because they were members of a large flock, numbering 1.65 million in 1998, not as well as the favoured group that followed them.

THE DEPRESSION BABIES (1930 TO 1939)
In hard economic times, many Canadians couldn't afford children, and so fertility declined. The lucky ones who were born then became the golden group of Canadian society. The children of the 1930s have lived a life of incredible good fortune.

The 1930s were a time of hardship for everyone, including young children. They lived through World War II, hardly a carefree time to be alive. Because of their youth, they didn't have to serve in the war. But once the war ended, everything went their way. Entering the workforce during the postwar reconstruction of the 1950s, they never had to worry about finding a job. On the contrary, they had their choice of jobs. They never had to worry about being promoted; rather, they were promoted faster than they ever expected to be. Because they were doing so well, they went out and got more of everything, including kids. The Depression kids gave us the boom because they could afford a house full of children on only one salary.

Most of them had three or four children, and that was the best investment they could have made. Their kids sent real estate prices into the stratosphere in the 1980s, and subsequently they boosted the value of their parents' stock market holdings. In the 1990s, some

Depression kids began cashing in these assets, using the proceeds to bolster their retirement nest eggs as well as for travel. Early retirement has been common among this group because they had the assets to afford it. As they enter senior citizenship during the latter half of the 1990s, their timing once again is flawless: they are claiming free banking, cheap movie tickets, and all the other breaks our society awards seniors, because the dispensers of these perks do not understand that today's youngest seniors are the cohort least in need of such advantages.

In 1998, 2.6 million Depression kids were living in Canada and still doing well for themselves. Those who haven't retired occupy many of the senior jobs in this country – in government, in business, in major educational and other institutions. Some of them are smart and capable and some of them aren't. Few of them realize how much they owe their success to being part of a small cohort that has always been in the right place at the right time.

WORLD WAR II (1940 TO 1946)

For those who postponed having children because of the Depression, the biological clock was running out by the end of the 1930s and the early years of the 1940s. Then the war kick-started the economy – and the fertility rate. Canada, away from the main arenas of war, was a pretty good place to be. Canadians had plenty of food and jobs were plentiful. And so maternity wards started to fill up again. The World War II generation numbered 2.2 million in 1998. They aren't as prosperous as the 1930s generation before them because more of them were born during each year. (The total number of Depression kids is larger because their cohort spans ten years, compared with only seven for the children of World War II.) On the other hand, the war babies haven't had nearly as much peer-group competition as those born in the following decade; so by comparison with everyone except the Depression kids, they've done extremely well.

Why did Canada experience a decline in births during World War I and an increase in births during World War II? A larger percentage of Canadian men went overseas during World War I than in World

War II, and many more lost their lives: 60,661 in World War I, compared with 42,042 in World War II. Moreover, in August 1918, almost
as many Canadians were killed by a worldwide influenza epidemic as
fell victim to enemy fire during the war. Both calamities reduced the
numbers of Canadians in the child-producing age groups. Another
reason for the difference was that while World War I followed a
period of prosperity and high fertility, World War II followed the
Depression. People had been postponing having families in the 1930s,
and those in a position to start having children during World War II
were eager to do so. Yet another reason was that Canada's economy
got a bigger boost from World War II than from World War I. During
World War II, Canada became a major producer of ships, cargo carri-
ers, aircraft, tanks, and other military vehicles. As a result, Canadian
incomes rose, and rising incomes always mean increased demand for
everything, including children.

THE BABY BOOM (1947 TO 1966)

Even people with no knowledge of demographics have heard of the
group born from 1947 to 1966. These are the boomers. Some members
of this particular cohort seem to think they are pretty special. To hear
them talk, you'd think they were the most innovative and creative
bunch of people Canada had ever seen, infusing all of society with
new ways of thinking and new ways of doing things. This is nonsense. In fact, when they were 20, boomers weren't much different
from the 20-year-olds who had preceded them. And now that many of
them are in their 40s and early 50s, they are behaving just as middle-
aged people have always behaved.

The only thing special about the boomers is that there are so
many of them. It seems hard to imagine now, but at the height of the
boom, Canadian women were averaging four offspring each. Canada
produced more than 400,000 new Canadians in each year of the
boom, peaking at 479,000 in 1959. But examining Canadian births
alone isn't sufficient to define the baby boom. The largest single-year
age group in Canada is those born in 1961, even though 3,600 fewer
people were born here in that year than in 1959. That's because the

1961 group includes immigrants born in that year somewhere else. The boom, both those born in Canada and those born elsewhere, totalled 9.9 million people in 1998, or 32.4% of the Canadian population.

Canada's was the loudest boom in the industrialized world. In fact, only three other Western countries – the United States, Australia, and New Zealand – had large booms. Part of the reason was that these four countries were immigrant receivers, and immigrants tend to be in their 20s, the prime childbearing years. The U.S. boom started earlier, in 1946, and it also ended earlier, in 1964. At its peak in 1957, the U.S. boom hit 3.7 children per family, nearly half a baby fewer than Canadian women were producing at the peak of the Canadian boom. The Americans started their boom earlier because more of their war effort was in the Pacific, and the Pacific war wound down sooner. The U.S. troops were brought home in 1945 and kids started appearing in 1946. Canadian troops came home later, so Canadian births did not leap upwards until 1947. As for the Australians, they never got much higher than three babies per woman, but they compensated by continuing their boom ten years longer than Canada did. That happened because Australians were slower to adopt the birth-control pill and because Australian women were slower than their North American counterparts to enter the workforce in large numbers.

Because the Canadian boom was so big, Canadian boomers are a slightly more important factor in Canadian life than American boomers are in American life. Almost one-third of Canadians today are boomers, and for that reason alone, when they get interested in a particular product or idea, we all have to sit up and take notice. It's not that the product or idea is so great, it's just that everyone seems to be talking about it. The result is that phenomena such as the return to "family values" are often mistakenly identified as new social trends rather than the predictable demographic events they really are. (There is nothing new or remarkable about 35-year-olds raising families being interested in family values.)

Why did the boom happen? A likely explanation is that during those 20 years, Canadians knew they could afford large families. The postwar economy was robust, the future seemed full of promise, and young couples wanted to share that bright future with a big family. A second reason was the high immigration levels that prevailed during the 1950s; immigrants tend to be people of childbearing age, and they made an important contribution to the boom. The combination of two ingredients – lots of people in their high fertility years and high incomes – is a surefire recipe for filling up maternity wards. But you need both: immigration levels were raised in the early years of the 1990s but the fertility rate didn't respond because incomes were falling, and Canadians, immigrants and non-immigrants alike, didn't think they could afford extra mouths to feed.

Why did the boom end? Towards the end of the 1960s, an increasing number of women were pursuing higher education or entering the workforce. As a result, they were postponing childbirth and deciding to have fewer children. The introduction of the birth-control pill made this easier than ever to achieve. The more rapid acceptance of the pill in the United States may explain why the American boom ended before Canada's.

Like the seniors, the boomers break down into separate subgroups. The front-end boomer, in his early 50s, with a bulging waistline and equally bulging Registered Retirement Savings Plan, doesn't share much in the way of cultural attitudes or life experiences with the Generation-Xer, in his mid-30s, whose career hasn't yet got off the ground and who has trouble scraping up rent money every month. But as boomers, they have one very important thing in common: they are part of a huge cohort. For the front-end boomers, this was an advantage they could exploit. For the back-end boomers of Generation X, it is the cause of most of their problems.

It's important to grasp this point because the mass media have thoroughly confused it. Newspaper articles, media pundits, and even Statistics Canada often confuse Generation X with the baby-bust generation that followed it. Even as the millennium looms, the media are still calling Gen-Xers "twenty-somethings" although all of them have celebrated their 30th birthdays. Some writers are so confused they seem to think Generation X is the children of the boomers. But it isn't. Most boomers weren't yet old enough to have children when

Generation X came along. To clarify matters, we'll look at the characteristics of each subgroup of boomers in turn.

The front-end boomers have done pretty well for themselves. There are a lot of them, so they had to compete for jobs when they entered the workforce over the 1960s. But the entry of vast numbers of younger boomers into the marketplace through the 1970s and 1980s created wonderful opportunities for the front-enders already entrenched in business and government. New products, new services, new government programs, new universities – it was a period of seemingly endless expansion. The front-end boomers got there first, so they are the ones in good jobs now in both the public and private sectors. They understand the needs of the boom because they are the leading edge of it.

Those born towards the end of the 1950s also understand the boom but, unlike the front-enders, they have been less well positioned to profit from that knowledge. Most members of this boomer subgroup have got a house and are in a career, but that career seems to be going nowhere because the rungs ahead of them are clogged with older boomers who are still 15 to 20 years from retirement.

Things are tough for the late-1950s group, but not nearly as bad as for the back end of the boom that arrived just after them. These are the 3.2 million people born from 1961 to 1966. They are the same age as the characters in Douglas Coupland's novel *Generation X*, which gave the early-1960s group its name. Many of them were still living at home with their parents at their 30th birthday because, faced with horrendous obstacles in the labour market, they had a terrible time getting their careers on track. That is why, while front-end boomers were earning 30% more than their fathers by age 30, back-enders were making 10% less than their fathers at the same age.

Gen-Xers' life experience has led them to distrust any sort of large institution, whether in the public or private sector. It didn't take them long to learn that, in an overcrowded world, they had no choice but to "look out for number one." On their first day in kindergarten, the Gen-Xers discovered there weren't enough seats for them. In elementary school, many of them were squeezed into portables. They have been part of a crowd ever since. Whether it was trying to enrol in a ballet class, get into a summer camp, or find a part-time job, waiting lists have been a way of life for Generation X.

The millions of boomers who preceded them drove up rents, drove up house prices, drove up interest rates, and claimed all the best jobs and opportunities. As if that weren't enough, the Gen-Xers entered the labour market in the late 1970s and early 1980s, just when a brutal recession gripped the Canadian economy. In the best of circumstances, there would have been few jobs; in the recession there were virtually none. And when economic recovery finally began to create new demand for labour, the Gen-Xers were told they were too old for entry-level jobs and too short of experience for more senior ones. They kept hearing the same story right through the 1990s.

One of the worst things the Gen-Xers have to cope with is their parents – the Depression generation. These are the 60-year-olds sitting at the top of the corporate ladder or recently retired from very successful careers and unable to fathom why their 35-year-old offspring still hasn't got a permanent job. Tension is tremendous in these families. Often the father is certain that his own success is based solely on his own merit while he sees his son's failure as a result of lack of drive and ambition.

THE BABY BUST (1967 TO 1979)

The commercial introduction of the birth-control pill in 1961 and the rising participation of women in the labour market led to declining fertility over the 1960s. The result was a decline in births and a smaller cohort, often called the baby bust. In 1998, 5.6 million Canadians were in this cohort. The baby-busters have done pretty well so far, especially the younger ones. They have been able to get into just about any school or summer camp they wanted. They had no difficulty finding babysitting, lawn-mowing, and other part-time jobs in high school, unlike their older brothers and sisters, who had less opportunity to earn money while in high school because they had so many competitors. During the 1990s, university entry standards fell, making it easier for busters to get into the school of their choice.

There is good reason for people in their 20s at the millennium to be both more realistic and more idealistic than those in their 30s. In fact, the baby-busters resemble the front-end boomers, who could espouse idealistic causes during the 1960s safe in the knowledge that a good job and a prosperous lifestyle would be there for the taking once they were ready for those bourgeois things. But the back-end boomers, as we have seen, had no choice but to look out for their own best interests. They were less idealistic than their elders, not because they were worse people but because they couldn't afford to be idealistic. In contrast, the baby-busters have had a pretty good life so far, and when the world has treated you well, you have the luxury of being able to pay attention to social issues, such as peace, the environment, and AIDS, and therefore are more inclined to do so.

That's not to say there are no similarities between the Gen-Xers and the baby-busters. Both groups started their working careers in tough economic times when corporations were more interested in

Born 1930s

Born 1960s

Cohort opportunities

trimming payrolls than in hiring new staff. As a result, the older baby-busters, having recently celebrated their 30th birthdays, face the same problems and frustrations that Generation X knows so well. But as the economy turns around, the 20-year-old with minimal experience will have better prospects than the 30-year-old with minimal experience. That's partly because employers usually prefer younger people for entry-level positions, because they are cheaper and more adaptable; partly because there are fewer busters than Gen-Xers; and partly because the busters are better equipped than the Gen-Xers with the computer skills that today's job market demands.

THE BABY-BOOM ECHO (1980 TO 1995)

These are the children of the boomers. The boomers began having children in the 1970s and by 1980 enough of them were reproducing to produce a mini-boom of their own. The boomers, however, never matched the reproductive prowess of their parents. At its peak, in 1990, the echo produced 406,000 babies from a population of 27.7 million, compared with 479,000 from a population of only 17.5 million in 1959. This generation is most noticeable in Ontario and western Canada. Quebec and the Atlantic provinces (except for Halifax) haven't had much of an echo because so many of their boomers moved to Ontario and the western provinces and had their children there. So the echo won't have as much impact on society in eastern Canada as it will in Ontario and the west.

As of 1998, there were 6.5 million members of the echo generation. The boomers haven't finished having children, but annual births had declined so much by 1995 that the echo had to be considered at an end. What is the outlook for the echo kids? It won't be quite as smooth sailing as the baby-busters have had, but it won't be as disastrous as for Generation X either. These echo kids are part of a large cohort and that's always bad news. They crowded nurseries in the 1980s, pushed elementary school enrolments up in the late 1980s, and did the same for high school enrolments in the mid-1990s. Like the boom, the echo has a front end, born in the 1980s, that will have an easier ride than its back end, born in the first half of the 1990s. The latter group, Generation X-II, will experience the familiar disadvantages of arriving at the rear of a large cohort. Think of a cohort as a group of people all wanting to get into the same theatre to see the same show. There is no reserved seating. So who claims the best seats? The ones who get there first. The back end of the echo generation, Gen X-II, will have a life experience similar to that of its parents, the first Generation X. Just as the first Gen-Xers have done, Gen X-II will have to scramble.

However, Gen X-II should be better prepared than its parents were to cope with high youth unemployment and other difficulties associated with a large cohort. That's because these kids have their Gen-X parents to teach them. By contrast, the original Generation X was the offspring of a small cohort that wasn't equipped to prepare them for the difficult world they encountered when they left home in the early 1980s.

THE MILLENNIUM BUSTERS (1996 TO 2010)

These are the millennium kids, the generation that is following the echo. As of 1998, just over 1 million of them had arrived. The women producing them are the baby-busters, a cohort 14% smaller in each year than the boomers and 44% smaller in total. That's why, in 1998, there were 67,000 fewer children under one year of age than 8-year-olds. Because of immigration, the millennium kids won't necessarily be 44% fewer than the echo kids, but they will definitely be a smaller group. As the new millennium approaches, it is clear that another small, and therefore favoured, cohort is emerging from Canada's maternity wards.

Chapter 2

The Real Estate Meltdown

No real estate development better mirrors the shifting demographics of the Canadian population than the Bay-Adelaide Centre in downtown Toronto. When the original version of this book was published in the spring of 1996, construction of the $1-billion office project had been halted for three years. What was supposed to have been the brightest jewel in Toronto's glittering downtown core was a six-storey bunker, its raw concrete exterior streaked and filthy. It had no roof and empty holes where its windows should have been. It looked more like war damage than what one would expect to see in the financial heart of Canada.

Of course, no bombs had dropped on the Bay-Adelaide Centre. The problem was a shortage of demand for office space in the 1990s when new entrants to the labour force were coming from the small baby-bust cohort. Because there weren't many busters, there was little need for new office buildings to accommodate them.

But just as one demographic shift is powerful enough to shut down a huge real estate project, so another shift has the strength to swing the construction cranes back into action. As the millennium approaches, the baby-boom echo, 6.5 million strong, will begin swelling the ranks of Canada's working population. Meanwhile, most of the 5.6 million baby-busters have entered the labour force. While these busters were going out to work, developers, scared off by high vacancy rates and low rents, added almost no new office space to downtown Toronto's existing supply during the 1990s. The result, by

1998, was that the vacancy rate had fallen below 10% for the first time since the 1980s. That meant that the Bay-Adelaide Centre finally made demographic sense. And because it made demographic sense, it also made economic sense. So, as the millennium edition of *Boom, Bust & Echo* went to press, TrizecHahn Corp. was planning to resume construction on a scaled-down version of the project.

The conventional explanation for the demise of the Bay-Adelaide Centre in 1993 was that it was the most visible symbol of the worst economic downturn since the Great Depression. But, in reality, even if the recession had not hit central Canada with the fury it did, Toronto did not need yet another major new office project in the mid-1990s. Real estate is about places for people to live in and work in. That's why real estate is driven more by demographics than by economics. A rapidly growing population requires more goods and services and more people to provide them. The new labour-force entrants need new places to work in. When new labour-force entrants are few, as they were in the late 1980s and 1990s, demand for new places to work in dwindles. And when they are increasing in number, as they will be in the new millennium, demand for new places to work in inevitably will rebound.

Other factors do play some part in the success or failure of a real estate venture. Location, quality, property taxation, and economic cycles are all important. But the significance of these factors is consistently overrated by the industry itself, which is why many real estate companies that were big players ten years ago have become small players or have gone out of business. These companies failed because their owners ignored the overwhelming power of demographics. They understood the sophisticated intricacies of big-time real estate transactions, but they did not understand the obvious: if you erect a new office tower when hardly anyone is entering the labour force, you take a huge risk. If you build a building for the busters, chances are it's going to be a bust.

Let's take a closer look at how demographic change affects the real estate industry. The baby boom started in 1947 and ended in 1966. The typical Canadian enters the labour force at about the age of 20.

During two momentous decades, from 1967 to 1986, more than one-third of the Canadian population entered the labour force and subsequently the housing market. In doing so, they transformed the skylines of Canada's cities. Until the boomers decided to leave home, Vancouver's West End consisted of rows of graceful old frame houses, and one of the few buildings more than three storeys high was the Sylvia Hotel on English Bay. Now the Sylvia is dwarfed by a forest of high-rise apartments in one of the most densely populated neighbourhoods in North America. Many would dispute whether this represents progress, just as others mourned the loss of many old buildings that fell to the wrecker's ball in the construction frenzy that reshaped the central cores of Montreal, Toronto, Calgary, and other Canadian and American cities.

Developers were not among the mourners. It was no accident that Canada, with the world's biggest baby boom, briefly boasted one of the world's great development industries. Olympia & York was the biggest office developer in the world, and others such as Campeau Corp., Trizec, and Bramalea made their mark right across North America. If these companies had paid attention to demographics, they would have known the boom could not continue. Just because there is a 30-year trend in an industry doesn't mean that trend will continue forever. That is especially true when the demographic realities that underlie the trend change significantly. In the case of commercial real estate, it was predictable at least 25 years ago that demand for new office space would stall over the last half of the 1980s because of the slowdown in labour-force growth. Yet even after the signs of drooping demand had begun to appear, developers continued to plan new office towers. Because they didn't understand demographics, they continued building for the future – a future when there would be fewer new workers needing new space to work in.

The recession of the first half of the 1990s loaded the deck even more against real estate because companies became more interested in firing than hiring. And at the same time, other factors were at work, with ominous implications. While the boomers were applying for their first jobs in the 1960s and 1970s, major Canadian employers had little incentive to automate, because armies of affordable workers were streaming onto the labour market every year. Why pay for expensive new machines when human labour can do the work for less? In the mid-1990s, the supply of new workers was shrinking at the same time as labour-saving equipment was dropping in price and rising in quality and effectiveness. These developments gave employers every reason to embrace technology.

How does this affect the real estate industry? A computer requires less space than a person and it never insists on having its own office. Moreover, computers in combination with new communications technologies make it possible for people to work at home, with only occasional forays to the office. All these trends contributed to cooling down demand for new office space. And of course, we have deregulation, globalization, and downsizing, three catchwords that translate into fewer jobs in both public and private sectors.

The one Canadian city where construction was still a growth industry in the mid-1990s was Vancouver. That's because Vancouver had faster population growth than the rest of the country, as a result of migration from other parts of Canada and abroad. However, since then the combination of a weakening economy in British Columbia and strengthening economic conditions in other parts of Canada has reduced the flow of migrants from other provinces. And of course Vancouver is not and never was immune from the impact of demographics – the baby-bust generation on the west coast is smaller than the baby boom, just as it is in the rest of the country. The result, by the late 1990s, was a drop in demand for new office space, accompanied by an increase in vacancy rates and a slowdown in new construction.

Reduced demand for office space, caused by demographic change, should not be cause for alarm on the part of anyone, save those who work in the land development industry. The prosperity of that industry and that of the rest of us are not one and the same thing. And an increase in a city's population doesn't necessarily mean that the incomes and well-being of the people who live there also increase. If it did, the citizens of huge cities such as Mexico City and Calcutta would be wealthier than those of smaller ones such as Vancouver and

Geneva. Economic growth can and does occur in the context of a stable population and in the absence of construction cranes. The point is
simply that without large numbers of new labour-force entrants and a
high rate of new family formation, real estate investments must be
very carefully chosen.

In this new environment, timing becomes crucial, as the con-
trasting fortunes of OMERS Realty Corp. and TrizecHahn Corp. illustrate. OMERS Realty, the real estate subsidiary of the Ontario
Municipal Employees Retirement Board (OMERS), one of Canada's
largest pension funds, was created in 1990 just as the demographic
shift was darkening the outlook for commercial real estate. OMERS
Realty plunged into the market, snapping up an average of $325 mil-
lion worth of property every year. But, to its disappointment, real
estate generated a negative return for OMERS between 1990 and 1995
while its stock portfolio returned an average of 7% and its bond
holdings 13%. By 1997, despite the beginnings of an upturn in the
real estate market, OMERS Realty's portfolio was worth less than the
original acquisition costs.

TrizecHahn Corp., the Toronto-based company controlled by
Peter Munk that is reviving the Bay-Adelaide Centre, also went on an
acquisition binge – but not until 1996, when the demographic shift
was poised to start working in real estate's favour once again.
TrizecHahn was able to buy when prices of top-quality office buildings had been beaten down below their replacement costs and just
before new demand, intensified by shifting demographics, was about
to drive up rents. The result has been steadily rising profits for
TrizecHahn.

But good timing is only one issue when it comes to real estate
or any other kind of investment. A project may be well timed to take
advantage of demographic realities, but that alone does not mean it
will succeed. Quality – in construction, management, and marketing –
is an essential ingredient of success. As well, investors must be careful
not to invest in a real estate product that may be in oversupply.

An example of a potential oversupply situation in the making
is the flood of new hotel projects on the west coast. As of early 1998,

some 3,400 new hotel rooms in ten new projects were proposed for the Vancouver area. In several cases, developers were employing a new financing technique, hotel strata ownership (HSO), to raise money for these projects. In an HSO project, a small investor can become the owner of a single room or suite in a hotel. The investor thus enjoys a flow of rental income without the tedious work of finding tenants, collecting rents, or playing landlord, tasks that are left to the hotel's managers.

Demographics would seem to favour investing in a Vancouver hotel project. Tourism is a growth industry in an aging population because middle-aged people have more money to travel, and older people have lots of time on their hands. Vancouver's profile as an international tourist mecca has risen dramatically over the past decade, so much so that *Condé Nast Traveler* magazine ranks it one of the top ten destinations in the world. The Open Skies air treaty between Canada and the United States that came into effect in 1995 has been a boon to the Vancouver tourist industry, increasing non-stop air services from the United States by 216%. In all, overnight visits to Vancouver from other parts of Canada and the rest of the world increased from 5.9 million in 1992 to 7.6 million in 1996.

In this environment, it is obvious that a demand exists for more hotel space, not just in Vancouver but in nearby Whistler and Victoria as well. However, investors must consider how many new hotels the market can accommodate before occupancy rates start to slip. And they must also satisfy themselves that occupancy and room rates will be high enough to produce a decent return on their investments. As always, demographics is only two-thirds of the story – the other third can be of crucial importance when it comes to the bottom line.

The impact of demographic change on residential real estate has been just as great as its impact on commercial real estate. Between 1967 and 1986, nearly 10 million Canadians left their parents' homes and set up households of their own. Inevitably, this created a phenomenal boom in rental and residential real estate, resulting in a 115% increase in the price of the average Canadian house between 1980 and 1989. It was just as inevitable that once the boomers were housed, the boom would end, which is why house prices rose only 7% between 1989 and 1997, failing to keep pace with even the low inflation of the 1990s. This stunning decrease in the rate of growth of Canadian house prices is the "real estate melt-down" in the title of this chapter. Because of demographic change, housing went from being a sure-fire investment to a risky investment. And boomers who had envisioned their houses as their pension plans had to think again.

To understand the future of residential real estate in Canada, we need to understand the normal behaviour of people, boomers or any-one else, when they enter the housing market. You leave your parents' house at the same time you enter the labour force, about age 20. But you don't buy a house then because you can't afford it and you are not ready to settle down anyway. So you rent. Over the next ten to fifteen years, you find a partner and establish a family. So you buy a house. In another ten years or so, in your 40s, you may be ready to move up to a better house or to renovate the one you have. You're also primed, if you can afford it, to buy a country property.

The movement of the huge baby-boom generation through these cycles has driven the real estate industry in Canada since 1967, Canada's centennial year. That year is fondly remembered for Mon-treal's wonderful Expo 67. But an even more significant event was going unnoticed at about the same time: the first boomers were tum-bling out of the family nest and into the housing market. Only a third of them had left home by 1975 but their impact was already enor-mous: apartment vacancy rates everywhere were in free fall, triggering an explosion in rents that in turn led to rent controls in all ten provinces. Demand continued to increase through the 1970s, but rent controls killed the market's ability to respond. As a result, in those parts of urban Canada most sought after by young boomers, key money – a chunk of cash under the table – was required for the privi-lege of renting even the most dismal basement suite. For the next ten years, vacancy rates stayed down and rents stayed up.

Then came 1986, the year the last boomers left home. For rental housing in Canada, that was a key turning point because the baby-bust generation that followed is 44% smaller than the boom cohort. So demand for accommodation, as was perfectly predictable, was about to drop. The inevitability of this development was independent of the recession that struck most of Canada in the 1990s. It would have happened even in an economic boom. By 1988, sure enough, vacancies were rising, especially at the high-priced end of the rental housing market, and through the mid-1990s most of Canada experienced a falling rental market instead of a growing one. The recession, by forcing people to double up or live with their parents, aggravated the plight of the rental business.

In this environment, few developers were eager to put new rental units on the market. Meanwhile, as the economy improved and created more jobs, people who had been living at home or doubling up started looking for places of their own. In the waning years of the old millennium, most of the baby bust was in the market for rental accommodation, as was part of the leading edge of the baby-boom echo. The combination of these factors pushed vacancy rates down so that, by the end of 1997, they were at their lowest point in seven years.

As the rest of the echo strikes out on its own over the decade to come, demand for rental accommodation will continue to increase. In cities like Toronto, Vancouver, and Calgary, where the echo is biggest, that demand will trigger construction of new rental units. But it's important to note that this phenomenon will take place only in those parts of the country – Ontario, the west, and Halifax – that actually have an echo generation. Other parts of Canada have experienced an exodus of boomers and, as a result, won't have a large group of boomer offspring needing apartments.

In real estate markets, factors other than demographics can sometimes delay the inevitable. That's what happened in the market for owner-occupied homes in the first years of the 1980s. The leading-edge members of the boom generation were moving into their 30s, when their thoughts should have been turning to buying houses. That didn't happen. One reason was that all of Canada was mired in recession. Another was that we had outrageous interest rates. Yet another

was that these same front-end boomers who should have been buying houses were occupying the best rent-controlled apartments and saw no immediate advantage to giving them up.

So the movement of front-end boomers out of rentals and into owner-occupied homes was delayed until the mid-1980s. By then, the first five years of boomers had accumulated enough money for a down-payment on a home. They had kids. They wanted backyards. The economy was growing again and interest rates were dropping. And the housing market went crazy.

Those days of houses selling for more than their asking price and then doubling in value seem like ancient history as the century draws to a close. In fact, they should have lasted longer than they did. The housing market should have continued to show growth right through to the early 1990s, because the late boomers were still entering their house-buying years then. Price increases would inevitably have slowed down because the late boomers, the Gen-Xers, are less numerous and less well off than the front-enders, and making the jump from rental to owning was harder for them.

But demand would have remained strong had it not been for the arrival in the early 1990s of a severe recession marked by high real interest rates. (The spread between interest rates and the rate of inflation is the "real" interest rate.)

As a result, many of the Gen-Xers – those born between 1961 and 1966 – were still waiting in the mid-1990s for a chance to buy their first houses. Moreover, because of the uncertain economy, not much new housing was built in the 1990s. That combination – lack of new supply plus pent-up demand – is always a volatile one. As forecast in the first edition of this book, it resulted in a mini-surge in house prices in the latter years of the 1990s.

Just as there are significant demographic differences from region to region, so real estate markets differ from region to region. In Toronto, prices climbed steadily through the 1980s as both local boomers and others who had moved to Canada's largest city in search of opportunity competed for real estate. The average price peaked at $273,698 in 1989. By then, however, most of the front-end boomers were housed. That fact, combined with a sharp economic downturn, turned boom into bust as prices plunged 25% in only two years.

Since then, however, Toronto house prices have been fairly stable, with the average fluctuating around the $200,000 mark. This is the behaviour of a normal real estate market rather than a speculative one. In Toronto, as in the rest of the country, a house is back to what it was before the boomers entered the market – a place to live in rather than a way to get rich quick.

The Calgary real estate market, unlike Toronto's, underwent neither dramatic price increases nor sudden declines. Instead, prices increased, gradually and modestly, through the 1990s. During this time, Calgary, with Canada's lowest unemployment rate, was a magnet for job-seekers from Saskatchewan and points east. The only restraint on Calgary house prices during the 1990s was the age structure of its population – most Calgary boomers were already housed and the bust in Calgary, as everywhere else, was relatively small.

In Vancouver, meanwhile, migration from the rest of Canada and abroad delayed the impact of demographic change on the real estate market. As a result, average prices continued to rise until 1995. Since then, however, diminishing demand has caught up and average prices have been sliding. It's important to remember, however, that a drop in average prices does not mean that all houses are cheaper. "Real estate is turning into a stock market," observes David Cork, an Ottawa stockbroker for ScotiaMcLeod, who creates investment portfolios for his clients based on a keen appreciation of demographics. "On any given day, some stocks go up and some go down," he says. "In real estate, we are seeing the same thing."

Factors other than demographics are often part of the reason for such ups and downs. For example, because the 1997 transition in Hong Kong from British to Chinese rule was less eventful than many had feared, fewer wealthy Hong Kong people are moving to Canada and some recent immigrants have moved back. Partly for that reason, house prices in affluent parts of Vancouver favoured by such immigrants have tumbled. But demographic trends are also part of the story. Because of population aging in Asia, immigration to Canada from that region was going to decline anyway (see Chapter 11). Meanwhile, because of pent-up demand from Gen-Xers, prices in some of the less affluent neighbourhoods of the Lower Mainland have been rising in the latter years of the 1990s.

In the long run, however, houses in the wealthier, long-established neighbourhoods of our major cities are the most likely to increase in value. That's because the front end of the boom, a large, generally affluent group, wants to live in these neighbourhoods. The older, large homes that are found there may need costly repairs and renovations. But that is their only disadvantage. On the plus side, they are spacious and have large yards. They tend to be close to the downtown core, a crucial consideration for time-starved boomers. Finally, their size makes them adaptable to the changes coming in the first decade of the next century, when the rental market will pick up while demand for large family homes drops. Many big houses in central neighbourhoods will then be converted into luxury flats. This phenomenon is already well advanced in Toronto's Rosedale.

Homes in these good, inner-city districts will continue to enjoy modest increases in value through to the end of the century. Meanwhile, once the Gen-Xers are accommodated, starter homes in the distant suburbs of the major cities will begin to decline in value or, at best, maintain stable prices. That's because the baby-bust generation, who will make up much of the market for starter homes in the years after 2000, is smaller than the boomer generation.

The slowdown in demand for starter homes means boomers aspiring to move up won't be able to extract high prices for the homes they are selling. That in turn will put a brake on prices of homes in the boomer-occupied areas. And once the bulk of the boom is in its retirement years, even homes in Canada's most desirable neighbourhoods – such as Shaughnessy (Vancouver), Rockcliffe Park (Ottawa), and Forest Hill (Toronto) – may decline in value. The conclusion is clear: even in Canada's best urban neighbourhoods, the days of rapid and huge increases in house prices are gone. The real estate boom is over.

But the end of a boom is not the same thing as a crash. There is no reason to fear a crash even when the pace of boomer retirement picks up in the second decade of the new century. Only about 20% of retirees move out of their homes when they stop work (and most don't move very far). The other 80% stay put because they enjoy their homes and gardens and because they know the extra space freed up when the kids moved out will come in handy in the future when grandchildren come to visit. Most people don't trade in their houses for more compact accommodation until they are in their 70s. When the first wave of boomers reaches that stage, around 2020, the echo generation will be ready to buy the houses the boomers put on the market. The existence of the echo, therefore, is the boomers' guarantee that their houses will retain value until they are ready to sell. But this guarantee will work best in places like Toronto, Calgary, and Vancouver, where the echo is largest.

Younger people generally like the bright lights of the big city. They want to be where the action is. That's why most rental accommodation is downtown or near colleges and universities. As the early boomers moved out of their parents' homes in the late 1960s and 1970s, the inner city became the place to be, and we celebrated the revival of Old Strathcona in Edmonton, Old Montreal, the Historic Properties in Halifax, and False Creek in Vancouver. In Toronto, affluent front-end boomers (also known as yuppies) transformed Cabbagetown into a new haven of chic, where drunks and street people watched in amazement as renovators lavished huge sums on old working-class houses. This was the ultimate in gentrification.

But did gentrification represent a value shift, as so many people assumed, a rejection of suburban conformity in favour of the free and easy lifestyle of the inner city? Not really. In fact, it was just young people behaving as they always have, but because there were so many of them it looked like a new trend. Gradually, over the 1980s, growth switched back from the urban centres to the suburbs. Again, people were doing what comes naturally. The massive boom generation was having kids and wanted bigger backyards as well as spacious garages for its minivans. So suburbanization replaced urbanization, a trend that continued well into the 1990s.

But the impact of suburbanization should not be exaggerated. A major reason why Canada's three major cities – Toronto, Montreal, and Vancouver – consistently place near the top in global rankings of urban liveability is their relatively healthy downtown cores. In the United States, by contrast, the demographic phenomenon of boomers heading for the suburbs combined with severe social and racial problems to turn some large cities into urban doughnuts – a hole in the middle where the centre used to be, surrounded by a ring of thriving suburbs.

The cores of Canadian cities will remain healthy for four reasons. First, the turn of the century will see 6.5 million echo kids start to move out of their parents' homes and into their own rented accommodation. Many of these young people will move from the suburbs into the city centres. Although there aren't enough echo kids to recreate the downtown boom of the 1970s and 1980s, there are enough of them to ensure that downtown remains alive. Second, Canada has high levels of immigration, and immigrants, as a group, tend to be younger than the Canadian-born. The housing preferences of young immigrants are the same as those of the young Canadian-born. Young new Canadians will settle in the inner city while their elders head for the burbs. Third, a small percentage of aging boomers – smaller than is commonly believed – will resist the call of the boondocks and trade in their large homes for downtown condos. These sophisticated older boomers will be a valuable addition to the mix that will keep our big cities good places to live as we head into the 21st century. Finally, Canada still has many young boomers – Generation X – without a lot of money. For them, buying an older house in a moderately priced downtown area and fixing it up may be more affordable than buying a newer house in a more expensive area.

The average age of first-time homebuyers is the early to middle 30s. This age varies by location, being lower in more affordable areas. The average age of those trading in their first home for something better is the middle 40s. That's where the front end of the boom is in the late 1990s. Their kids, the echo generation that started arriving on the scene in 1980, are teenagers. Many of these kids are noisy and annoying – in other words, typical teenagers. They are demanding more space and more independence. Mom and Dad, who could use some peace and quiet, would love to give it to them. That means a bigger house where the two generations can practise peaceful coexistence. The real estate revival of the late 1990s has been fuelled in part by the phenomenon of boomers moving into bigger houses to make room for their teenagers.

Some boomers find they can't get the price for their existing homes that they need if they are to afford something much better. As an alternative, they decide to stay put and renovate or build an addition. The result in the late 1990s has been boom times for the renovation business. That has been good news for the profession of architecture, which went through some hard times in the first part of the decade. Some firms closed, others downsized, and talented people left the profession. No major rebound is in sight because real estate is no longer a growth industry. But architects who make quality renos a specialty have a good chance to prosper in the years to come. But the

A home becomes a castle – eventually

key word here is quality. These front-end boomers are a demanding lot and they won't tolerate shoddy workmanship (see Chapter 5). Architects and building contractors who can deliver good work on time will do well. The other kind won't.

In 1998, Canadians spent about $24 billion on home renovations, more than the value of new home construction. This boom is not confined to the major cities. Laverne Brubacher, president of Menno S. Martin Contractor Ltd., serves customers in several small-to-medium-sized Ontario centres, including Kitchener-Waterloo, St. Jacobs, Guelph, and Cambridge. He finds that his clients, who are mainly in the 45-to-55 age group, are less price-conscious and more quality-conscious than ever before. "If it costs a few thousand more, so be it, as long as they can rest assured that it's going to be done properly," he says. People are renovating to improve their lifestyles, rather than with a view to increasing the value of their real estate investments. "When they become empty-nesters, often they will remove walls to make a larger family room out of a couple of bedrooms and they will redo kitchens and bathrooms," says Brubacher. "Sometimes they will expand the house a bit but often it's putting bells and whistles on what they already have."

A third response to the need for space is the second house, the cottage by the water or the condo near the ski slopes. Most Canadians live in large cities, but the call of the wild remains deeply ingrained in the Canadian psyche. As the boomers' kids move into their teen years, their parents' desire for a country retreat becomes more intense. Partly this desire is based on the hope that the pull of the recreational property will counteract the natural tendency of teens to drift away from the family as they begin the difficult process of becoming adults. Conversely, the second home is also a way to maintain family harmony through the strategy of providing more space. Mom and Dad get some peace and quiet in the country while their teenagers enjoy the independence of being home alone in the noisy city for the weekend.

"The thrill of living shifts from the erotic intensity of the central city to that of field and stream," writes William Thorsell of the

Globe and Mail. "Subtly but suddenly, the rising of the moon and the soaring of the hawk excite the spirit, and the taste for a cottage or country house is born."

Whatever the motive, we know that the over-45 age group contains the largest number of owners of country properties, and we know that, in the 1990s, the boomers have been streaming into that age group. That's why leisure and recreational property will be a strong segment of the real estate market for the future. This won't be a boom such as rental housing had in the 1970s or owner-occupied housing enjoyed in the 1980s. That's because, although everybody has to have a home base, only a relatively affluent minority can afford a second home in the country. But there will be enough of these to put considerable pressure on the price of recreational property located within a reasonable distance of our major cities. Currently only 8% of Canadian households own a leisure property. In the new century, a significantly higher percentage of Canadians will own second homes.

While the biggest Canadian real estate companies were being hammered by recession during the first years of the 1990s, one company, Vancouver-based Intrawest Corp., continued to prosper. That was partly because most of Intrawest's assets are on the west coast, which has had rapid population growth and which avoided the worst of the recession. Another reason is that Intrawest's managers have a keener understanding of the realities of Canadian demographics than most of their competitors. Intrawest has always understood what the boomers needed and when they needed it. That's why its stock more than doubled between 1992 and 1997, a period during which the Toronto Stock Exchange's index of real estate companies lost almost half its value.

Because it knows where the boomers are headed, Intrawest has decided to concentrate on the resort business. "The last frontier of real estate in this century is vacation homes," says Joe Houssain, Intrawest's chairman. The company's attention to the impact of demographic change on real estate was evident in 1997 in its advertising campaign for a real estate project at Sun Peaks, a four-season mountain resort near Kamloops, British Columbia. "A rare opportunity to enter the market at the front of the boom – the baby boom, that is!" proclaimed the ad. Another indication that Intrawest is in tune with the demographic shift is its increasing emphasis on golf, a sport with greater appeal to older athletes than skiing (see Chapter 6). In 1998, the company announced it was acquiring Raven Golf Group, a golf course developer based in Phoenix, Arizona.

The managers in charge of developing the land around Intrawest's four-season resort at Mont Tremblant, in the Laurentians north of Montreal, have been surprised at the number of people interested in having their larger house near the mountain and keeping a smaller home in city – the reverse of the normal pattern. Some of these people will be able to continue their working careers in a mountainside home office (sometimes called a "hoffice"), with periodic visits to see clients or other key contacts in Montreal. This is a variation on a trend that is going to accelerate into the new century: the movement of the boomers away from the urban areas.

This shift away from the big cities means that the outlook is very promising for Canada's smaller cities. Some early and pre-boomers in the B.C. Lower Mainland were already cashing in their city homes for big profits in the mid-1990s and moving to the interior of the province. This was an early manifestation of what will be an important trend by the next century, when large numbers of front-end boomers start to take early retirement. Meanwhile, the Toronto metropolitan area experienced a net outflow of 87,400 people to other parts of Canada between 1991 and 1996. Most of these people, according to Statistics Canada, relocated to small cities and towns within commuting distance.

As the phenomenon of boomer retirement picks up steam in the first decade of the new century, there will be a movement from greater Toronto to more distant, smaller cities such as Guelph to the west, Collingwood to the north, and Kingston to the east. In addition, some retirees who, as young adults, moved away from idyllic surroundings in such places as Prince Edward Island and Newfoundland in search of economic opportunity in the big city will head back home. As stated above, only about 20% of retirees pull up stakes when they quit work, but 20% of 10 million boomers is a lot of people. Canada's smaller cities, therefore, will have a chance to attract an influx of well-educated, affluent retirees who will expand the local tax base and make a positive contribution to the community – for example, by supporting cultural and charitable causes. On the other hand, local municipalities will be faced with new costs associated with providing the serviced land and other requirements of an expanding population.

These retiring newcomers won't want to settle in the centres of their new small cities. Many will be looking for larger lots and a convenient drive from the town centre. Others will be attracted by new residential communities built around golf courses. Their arrival will create a major challenge for local politicians and planners: how to expand without falling victim to the sort of urban sprawl that would destroy the small-city charm that is among these cities' chief assets. The front-end boomers will want a small-town atmosphere, but at the same time they are unwilling to give up such urban amenities as good restaurants and shopping. The cities with the best planners, who can figure out the best ways of balancing these conflicting demands, will win the contest to attract retiring boomers to the local tax rolls.

Perhaps most important of all as the massive boom generation enters its 50s and 60s will be health care facilities. Boomers are less likely to relocate to a community that lacks a top-notch hospital. Hospitals that are viewed as a financial burden as we approach the millennium will be an important economic development tool for some small cities and rural districts after the turn of the century (see Chapter 9). That is why the policy of some provincial governments to cut health care funding in small communities may be short-sighted. Huntsville, Ontario, is a good example. A town of 16,000 located in the Muskoka vacation district about two hours north of Toronto, it is expected to attract a stream of retirees over the next two decades, some of whom will sell their city homes and live full-time in lakeside cottages they already own. Yet Huntsville's hospital has had to cut service because of reduced provincial grants. This policy puts the town's future prosperity at risk, according to David Selby, Huntsville's economic development officer. From his conversations with real estate agents and retirees, Selby knows that the presence of a good hospital is crucial. "Having a thriving full-service hospital and other health services plays a big part in attracting people here," he said.

The demographics-driven movement back to small-town and rural Canada also has important environmental implications. Rural land surrounding small cities is going to rise in value. Providing sewage, fire, and police services in formerly rural communities will be difficult. The pressure on farmland will increase. So will the pressure on forests and aquifers. These are priceless resources that must be protected for the generations to come. That should be done before the newcomers arrive, because once they are installed it will be much harder to impose new regulations. It's time to start preparing for the movement of the boomers from the big cities to the small ones. Let's not wait to be surprised by the inevitable once again.

Chapter 3

Investing for the Long Term

I n April 1996, the *Globe and Mail* launched its "boomer portfolio": $100,000 worth of stocks in companies believed well positioned to benefit from the changing needs and demands of the boomers. The idea behind the portfolio was that, since the boomers are the largest cohort of the Canadian population, above-average gains could be made by investing in companies selling services and products that boomers would be most likely to use as they moved through their 40s and 50s.

Two years later, the theory was looking good. The portfolio (which exists on paper only) was worth $169,173 – a robust gain of 67.4%, better than the Toronto Stock Exchange's 300 index (up 49.6%) and the Dow Jones index of U.S. stocks (up 59.3%) and just behind another American index, the Standard & Poor's 500, which was up 69.7%.

These are precisely the results a demographic analysis of the current investment climate would predict. Such an analysis points to a long-term upward trend in stock prices powered by the movement of the boomers from their spending to their investing years. The boomers are discovering stocks, just as they discovered other products and services when they needed them – baby food shortly after they were born, then hula hoops and other toys, then schools, beer, apartments, houses, minivans, and more recently Prozac and sport utility vehicles.

Because the big generation is focussed on the stock market,

stocks in general are in demand, leading to higher average stock prices. And the stocks of companies whose businesses are favoured by the demographic shift should be at the head of the parade. That's why a boomer portfolio outperforms even a rising stock market. The validity of this approach was confirmed by the performance of a boomer-oriented fund that actually invests real money. The CIBC North American Demographics Fund, launched in 1996, scored a 43.2% increase during 1997, more than three times as much as the TSE 300.

Nevertheless, investors should proceed with caution because demographics explain only two-thirds of a story, and the other third is also important. "Sometimes you pick a bad company in a good niche," says Stephen Northfield, the *Globe* writer who designed the boomer portfolio. An example is Northfield's pick of White Rose Crafts and Nursery Sales Ltd., of Unionville, Ontario, down 43% in the portfolio's first two years despite the growing popularity of gardening in an aging population. Unfortunately, says Northfield, White Rose's management hasn't been able to exploit a favourable demographic environment. A couple of Northfield's other picks, nursing home operator Extendicare Inc. and funeral company Loewen Group Inc., also performed poorly on the stock market – but then neither really belongs in a boomer portfolio at this time because boomers don't yet need their services.

On the other hand, huge gains by MDS Inc. (up 151%) and Trimark Financial (up 139%), companies that benefit from the growing demand among middle-aged boomers for medical and financial services respectively, compensated for the poor performance of White Rose – an example of the benefits of the diversity that a basket of stocks such as a mutual fund provides.

Northfield figures it will take five years to determine conclusively whether the demographic theory of investing is valid. He hopes to keep the portfolio going that long because the newspaper's readers are fascinated by the notion of investment based on the demographic shift. "I'll write 20 stories in a row without getting a single phone call and when [the monthly update on the boomer portfolio] comes out, I get tons of response. It's an approach people can understand. They say, 'Oh yeah, other people are like me, we're all buying recreational vehicles and we're all travelling and gardening.'"

The boomer portfolio, like most other stocks, plunged when the markets turned downward in August 1998. But as *Boom, Bust & Echo 2000* went to press, the portfolio was still up almost 20% since its inception – much better than the performance of the Toronto Stock Exchange's 300 index or that of fixed income investments during the same time period. Demographic phenomena express themselves over the long term and, in investment, the long term is at least five years and preferably much longer. Corrections are a normal, even necessary, part of stock market behaviour, and short-term gyrations in no way invalidate the usefulness of demographics as an investment tool.

Stocks, of course, are not the only available investment vehicle. Three other asset classes exist – real estate, fixed-income investments (including bonds, treasury bills, and bank deposits), and collectibles (such as art, antiques, classic cars, stamps, and coins). But in an aging population, stocks are the most promising. This chapter will examine the reasons why the stock market has a bright future in Canada and will suggest what sorts of stocks are most likely to do well as the population ages. There are plenty of potential stocks like Trimark and MDS out there. You just have to know how to spot them.

For David Cork, an Ottawa stockbroker and author of *The Pig and the Python* who bases his investment philosophy on demographics, the case of Chrysler is particularly instructive. The minivan, the wheels of the boom, turned Chrysler into a profitable carmaker. Yet at the time this new vehicle was being developed, Chrysler's stock was worth only US$2 and its management was begging for government help to fend off bankruptcy. At the same time, General Motors and Ford also had minivan prototypes in the planning stages. But Chrysler moved first, launching the MagicWagon in 1983. In early 1998, after Chrysler Corp. announced it would merge with Daimler-Benz AG of Germany, its stock was trading at around US$50.

In North America, Chrysler was in the right place – the

minivan – at the right time, just as the boomers were producing children and needing roomier, but not too expensive, cars. Being in the right place at the right time has always been the secret to successful investing, but it's much easier said than done. The advantage of demographics is that they give us a road map to find that place and time. When you live in a country where almost a third of the population is reaching the same stage of life over the same 20-year period, then you own an investment road map drawn on a large scale.

At the millennium, however, Chrysler has a problem that can be summed up in three words: the baby bust. Because the bust is smaller than the boom, says Cork, "Chrysler has a head count problem," which may explain its eagerness to strengthen its position by merging with Daimler-Benz, whose luxury vehicles appeal to wealthier boomers who have passed the minivan stage of life.

The merger – and others that industry observers are predicting for the future – was not surprising given the problems the demographic shift presents for the entire auto industry (see Chapter 5). So far, however, Chrysler's strategy, which is to design different vehicles for different demographic cohorts, has been successful. Jeeps and Durango trucks are popular with boomers and pre-boomers who have outgrown minivans. Meanwhile, the MagicWagon minivan retains its appeal to boomers raising families, while the Neon is doing well with younger buyers who don't yet need a family vehicle. This latter market, for smaller, cheaper cars, will rebound over the next two decades as members of the echo buy their first cars.

To understand why Chrysler and other stocks have soared so high in the 1990s, it helps to remember what happened to the asset class that captured the boomers' attention in the 1980s – real estate. In retrospect, it seems amazing that so many of us were surprised by the real estate boom of the 1970s and 1980s. Starting in the late 1960s and continuing for 20 years, more than 9 million people left their parents' homes and needed places of their own to live in. We knew they weren't all going to pitch tents on rural communes. We knew most of them would want apartments and houses in the major cities of Canada. We knew that the supply of land, and therefore of apartments and houses, in those cities was limited. Finally, we knew, or should have known, about the law of supply and demand, which states that if demand for a commodity increases faster than supply, the price of that commodity will rise. So when apartment rents and house prices soared, why was anyone taken by surprise?

The Canadian real estate boom was not only predictable, it was inevitable (see Chapter 2). People whose eyes were open to the obvious made fortunes buying and selling urban real estate in Canada. During that period, when the members of a generation as large as the entire population of Ontario were all singing the same tune – "Gimme shelter" – real estate was the best asset to invest in. But by the 1990s, most of the boomers had made their entry into the real estate market. As a result, demand dropped and the real estate market went flat. Those who were caught holding highly leveraged real estate invest- ments were punished for ignoring demographic reality. When demand moves on, the bubble bursts. That too is demographics-based investing.

In a young population, money, like real estate, is a commodity in demand. In the 1970s and 1980s, some commentators expressed despair that Canadians, renowned for their tendency to save, had sud- denly become big spenders. This was an example of how easily a phe- nomenon based purely on demographics can be mistaken for a value shift. In fact, people in their 40s and 50s were still saving during those decades. But at the same time, almost 10 million young adults were entering the job and housing markets and buying their first cars, furni- ture, and appliances while many of them were also trying to pay off student loans. How and what were they supposed to save?

Just as the price of real estate went up because a huge number of people wanted it at the same time, so did the price of money. That's why we witnessed the spectacle of Canadian banks paying double- digit interest rates on savings accounts. But by the mid-1990s, the boom generation had bought most of the houses, appliances, and cars it needed. The baby-bust generation that entered the labour and rental housing markets during the 1990s is smaller than the boom, and many of them, because of the shaky job market, have had difficulty qualifying for credit. As a result, the demand for money has flattened and interest rates have declined.

Canadians are still great savers, and many older investors cling to the hope that the lucrative interest rates of 1981 will soon return. Demographics say that won't happen. Older people lend to younger people as well as to companies and governments. Through the 1970s and into the 1980s, many younger people were putting tremendous pressure on the money of a much smaller number of older people. But, as the millennium approaches, the boomers are transforming themselves from a generation of borrowers to a generation of savers, lenders, and investors. The result is that per capita debt levels will decline in the years ahead. At the same time, because both the boomers and the generations that preceded them will be competing to lend to a smaller number of young borrowers, interest rates will stay low.

In general, the incomes of people under 40 are completely committed to raising families and paying down debts, while people over 40 gradually have more discretionary income. By 2006, the entire 9.9-million-strong boom generation will be in the 40-to-60 group of savers. Both the boomers and the World War II generation have two strong incentives to save for retirement: an unwillingness to be totally dependent on public or company pension plans, and the tax advantages available to those who invest in Registered Retirement Savings Plans (RRSPs).

Some analysts have questioned the notion that the boomers are becoming savers, pointing to a sharp decline in the savings rate during the 1990s. But the savings rate, as defined by Statistics Canada, is not a useful measure of what is actually happening in the financial lives of Canadians. Statistics Canada defines the savings rate as after-tax income minus expenditures as a percentage of after-tax income. The flaws in this definition are that it ignores capital gains and counts money spent to reduce debt as an expenditure. These flaws are the reason for an apparent anomaly of recent years – a decline in the savings rate at the same time as Canadians were increasing their total net worth.

To understand boomer behaviour, in the financial or any other aspect of their lives, it's always important to keep in mind one salient fact – the boomers are getting older but they are not yet old. All but a handful of the eldest are still in their 30s and 40s, with the peak of the boom in 1998 being 38. This means many boomers still have children who are costing them a lot of money. It also means many of them still have mortgages. Yet, as their disposable incomes increase, they are paying down their mortgages at a rapid rate. Because mortgage interest is paid in after-tax dollars, paying down the principal of a mortgage is an excellent investment. And, although such payments are technically expenditures, in the long run they save the payer a great deal of money.

In addition to getting rid of their mortgages, older boomers have begun investing in the stock market in a big way, primarily through mutual funds, which have grown at a blistering rate, accounting for 11.2% of Canadians' assets by 1997, compared to only 0.9% in 1981. Many of these assets are invested in stocks that have appreciated substantially during the 1990s. Real estate, especially homes bought by older boomers in the 1970s and early 1980s, has also risen in value. And while these capital gains are not recognized in the savings rate, it's a fact that people whose homes and investments have become more valuable are richer and often act that way. Jim Davidson, who has a bustling business buying cars for boomers too busy to do the job themselves (see Chapter 4), finds that his customers are increasingly opting for fully loaded vehicles costing much more than the cars they are trading in. "A lot of it has to do with the stock market," he says. "They don't necessarily sell stocks to buy a car, but the fact the stocks have gone up makes them feel richer."

But while they might splurge every six years for a car, as they get older the boomers will be investing more and spending less. What does this changed demographic environment mean for the future of interest rates? In answering that question, one should keep in mind that loan demand is not the only factor that determines interest rates. Government fiscal and monetary policies, domestic political uncertainty, and economic and political events outside Canada all play a part. But those are usually short-term phenomena. Over the long term, the composition and economic behaviour of the population are the most important determinants of the price of money. Demographics tell us that for the foreseeable future Canada will have more savers and fewer spenders, and that means the price of money – the interest rate – will stay low.

We will be living in this low-interest-rate world for many years to come. But it does not follow that Canadians should abandon all fixed-income investments. In fact, in a period of falling interest rates, long-term bonds are an attractive investment. Bonds do poorly in inflationary times because inflation reduces the value of both the principal and the income. Bonds also react negatively to rising interest rates, which make the yields of existing bonds less attractive by comparison. Conversely, low inflation and falling interest rates make bonds more valuable. For demographic reasons, the North American economy at the end of the 20th century is in the midst of an era of low inflation and falling interest rates. Moreover, because governments have balanced their budgets, they do not need to issue new bonds, a circumstance that further enhances the value of existing ones. The prospect of long-term low inflation, therefore, means that bonds offer good real rates of return as well as a chance for capital gains, with low risk.

As the millennium approaches, Canadian governments find themselves in the exhilarating situation of enjoying balanced budgets and, in some cases, surpluses, at a time when an aging population is accumulating surplus capital that needs a home. The demographic shift thus provides Canada with an opportunity to repatriate its foreign debt, which in 1997 stood at $417 billion for all levels of government and their enterprises. When the government's creditors are in Canada, the interest they earn is spent in Canada, creating growth and employment. Moreover, if we don't need other people's money, we won't need to raise our own rates whenever the United States or some other foreign creditor raises its rates. In an interdependent world of global capital flows, we will never have interest rates made entirely in Canada. But as savers bring more of the national debt back home, they will also increase Canadian control over Canadian interest rates.

Although low interest rates are good for the national treasury, they are not good for people saving for retirement. If all a person's money is in guaranteed investment certificates paying 5% or less, her savings won't grow quickly enough to deliver the income she will need to enjoy her retirement years. Savers need to find investments that offer a higher rate of return. Increasingly, they have been turning to the stock markets, which went from strength to strength during the 1990s until a major correction took place in August 1998.

When the first edition of *Boom, Bust & Echo* appeared in the spring of 1996, the TSE 300 composite index stood at 5,000. Two years later, the index was hovering just below 8,000. The comparable U.S. index, the Dow Jones, has surged even higher. Front-end boomers are propelling markets in both countries by putting an ever larger portion of their retirement savings into stocks. Why? Because, given the low returns available on real estate and cash, they have no acceptable alternative. And because they have little time and want their money professionally managed, they are focussing their attention on mutual funds. The first edition of this book declared that equity mutual funds would be Canada's next investment boom. That forecast has been borne out and the boom is a long way from over.

The future doesn't just arrive suddenly one day. There are always early warning signs. House prices in parts of urban Canada spiked up as early as 1974, even though only a handful of front-end boomers had yet acquired enough cash for a down-payment on a house. That was the real estate boom announcing itself well before it arrived in full force. Similarly, 1993 was an advance signal of the future of equity mutual funds. Interest rates were lower and stocks were enjoying a banner year. "GIC refugees" bailed out of fixed-income investments and poured huge sums into equity funds. For many, this was their first experience with an asset that carried the risk of loss of capital. Sure enough, the next year saw a sub-par performance by the stock market, scaring some of the refugees back to GICs. But as Canadians become older and more knowledgeable, they are learning that over the long term, common stocks outperform other investment vehicles. Despite the nerve-racking ups and downs that are a normal part of equity markets, anyone who held stocks for any 15-year period between 1924 and 1997 enjoyed a positive return. Moreover, dividends from stocks get more favourable tax treatment than interest from bonds, treasury bills, or GICs.

As any reader of the daily financial pages knows, there is never unanimity about the future of the stock market. Some analysts, noting that price-earnings ratios have risen to the 20-times range, more than twice what they were in the 1970s and 1980s, suggest that stocks are overvalued. But stock prices were low in the 1970s and 1980s because the boomers had driven interest rates to record highs. Why own stocks when government bonds are yielding almost 20%?

The surge in stock prices in the 1990s is just as boomer-driven as the high interest rates of the 1980s. "What's going on now surprises a lot of people because they have never witnessed this in the market before," says David Cork. "But it happened in schools and in real estate. It can't be accidental that this is happening when the boom comes of age in the 1990s. So the issue becomes 'How old are the boomers and did they just start investing or are they well into it?' I say they just started. Most boomers have not yet passed 45. So it's during the next decade that they will really concentrate on investments. We are not too late to the party."

The nearly 7.5 million Canadians born before the boom are also doing their bit to keep stock markets afloat. Historically, older people are more likely to be savers than investors. But the combination of rising life expectancy and low interest rates is modifying that behaviour. With interest rates in the cellar, some retired Canadians face the danger of outliving their assets. So they are putting more of those assets into stocks in search of dividends and capital gains. The need of older Canadians for investments that offer both growth and capital protection explains the growing popularity of segregated mutual funds, which come with a guarantee that limits potential loss to the investor. The guarantee typically covers at least 75% of the money invested.

These demographic trends, in combination with the improved

competitiveness of North American industry over the past decade, favour a continuation of the stock market advance, although there are certain to be retreats along the way. "No one can ever predict what the market will do on a given day," says Cork. "What we can do is be reasonably accurate over longer term periods. All people need to accept is the fact it is going a lot higher – we don't know when, but we know it will unfold over the next 10 to 15 years. Considering that no one has been successful at timing, I don't take seriously the notion that it's dangerous to get in when the Dow is at 9,000 because it could go back to 7,000. It could also go to 11,000. There is greater risk being out than in and greater risk trying to tell when to get in."

Investors, however, must not assume that the spectacular returns of some recent years will be the norm. Just as the price of houses rose during the 1980s more than demographics would have predicted, so the price of some stocks and value of some mutual funds have risen higher than demographic analysis would have forecast. Stock markets attract speculators who sometimes drive share prices to

A winning approach

unreasonable levels. Then the speculators take their profits, which drives prices down again. Meanwhile, various sectors of the economy have their ups and downs as do different regions of the world; Asia's economy, for example, boomed through most of the 1980s and 1990s but was mired in crisis at the end of the 1990s. Such short-term fluctuations cause serious problems for short-term investors. They should not trouble long-term investors.

When is the best time to invest in stocks? "When you have money," advises legendary investment manager John Templeton. Both Templeton and the equally renowned Warren Buffett believe in buying well-managed growth companies when the price is right and holding them for the long term. This philosophy fits well with a demographic approach because demographics point to trends that unfold over long periods. Moreover, the buy-and-hold approach has the important advantage of deferring tax payments on capital gains, further increasing the investor's returns.

It's one thing to decide to buy and hold. It's another and more difficult matter to decide what to buy and hold. It was easier for the boomers' parents. They bought houses to live in and watched them appreciate in value by ten times and, in some cases, much more. They put their extra cash into risk-free, fixed-income investments that earned double-digit returns. But this passive investment strategy doesn't work any more because there is no baby boom to drive up the price of money and real estate. And while it's true that the stock market as a whole rises in value over the long term, that doesn't mean choosing stocks at random is a reliable strategy.

Currently, most new investors are putting their money into mutual funds, thereby hiring professional investors to choose their stocks for them. But professional help is costly. Some mutual funds take 3% up front as a purchase fee and a further 2.5% as an annual management fee. These fees are easy to stomach if the fund consistently outperforms the market. But few funds do that, and the fees reduce long-term returns. The advantage of buying stocks directly is that the only fees are brokerage commissions, paid when the investor buys and sells. These costs can be minimized by trading through a discount broker and minimized still further by issuing buy and sell orders by computer rather than by telephone.

Using the demographic shift as a basis for stock selection is no guarantee of success, as the case of White Rose illustrates. But choosing companies well placed to serve the needs of aging boomers helps steer the investor towards growing businesses and away from cyclical stocks where success requires getting in and out at the right time. Cork has his own fictional boomer portfolio, published in the *Toronto Star*. It contains twelve stocks, six Canadian and six American. They are Canadian Imperial Bank of Commerce, C.I. Mutual Funds, Travelers Group, Franklin Resources, and Charles Schwab & Co. (all in the financial services industry), Loblaw Companies (a grocery chain), Chapters Inc. (books), Sleeman Breweries Inc., Harley-Davidson Inc. (motorcycles that appeal to hip boomers), Estée Lauder Cosmetics Inc., Callaway Golf Co., and Bombardier Inc.

Eleven of these companies are obviously in fields favoured by middle-aged boomers. But what about Bombardier? The Montreal-based manufacturer makes a wide variety of transportation equipment, from snowmobiles to executive jets. It has products that are used by every age group. So why is it a boomer stock? Because the front end of the boom is at the stage of life when time is in short supply. Just as Chrysler's minivan was the right product at the right time in the 1980s, so Bombardier's Regional Jet is the right product at the right time in the 1990s. The Regional Jet is a 50-seat plane that for the first time allows airlines to make a profit on non-stop routes connecting small and medium-sized cities to big ones. Before Bombardier invented the plane, travellers from Ottawa had to change planes at the Toronto "hub" to get to New York or Chicago. Now they can fly non-stop in a Regional Jet. "The Regional Jet is a hub-buster, and that's how it fits into the portfolio," says Cork. "Boomers want speed and convenience."

The movement of Canadians' savings into mutual funds is accelerating every year and is having a profound impact on the financial services industry. Forty-five is the age at which an individual's attention typically starts to turn away from spending and towards saving and investing. At the start of 1992, the year the first wave of boomers turned 45, the total amount invested in equity mutual funds (including balanced funds that mix stocks and bonds) was $28 billion. By the end of March 1998, the total had swollen to $254 billion, a 900% increase. The banks set up mutual fund operations to grab a share of this fast-growing business, and other new players arrived on the scene. The result was to present consumers with a wide and often confusing array of new investment products.

Jonathan Wellum, manager of the AIC Advantage Fund, which invests in money management companies, predicts that Canadians will have $500 billion invested in mutual funds by 2002. Wellum's investment strategy is based on the demographic fact that by 2000, half of the Canadian population will be 37 or over, and increasingly relying on the financial services provided by the companies that his fund holds. "That's savings age, a fabulous population distribution for wealth management companies," he says. The Advantage Fund's success propelled AIC from the 23rd largest mutual fund company in 1996 to 12th largest in 1998; assets under its management went from $300 million to $7.3 billion. The CIBC jumped on the bandwagon, creating a financial services fund of its own.

As for AIC, investors poured so much money into its Advantage Fund that in some cases it was running up against the limit one fund is allowed to own of any stock. It got around the problem by starting another fund, Advantage II, to invest in many of the same companies, but AIC's problem foreshadows one that may cause problems for many Canadian investors in years to come: a shortage of good stocks to buy. The policy of some companies of buying back their own shares and the mergers of major companies, such as the ones proposed by four of Canada's biggest banks, reduce the number of shares on the open market. The supply problem is aggravated by the federal government's policy of limiting the foreign portion of RRSPs to 20%. This has the effect of increasing competition for good Canadian shares, driving up their prices. The government's plan to invest the Canada Pension Plan's funds in the market will put still more upward pressure on the prices of Canadian stocks.

Large investors like the CPP are attracted to large companies with large numbers of shares. For this reason, the stock of Bell Canada, the banks, and a handful of other major companies will be in ever greater demand. Increasingly, the price of such stocks will outpace the earnings growth of the companies whose ownership they represent. In other words, stock prices will be more reflective of the demand for stocks than of the ability of a company to produce dividends.

Many companies are rushing to cash in on the demand for stocks by issuing shares on the public market for the first time. However, these initial public offerings (IPOs) are risky investments. In 1997, a winning year for the market as a whole, almost half the new stocks on the Toronto Stock Exchange were worth less than their offering price at the end of the year. The quickest available solution to the problem of the stock shortage is for the federal government to raise the 20% limit on foreign equities in RRSPs. As the flood of boomer money into RRSPs becomes a torrent, a system that squeezes 80% of Canadian retirement savings into the $2^1/2\%$ of the global total of equities represented by Canadian stocks will be increasingly untenable.

The danger inherent in the 20% rule, says Cork, "is that of a balloon filling up too quickly. It can pop. In other words, the downward corrections could be greater. So let people invest elsewhere. Money should not be trapped. Otherwise, markets in Canada could go too high the way they did in Japan, where investors bid Japanese stocks way beyond any reasonable level."

Japanese stock prices eventually came down to earth with a thud as retired Japanese started to sell their equity holdings. Canadian stocks are no more likely than Japanese stocks to move in only one direction. That's why wise financial planners advise their clients to maintain balanced portfolios, whose proportion of equities diminishes as the investor approaches retirement.

The similarities between the investment environments of Japan in the 1970s and Canada in the 1990s should not be exaggerated. A major difference is that Canadian real estate, unlike Japanese real estate, is affordable to the average income earner, with the result that Canadians will continue to keep a large part of their assets in houses and cottages. Nevertheless, there is room for a major increase in stock buying by Canadians. Annual RRSP contributions rose from $15 billion in 1991 – just before the mass of boomers were about to enter their prime savings years – to $26.2 billion in 1996. Yet Canadians as a whole still contribute only a small proportion of the maximum allowable amount to their RRSPs. By 1997, they had accumulated a total of $168 billion of allowable contributions that had not been used in previous years. As more and more boomers hit 50 in the coming years, a large part of this unused contribution room will be used up.

CHOOSING INVESTMENTS

Let's look more closely at what investments stand to benefit most at the millennium from the demographic shift. Companies operating in such industries as financial services, pharmaceuticals, health care, and gambling are in the right place at the right time as the boom generation moves into its fifth decade. But the non-boomer majority also has needs to be filled. As the offspring of the boomers turn 20, companies offering cheap products with youth appeal will have an edge in the marketplace they didn't possess a few years ago. It should also be remembered that as the front-end boomers get older, increasing numbers of them will die. This will boost the relative importance of younger Canadians – Generation X (the back-end boomers), the baby bust, and the echo – in Canadian society. Finally, let's not forget that Canada is a trading nation that sells its products all over the world. This means that a Canadian company whose products appeal mainly to young people is not necessarily a poor investment if it can export successfully to countries with young populations.

In considering investments in industries well placed to benefit from demographic change, it must never be forgotten that demographics-based investing is not a way to get rich quick. Rather, it is a strategy for identifying long-term trends that will lead to long-term growth in various sectors of the economy. It is also a useful analytical tool for the investor. But it is only a useful tool if the investor understands the significance of demographic data and the importance of correct timing. A good example of the dangers of getting demographics wrong was found in the *Globe and Mail* in February 1998, in the "Stars and Dogs" column, which contrasts rising stocks with falling ones. The writer was dumbfounded by the decline in the shares of the nursing home operator Extendicare. "Let's see here," the columnist wrote. "Nursing homes, aging population. Sounds like an investment opportunity." This columnist is confused. While it's true that the average age of North Americans is rising, the largest cohort, the boom, was 32 to 51 in 1998, still many years away from needing nursing homes. In fact, at the millennium, only a small percentage of the North American population needs Extendicare's nursing home services.

Compounding the *Globe* columnist's confusion was the steady rise on the New York Stock Exchange of La-Z-Boy Inc., a manufacturer of reclining chairs that "have all the trendiness of Hush Puppies and cardigan sweaters." Yet the demographic situation at the end of the 20th century favours a company like La-Z-Boy. That's because resting is one of the fastest-growing leisure activities (see Chapter 6) and La-Z-Boy makes good resting equipment.

It is a sad fact but true that most people do more research before buying a car than before making an investment. In a time when governments are under severe pressure to modify the public pension scheme, people who want to enjoy their golden years in comfort and style had better start accumulating some gold. To be successful, both investments and investment advisers should be chosen very carefully. Some of these advisers charge commissions on every financial transaction. This gives them an incentive to trade securities in a client's portfolio frequently. But demographics-based investing is founded on the idea of selecting solid companies in industries certain to grow over the medium to long term because of demographic change and holding on to them. Such an investment strategy is ill-suited to frequent buying and selling of stocks. The investor basing his moves on demographics would be better off with an investment adviser who is rewarded on a fee basis rather than by commissions.

With those caveats in mind, let's look briefly at some of the industries that can't help but grow as a result of demographic change at the millennium. The following is the demographic big picture that points the way to areas of the economy that will grow as the age structure of the population changes. The actual stock picking is up to individual investors and their financial advisers.

FINANCIAL SERVICES

As they age, people's financial priorities change. They move from debt management to asset management. When you are young, you are a borrower. In your 30s, you are earning income to pay off the money you borrowed in your 20s and early 30s. In your 40s and 50s, you are trying to build a nest egg for retirement. Except for Generation X, all of the boom will be over 40 by 2000. This means the financial services industry has a huge new customer base. Not only have these people reached the stage where they can let some of their earnings accumulate, but many of them will be coming into inheritances as their parents die.

It's estimated that $1 trillion will pass from Canadians now over 55 to younger generations. But the economic impact of these inheritances should not be exaggerated. For one thing, the total may not reach $1 trillion; many people spend large sums on health care in their last few years, and older Canadians may be spending more because of cutbacks to the health care system. And this transfer of assets, large though it may be, may do little for the economy if the bulk of the inheritances goes to the boomers. Money willed from an 85-year-old to a 55-year-old merely passes from one saver to another. The money is already in the economy, and it won't stimulate much new economic activity beyond fees for lawyers and brokers. Moreover, these legacies will be split up into several pieces and so into relatively small amounts. After all, the reason Canada had a baby boom was that, for a 20-year period, Canadian couples were producing three and four children each. On the other hand, money that passes from grandparents to grandchildren, from people born before 1940 to people born after 1967, will give a boost to the economy. This money will flow to baby-busters or to members of the echo generation, who will spend it on cars, houses, and other necessities of life. Money that is willed to charities will also tend to stimulate new economic activity because much of it will fall into the hands of poor people, who are spenders.

People acquiring large sums of money in one lump sum need advice to help them invest it wisely. Some money will be moving out of real estate owned by parents and into mutual funds and other investment vehicles sold by the financial services industry. As a result, investment dealers, law firms, mutual fund companies, financial planners, and banks are poised for major growth over the next two decades. Finally, insurance will also benefit from demographic trends. An older population has accumulated a lot of valuables that need insuring. An older population also produces a large number of travellers, who need travel insurance.

The stocks of well-managed players in the financial services industry will grow in this climate although there will certainly be setbacks along the way – shares in financial services companies often suffer above-average volatility. In deciding whether to invest in this industry, one key question needs to be answered: Has the average 35-year-old bought all the mutual funds he is ever going to buy, or has he just started? The investor's answer to that question will determine whether he decides to invest in the financial services industry.

HEALTH CARE SERVICES

"The aging baby boomer population wants to remain young and is very willing to use drugs that counteract some of the ravages of aging," pharmaceutical analyst Jack Lamberton told *Business Week* in May 1998. And, he might have added, the drug industry is very willing to spend vast sums of money to give the boomers what they want because the potential rewards are huge. One of the "ravages" some aging boomers were eager to reverse was a decline in sexual performance. Viagra quickly became a household word in the spring of 1998 when Pfizer Co. released it onto the U.S. market as the first effective drug therapy for impotence. Wall Street analysts predicted that sales eventually could reach as much as US$11 billion a year – a fantastic sum considering that, at the time of Viagra's release, annual sales of all pharmaceuticals worldwide totalled US$300 billion.

Not surprisingly, the success of Viagra boosted Pfizer's share price. Patent protection and the inevitability of rising sales for both established products and new ones make drug companies a promising investment for long-term growth. Driving this growth will be a new wave of blockbuster pills, many of them directed at age-related ailments. The new medicines target such ailments as elevated cholesterol, arthritis, diabetes, and osteoporosis. Other new drugs will attempt to moderate, if not cure, less serious afflictions of middle age such as baldness and wrinkles.

The instant popularity of Viagra highlighted a new direction for the pharmaceutical industry. Previously, researchers concentrated on trying to cure or control severe illnesses. Now, an increasing amount of attention is focussed on ailments of middle age that are neither life-threatening nor even debilitating. This phenomenon is driven by demographics, namely the movement of the huge boom generation into middle age. Because the boomers are such a large market, the drug companies have every incentive to pour big dollars into treatments that could help them cling to the health and vigour of their youth. An unfortunate result of this demographic phenomenon is that more money is being spent finding ways to preserve the skin, hair, and sex lives of millions of middle-aged boomers than trying to find cures for other, more serious health problems – for example, Hepatitis C, a sometimes fatal disease that afflicts 400,000 Canadians and 4 million Americans and is notoriously under-researched.

This is not to suggest that all health preoccupations of middle-aged boomers are trivial, because they most definitely are not. For example, every man over the age of 45 has some degree of enlargement of the prostate gland. After the age of 60, one in ten men suffers serious urinary problems as a result of this disorder. Drugs and medical devices that can reduce the need for surgery to correct these problems will find a huge market. Diabetes (see Chapter 9) is another serious problem that worsens in an aging population. Type II diabetes occurs in overweight, middle-aged adults. The boomers, who lead a more sedentary lifestyle than previous generations, are vulnerable to this disease, which will reach epidemic proportions over the next 20 years. If not managed effectively, diabetes can lead to severe complications such as kidney failure, heart disease, and blindness. Products that help diabetics manage their disease will be in increasing demand.

Drugs are just one part of the health services industry. Important investment opportunities also exist in the health care delivery business. The boomers' bodies are starting to wear out just as governments are putting a lid on health care expenditures. Partly to cut costs and partly in response to changes in medical practice, hospital stays are being shortened. This means that care formerly delivered in publicly funded hospitals is being transferred to the home. Some of this care will be delivered free by relatives of the patient – that's why the move to home care is such a popular cost-cutting device for provincial governments.

But there is a gap between the services that hospitals used to provide and the services that families of sick people are capable of providing. These missing services could include follow-up treatments, health maintenance, or physiotherapy as well as delivery of meals, doing laundry, and housecleaning. Health care entrepreneurs will develop systems to deliver these services profitably in ways that will allow new companies to grow to meet the surging demand for home care. These new businesses will employ health care consultants, doctors, nurses, physiotherapists, pharmacists, chefs, nutritionists, and house cleaners. Where will the demand come from? These services are already needed by people in the fast-growing over-80 population, the parents of the front-end boomers. But the big growth, as always, will come from the boomers themselves. They won't fall apart all at once, but a person's need for health care increases after the age of 50. The boomers started turning 50 in 1997, marking the beginning of an extended period of growth for the home health care delivery business.

At first, the greatest demand will be for the services of doctors and other caregivers. Later, it will be for services previously provided in hospitals. While politicians and the medical establishment debate whether and how private enterprise should be allowed to supplement the publicly funded system (see Chapter 9), the existing private tier is growing quickly.

London Eye Centre Inc., which does laser eye surgery to correct nearsightedness and other eye problems, had only a New Westminster office when the first edition of *Boom, Bust & Echo* came out in 1996; by 1998 it had expanded to downtown Vancouver and Honolulu and was eyeing Japan. King's Health Centre, a luxurious private clinic in downtown Toronto that offers non-insured medical services as well as services paid for by medicare, had plans to issue stock and to open branches in several Ontario cities.

Croft Clinic, due to open in 1998 in Coquitlam, east of Vancouver, is an example of how the private sector plans to exploit service cuts in the public sector. One of its services will be postoperative care for patients who don't want to return home after surgery and would prefer to recuperate in comfort while attended by doctors and nurses. This service is not covered by medicare and so can be freely offered by a for-profit health care company. As well, like other private clinics, Croft will be able to offer a full range of health services to foreigners.

As the millennium approaches, the most controversial issue in health care is whether the private sector should be allowed to offer medically necessary services covered by medicare to Canadians prepared to pay extra for faster or better care. Under the Canada Health Act, doctors who operate within the Canadian medicare system are not allowed to charge patients directly for medically necessary services. Those who do must opt out of medicare. Private clinics in Manitoba and Alberta, which had been billing provincial health plans for covered services and then charging patients an extra fee for using a private facility, were forced to stop that practice as a result of financial penalties imposed by Ottawa on the respective provincial governments. Potential investors in new private clinics should satisfy themselves that the business plan is not predicated on a change in federal policy that may not take place.

Population aging will also create opportunities for real estate developers, although the big growth won't commence until after 2010, when the early boomers are entering their 60s. Only a minority of seniors live in retirement homes; most live on their own or with their children. The boomers, many of whom see themselves as perennially young, are not likely to embrace conventional retirement villages. The winners among real estate companies will therefore be the innovators who figure out how to provide for the boomers' changing needs without making them feel old. A successful housing community for aging boomers will grow and develop along with its residents. It might start as a village of houses with a golf course and other recreational facilities. Later, hostel-type accommodation could be built for widows and widowers who need a greater level of service. Later still, nursing homes could be constructed as they are required.

Dr. James Swanney, chairman of Specialized Surgical Services Inc., operator of the Croft Clinic, would like to get together with a developer to create a chain of clinics integrated into new housing developments aimed at people with special health care needs. He had the idea after he paid $2,000 for a nurse to stay with a sick elderly relative for two days. This patient did not really need a nurse with him at all times, but he did need one who could be at his bedside within a few minutes. What if people could live in private homes in a residential development that contained a clinic with professional staff? "That is the sort of new thinking we are going to need if we are going to prevent the massive warehousing of older people. It would be so much better if people could live in their own homes, with their dog, cat, and visiting grandchildren – and have medical care immediately available."

Such an arrangement would be of interest not just to older people but also to young families with severely disabled children. "A child who has Duchenne's muscular dystrophy at the age of 7 is a bigger burden on the family than a geriatric who has had a stroke at 87. If the health facility were there, the family could have a much more normal life. You would no longer have to turn the home into a mini-hospital."

LEISURE AND RECREATION

Gambling, one of the fastest-growing leisure activities in North America, is a relatively easy industry for the investor to follow. Both serious and recreational gamblers tend to be people in their 50s and 60s who have enough discretionary income to afford this pastime. The boomers are about to move into their gambling years (see Chapter 6). Several major casino companies as well as hotel chains deeply involved in gambling are listed on the New York Stock Exchange.

Other parts of the leisure and recreation sector require more research on the part of the investor. Gardening, for example, is already blossoming spectacularly and will continue to do so. This is the classic case of an activity that the 20-year-old has no time for and the 50-year-old loves. Gardening is an excellent business because gardeners need a constant supply of things, bulbs and seeds and fertilizers and

A growing activity

tools and books. Someone is going to do such a good job of supplying these things that her operation will become the Body Shop of the gardening business.

Upmarket travel will be yet another major growth area as the boom ages (see Chapter 6). But this is a complex, risky, and highly competitive business, and only the most capable players will be able to exploit that growth for steady profits. Innovative niche marketers who can deliver quality and service will probably show stronger growth rates than volume merchandisers. While a 30-year-old buys a plane ticket on a charter to Cuba, a 55-year-old is ready for something at once more exclusive and exciting, like a cruise for 20 people down the coast of Antarctica with naturalists on board to explain the sights.

Home fitness will continue to enjoy growth but the heyday of the fitness club is over. Younger people frequent fitness clubs, which is why this business grew rapidly during the 1980s. Older people can save time by buying their own equipment, and they can afford it. That's the reason for the growth of the home fitness industry over the 1990s; it will enjoy solid growth into the new century.

RETAILING

This will be one of the most volatile areas of the economy over the next decade as retailers respond to growth in both the over-50 and twenty-something segments of the population. As Chapter 5 explains, these two segments have different needs. The older consumer is more interested in quality and service while the younger one wants low prices. Although the older consumer is willing to spend more money to get what he wants, he has already satisfied most of his material needs. Because aging boomers are such a dominant force in the Canadian retail marketplace, storekeepers will increasingly have to rely on margin, rather than volume, to find their profits. But customers will accept high margins only if the retailer is delivering added value. They will look for that added value in a smaller store, either independent or franchised. The big store is likely to become increasingly alienating to the older customer who prefers careful service in a calm atmosphere.

On the other hand, stores offering low price and high fashion can profit from the shift of the echo generation into its young adult years. The maturing of the echo kids is especially good news for the apparel industry. We are all retail analysts, because we all inspect retail stores on a regular basis. Investors will have plenty of opportunity to decide which ones have what it takes to exploit the demographic shifts taking place at the millennium.

FUNERALS AND CEMETERIES

Everybody uses this service eventually, which is why the bereavement industry has long been a favourite of some investors. But one has to be careful. In the late 1990s, the fastest-growing segment of the Canadian population is the over-80s, which means funeral services are temporarily a growth industry. But a much smaller cohort will enter that age group over the next 20 years, resulting in slower growth. The real boom in this business is three decades in the future, when large numbers of boomers begin to expire. Post-boomers who time their investments well should be able to profit.

COLLECTIBLES

There's one other asset category that is a lot more fun to own than stocks or bonds. Collectibles, which include a wide array of items from classic cars to old guitars to postage stamps, are likely to increase in value as the boomers reach the age in which discretionary income increases. Only a small portion of an individual's wealth should be invested in collectibles, and no one should make a major investment without first acquiring expertise in an area of interest. The disadvantage of collectibles is that they must be insured and protected from theft or damage. The advantage is that they add valuable diversification to an investment portfolio. Best of all, such things as fine art, antique books, or jewellery can be used and enjoyed while they appreciate in value.

Chapter 4

Jobs and the Corporation

I n the 1980s, something terrible happened to thousands of hard-working Canadians on their way up the corporate ladder: they got stuck. These weren't nine-to-fivers only putting in time to draw a weekly salary. They were people whose jobs were central to their lives and to their definitions of themselves. They were good at what they did and were making important contributions to the companies they worked for. They had fully expected to progress steadily upwards, at the very least into the ranks of middle management. But as the 1980s progressed, it gradually dawned on them that they weren't going to get even that far. They had plateaued.

By the mid-1980s, steady progress up a corporate ladder was no longer possible for many people who could have aspired to it in previous decades. Nor was a tall corporate ladder with dozens of rungs any longer necessary or desirable for most companies. The phenomenon of plateauing, or career blocking, was an early sign that the corporation as we had known it was about to undergo a major transformation. Plateauing was a result of demographic change intensified by the rapid development of labour-saving technology. As the millennium approaches, corporations are still engaged in the painful process of remaking themselves to adjust to these profound changes. At the same time, the nature of work, both within and outside the corporate world, is being redefined.

During the 1990s, small business, not large corporations, was where much of the action was in Canadian business. Small businesses were inventing new innovative technologies, developing new services, and creating new jobs. One important reason for this development was the changes, partly driven by demographics, that transformed the large corporations. Some of the best talent in these corporations either left in frustration or was downsized out of a job, thereby making a priceless new pool of talent available to small business.

Corporations don't grow and develop in isolation from the rest of society. They are social organisms and as such reflect the demographic structure of the country in which they operate. Because Canadian couples had always produced more than enough offspring to replace themselves, Canadian corporations evolved over the 20th century to accommodate a rapidly growing workforce. But after 1960, the Canadian fertility rate dropped and by the late 1960s Canadian couples were averaging fewer than two children each. Canadians were no longer replacing themselves. Consequently, 20 years later, workforce growth slowed down. At the same time, computer technology was reducing the need for labour, especially the kind of labour needed to do the routine tasks typical of entry-level jobs.

Think of the baby boom as a rectangle while the corporate structure looks like a triangle or pyramid (see Figure 2). We tried to promote a rectangle up a triangle, and it couldn't be done. The rectangle was there because a huge number of boomers entered the workforce in the 1960s and 1970s. By the mid-1980s, they were clogging up the corporate hierarchy. There weren't enough openings for them at the top, nor were there enough people for them to manage at the bottom. So they were stuck in the same old jobs.

A triangular corporate structure works when there is a large and continuing flow of new workers at the entry level, constantly maintaining the large base of the triangle. In such a context, there is a close association between age and level in an organization. The 60-year-olds at the top direct the 40-year-olds in the middle and they manage the 20-year-olds at the bottom. This system works when there are more younger than older employees, which was exactly the case over most of the 20th century in North America as the modern corporation took shape. Even during the 1930s, a period of relatively few

FIGURE 2: CANADA'S WORKING-AGE POPULATION, 1981

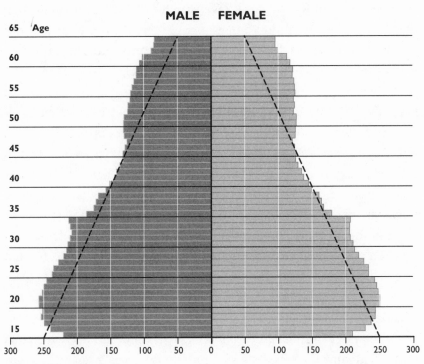

MALE   FEMALE

Population in thousands

Source: Based on Statistics Canada, *Revised Intercensal Population and Family Estimates, July 1, 1971-1991*, catalogue 91-537 occasional (July 1994).

births, the fertility rate stayed above replacement, at about 2.5 children per family. At the peak of the baby boom, it was four children per family. When the boomers grew up and went out to work, labour force growth took off in Canada, maintaining a pace of more than 3% a year, faster than any other country in the developed world. By comparison, European countries during the same period had annual labour force growth of around 1%.

Canada's economic policies in the 1960s and 1970s focussed on job creation, and these policies were successful. Canada created jobs faster than all other developed countries. Then, during the 1980s, it was the turn of the baby bust, the smaller generation that followed the baby boom, to enter the labour market. Labour force growth fell to 1.5% a year, half what it was during the 1960s and 1970s.

What do you do when there are too many people in their 40s looking for management jobs and too few in their teens and 20s to fill out the bottom of the organizational structure? Some companies tried to get older people to do younger people's work. But a 29-year-old doesn't want to do a 19-year-old's job. He thinks he's beyond that. And a 39-year-old certainly doesn't want to do a 29-year-old's job. The result was an increasingly frustrated workforce. Mid-management people were telling employees below them that they couldn't progress in their careers as quickly as they, the middle managers, had done. The implication was that the less senior workers weren't as good, when in fact their only major flaw was that there were too many of them. At the same time, information technology was enabling companies to dispense with middle managers whose major function was seen as channelling information between the upper and lower echelons. This function could now be done more directly and more quickly, but not necessarily more effectively, without human intermediaries.

During the 1980s, senior management perceived that the old organizational structure wasn't working and articles started to appear about the need for re-engineering the corporation. In most cases, this meant flattening the corporate structure. In the private sector, this was called delayering. In the public sector, it was called broad-banding, meaning putting more jobs in the same salary category or level.

Companies such as IBM Canada that took the need for change seriously went from about ten levels on the corporate hierarchy to four or five. This was the right response to the new demographic reality, because the only way to promote a rectangle up a triangle is to flatten the triangle. The companies that didn't flatten as much dumped experienced employees, laying them off or offering them early retirement or severance packages. The downsizing trend helped push the median retirement age of Canadians in 1998 to 62, which was $2^{1}/_{2}$ years lower than it had been a decade earlier. These organizations also reduced hiring during the 1980s and 1990s, and in the mid-1990s they had to tell 35-year-olds to do jobs that 25-year-olds used to do. Was it surprising that these employees were increasingly difficult to work with and increasingly disloyal to their employers?

Or that many of the most talented workers chose to sign on with flexible, small businesses rather than big corporations?

The difference between these two responses to demographic and economic change is the difference between delayering and downsizing. The latter is just reducing the workforce, and it can be done whether the corporate structure has been flattened or remains hierarchical. It is not necessary to downsize in order to delayer. A downsized employee doesn't just disappear. She may stay unemployed, or she may launch a new career as an independent contract worker. Or she may become one of the thousands of Canadians who have started new small businesses in recent years. As either a contractor or an entrepreneur, she has more independence than she enjoyed before, but she now lacks the security and fringe benefits associated with full-time employment in a large corporation.

The re-engineering of the corporation in response to demographic shifts has dramatic implications for careers. Let's take a look at the four basic career paths – linear, spiral, steady-state, and transitory –

Boomer bottleneck

and examine how each has been affected by the re-engineering of the corporation.

The linear career path is one of upward mobility towards the top. A typical case would be an engineer in a large hydro company who moves through a succession of jobs, each carrying more responsibility and a higher salary, and eventually winds up in a senior management position. This career path is associated with tall corporate pyramids. These companies, with lots of levels, are the ones we are most familiar with. Their reward system is based on promotion up a career ladder. Sometimes they add a few rungs to the top of the ladder, allowing them, in effect, to demote people while pretending to promote them.

In the spiral career path, an employee spirals up the corporate structure. In other words, lateral moves are mixed with promotions. Each lateral move involves some change of occupation: for example, a move from sales to marketing or from nursing to computer programming. Typically, an employee would have four or five of these lateral moves over a working lifetime. Some of them would be within the same organization and some would be between different organizations. In organizing a corporation to make this kind of career possible, the triangle is retained for promotions, but it must be flattened out, resulting in a much broader base and more opportunity for lateral moves. In contrast to a company using linear career paths, a corporation like this has only a few levels in its hierarchy. Its reward system is focussed less on promotions and more on the satisfaction that employees get from mastering new challenges through re-education and lifelong training. Education becomes a lifelong process (see Chapter 8).

The steady-state career path is one occupation for a lifetime: the doctor, professor, or member of the clergy. To the extent that such people work in an organization, it is one with a largely rectangular structure: the Roman Catholic church, for example, with one pope at the top, a sprinkling of archbishops and other senior clergy, and a massive rectangle of priests below. A university has a similar structure, with a president, a few vice-presidents and deans, and many professors. In these organizations, the reward system is based on autonomy, fringe benefits, and tenure. Disputes frequently occur over such things as autonomy, a larger office, or attending a conference overseas.

A worker who follows a transitory career path adopts whatever occupation is necessary to get a job. He could be a receptionist, a bicycle courier, a film editor, a management consultant, or a computer programmer. This worker might be hired by a company to work on a temporary project, be part of a temporary team brought together to solve a particular problem, or be a member of a "virtual organization" consisting of various specialists operating under a coordinator, who calls on particular members of the organization whenever their special skills or expertise are needed. This kind of self-employment – an individual working on his own – grew by 5.3% per year on average from 1990 to 1996, while paid employment grew by only 0.2%.

In the future, the fastest-growing career paths will continue to be the spiral and the transitory, although the steady-state career path will always be with us. These two paths best fit the new economy that has been shaped by demographic and technological change over the 1980s and 1990s. Transitory workers will be freelancers. Spiral workers will work in companies with flattened corporate structures. Because of demographics, the flat structure will replace the vertical organization as the norm in North America.

The growth in spiral career paths is driven by corporations deciding to flatten. The growth in transitory career paths is driven, in part, by corporations deciding to downsize. Many corporations are deciding they can no longer afford to keep a public relations specialist or an engineer on staff. But they need the services that only those specialists can provide, so they purchase them from freelancers, many of whom are former corporate employees who have become transitory workers either by choice or of necessity. Some of these former employees start out working alone and end up forming a larger business and hiring staff of their own. Both the spiral employees and the transitory freelancers are generalists more than specialists, flexible enough to adapt quickly to rapid changes in demand for their services. This does not mean that specialization is obsolete. Specialization is still important, but it has to be part of a broader context. The person who can offer a range of services within a broad specialty is the one most likely to prosper in the organization and economy of the future.

THE LATERAL ORGANIZATION

Smart corporations know they have to flatten the organizational pyramid, but that's not all. To make the new system work, a company has to install a new reward system based on providing challenging opportunities that require re-education and retraining instead of promotions up a ladder that no longer exists. This in turn requires a commitment by both employer and employee. It is futile for a company to flatten its structure and at the same time cut its retraining budget – yet that is exactly what many organizations did during the 1990s. Moreover, it is also insufficient merely to send employees on courses. The best-managed companies understand that much retraining must take place on the job, whether through apprenticeship programs, mentoring, or other kinds of training.

In a flattened organization, the employee has to move from a linear to a spiral career path. That means new duties and new responsibilities. How can people take on work they have never done before without education and training? Unless management increases the re-education and retraining budget, the flattened corporate structure will not work.

Companies that abandoned the vertical structure also need to abandon vertical thinking. A lateral company doesn't need a database listing people's academic degrees. That's appropriate for a tall corporate structure where people are going to stay in the same occupations until they go into management. Instead, a lateral organization needs to know people's job preferences, help them plan their career paths, and give them the training they need. Of course, this approach to employee management is a caring one that differs from the lean-and-mean approach that became fashionable in the 1980s and 1990s, an approach that regarded employees as interchangeable units of production needing no motivation other than fear of losing their jobs.

The mean approach is self-defeating, because companies that

invest in worker training are more profitable than those that don't. That was the conclusion of a major study conducted in 1995 for the United States Department of Labor by researchers at the Harvard and Wharton business schools and the Center for Business Innovation, a Boston research organization. "It's a landmark study demonstrating that a company's surest way to profits is to treat employees as assets," said Robert Reich, an economist and a former U.S. secretary of labour.

Matthew Barrett, chairman of a hugely profitable Canadian company, the Bank of Montreal, has revived not only the bottom line but the morale of the bank by following that philosophy. "I always find myself a bit uncomfortable when I read about some CEO who says, 'Look how macho I am, I've just laid off 10,000 people,'" he told the *Financial Post*. "My view is that when you see massive amounts of restructuring happening quickly and suddenly, that's a reflection of management asleep at the switch."

If employees are assets, it makes more sense to keep them than to get rid of them. That's why delayering is a better strategy than downsizing. That's now the opinion of Michael Hammer, the management guru whose ideas, according to the *Wall Street Journal*, "launched tens of thousands of pink slips." Hammer is the co-author of *Reengineering the Corporation: A Manifesto for Business Revolution*, one of the most influential management books of the 1990s, which advocated smashing corporate hierarchies and replacing them with teams of people that use computers to combine tasks and dispense with most supervision. In 1996, three years after the book was published, he admitted that he had paid insufficient attention to the human dimension of corporations.

Many corporations had come to the same conclusion because of the backlash against downsizing and the constant upheaval caused by misapplication of the notion of re-engineering. At a conference in Boston in 1996, Hammer pointed to Fanuc Automation North America, a joint venture of General Electric Co. and Fanuc Ltd. of Japan as an example of successful re-engineering. This company reorganized without laying off workers. Instead, it boosted employment by 3% while revenues shot up 18% over two years. The point of changing corporate structures, Hammer told the conference, "is not so much getting rid of people. It's getting more out of people."

One Canadian employer that appears to have gone overboard in downsizing is government. Since its peak in 1992, public sector employment in Canada has dropped by more than 197,000 jobs – more than the entire populations of such medium-sized cities as Regina, Sherbrooke, and St. John's. The downsizing of the public sector was implemented through a combination of early retirement, attrition, and not hiring young workers. The result of this policy in the federal public service has been to create an extremely unbalanced workforce, top heavy with older boomers. Most of the male civil servants are in their late 40s; most of the females are in their early 40s. There are few older people and almost no one under 30. This is an unhealthy situation. The absence of young civil servants means that the attitudes and perspectives of the young are shut out of government. If we want government to be irrelevant to younger Canadians, this is the way to do it. Moreover, the lack of demographic balance reduces the effectiveness of the public service. For example, in 1998 a priority of the federal government was to update its technology. Yet the absence of workers under 35, who are the most adept and up to date when it comes to technology, makes this goal far more difficult to achieve than it should be.

Workplaces that flatten must make horizontal mobility possible. Suppose a member of the legal department wants to work on health and safety within the human resources department. She needs some courses to make that career switch. In a vertical organization, there is no incentive for the vice-president of legal affairs to pay for these courses in order to lose an employee to another department. Once you flatten a corporate structure, major changes in human resource policies and procedures must follow. This is one area where the conventional wisdom in favour of pushing decision-making down the line is inappropriate. Since lateral moves are made for the well-being of the organization as a whole, the decision to make them must come from those at the top of the hierarchy charged with looking after the interests of the organization as a whole. Most companies that have started out on this path have much work to do to make the new system work.

Another area in need of reform is compensation. Employees should get paid more for lateral moves when those moves improve corporate and individual productivity. In this corporate world, salary should bear little relationship to one's place in the hierarchy. Someone who has moved laterally a few times may end up earning more than the person who has just moved up one level. But one shouldn't expect automatic raises for lateral moves – raises should go to those who have earned them.

The flat organization with a spiralling workforce confers benefits on company and workers alike. Employees motivated by new challenges and new learning opportunities are more productive than employees who feel themselves stuck in a rut with no prospect of change or promotion. As well, people who move laterally to another department seldom carry any occupational burdens or past obligations with them. All of a sudden, new ideas come rushing up to the surface. In one company, an MBA became head of the engineering division because of a lateral move. One of his first tasks was to improve the traffic situation in the loading area where, for 40 years, trucks loading and unloading had crossed one another through two gates. He said, "I know nothing about this. I'm willing to take any advice." An hourly paid worker who was directing traffic said, "If you moved one of those gates, the trucks wouldn't have to cross and we'd save several minutes a day."

That simple change saved a lot more than several minutes; over a week, it added up to several hours. It happened because the new MBA at the top had no commitment to the past policies of the division and was a lateral thinker, willing to admit that the person directing traffic knew more about the problem than he did. At the same time, the previous head of the department, with his knowledge of the division's history, remained in the company directing another division and was available for consultation when necessary. Because of their own positive experiences, both managers encouraged other lateral moves throughout the organization. Employee bragging rights in this company now focus on how many assignments one has had rather than one's level in the flattened hierarchy.

This kind of organizational structure puts a greater premium on such intangible employee characteristics as flexibility and motivation – qualities that are required if companies are to respond successfully to rapid changes in their business environments – and places less value on more tangible assets such as experience and qualifications. Rigid job descriptions are inappropriate in such a workplace. At many progressive companies, employees speak of "owning problems" rather than occupying specific jobs.

EDUCATION AND THE CHANGING CORPORATION

The changes being forced on corporations are at once a challenge and an opportunity for the educational system. Universities and colleges are logical candidates to provide the continuing education and retraining that spiral and transitory workers need, but offering a course every Monday afternoon for eight months is not going to help people who have to be retrained in a month. They need a course that is offered in concentrated form over three weeks. And it has to be delivered so that the knowledge can be applied immediately in the workplace. Spiral workers will need such courses in a huge variety of subject areas, from industrial relations to insurance law to ethics to plumbing.

A huge new adult clientele can be attracted to educational institutions, some of which experienced falling enrolments during the 1990s. But to win this business, these institutions will have to change some of their ways. Their new students will be there not to get a degree but to learn. The educational institution should not put bureaucratic roadblocks in their way. It should not tell a 40-year-old that he will be admitted only if he has a B+ in his undergraduate transcript. After 20 years of work experience, that 20-year-old transcript is irrelevant today, and because of grade inflation, his C could have been the equivalent of a B+ anyway. Decisions to admit should be based on the work record, experience, needs, and goals of the student. Educational institutions should also adapt their offerings to the changing needs of these mature students. If corporations, because of demographic and technological change, are placing more emphasis on teamwork and less on leadership, then courses on teamwork should be substituted for courses on leadership.

To succeed in adapting to the new world of lifelong education, educational institutions will have to understand that their new clientele is not the same as the youthful full-time students they are used to. The full-time student has plenty of time; the adult in a full-time job doesn't. The old ways of doing things are not where the marketplace is at the millennium, and the marketplace for re-education and training is no different from any other marketplace – it demands quality and service (see Chapter 5). That means a course compacted into a short time period that is easily accessible (where numbers warrant, it could be delivered right in the workplace), provides a mixture of theory and application, and is of the highest quality. One of the biggest issues as lifelong learning becomes essential to the functioning of the Canadian economy is whether traditional educational institutions can meet these challenges.

THE FUTURE OF JOBS

At the end of the 20th century, young people are entering a volatile, uncertain, and unsettled job market. These new entrants are the back end of the baby-bust generation and the eldest representatives of the echo. Both of these groups are fewer in number than Generation X (the back end of the boom) that preceded them. For this reason, they should be expected to do better in the job market than Gen-X has done. And, in fact, unemployment among youth was lower throughout the deep and prolonged recession of the early 1990s than it was during the milder recession of the early 1980s. To that extent, being members of a small cohort has helped the baby-busters. The Generation-Xers were the new labour market entrants in the early 1980s, and they had a tougher time.

But knowing it was worse in the early 1980s doesn't do much to cheer up an unsuccessful job-seeker in the late 1990s. Canada is coming to the end of its fourth consecutive decade of rising unemployment. During the 1950s, unemployment averaged 4.2%, rising to

5% in the 1960s, 6.7% in the 1970s, 9.4% in the 1980s, and 10.1% in the 1990s. As the recession ended in the mid-1990s, the term "jobless recovery" was coined to describe the odd phenomenon of a rebounding economy combined with slow job creation.

The reasons for this situation are well known. Shoes and fridges and tires and countless other things that once were made by Canadians for other Canadians are now imported from whichever country can make them cheapest. Canadian employers trying to survive in this world of global trade must cut costs wherever and whenever possible to be more competitive. Cutting costs often means cutting jobs.

Labour-saving technology was first embraced for demographic reasons in the 1960s and 1970s by Japan, when it was trying to compensate for labour shortages caused by falling birth rates in the 1940s. Since then, technology has taken on a life of its own. Computerized machines are used everywhere in the economy, from the checkout counter of the supermarket to a mine shaft deep below the earth. Technology continues to develop at a staggering pace, getting better and cheaper as each month goes by. The power of computers to store information and speed operations doubles every 18 months, and the cost of computing is cut in half every three years.

What does this mean for jobs? As recently as the early 1980s, it was cheaper to add workers than to add machines. But by the 1990s, the cost of labour in Canada was twice the cost of machines, according to a report published by the Conference Board of Canada in 1995. So companies added machines instead of labour. The result was improved productivity but increased unemployment. The conventional wisdom in the 1980s was that technology would eventually create as many jobs as it took. Although the jury is still out on this question, the optimistic view is increasingly being called into question. Technology continues, at a relentless pace, to destroy far more jobs than it creates. This is happening not only in Canada but right across the developed world. "Sophisticated computers will likely displace humans in the same way that work-horses were eliminated by the introduction of tractors," warns Nobel Prize-winning economist

Wassily Leontief. And in his book, *The End of Work: The Decline of the Global Labor Force and the Dawn of the Post-Market Era*, Jeremy Rifkin estimates that 90 million jobs in the United States out of a potential labour force of 124 million are vulnerable to elimination by machines.

The first jobs to go were the ones requiring minimal skills, such as routine recordkeeping or data transfer or repetitive assembly-line tasks that can be done quicker, better, and cheaper by robots. Yet these were the sorts of jobs that young boomers in the 1960s and 1970s were able to occupy with high school educations or less. The ambitious among them had plenty of opportunity to increase their skills while working their way up to better-paying, more responsible jobs.

Those unskilled entry-level jobs leading to middle-class security no longer exist. That is why the labour force participation rate for people between 15 and 24 fell to a 20-year low in 1997. Rather than jump into a labour market that has only dead-end jobs to offer the unskilled and undereducated, young Canadians are staying in school or going back to school. This is a wise decision. In 1997, 167,000 jobs in Canada disappeared for people with high school education or less, while 431,000 jobs were created for workers with postsecondary education. Virtually everybody with a postsecondary degree who enters the job market gets a job, although not always in their area of expertise (see Figure 3). Employers' preference for educated workers is entirely understandable. One of the impacts of the advance of technology is that many jobs that once required only manual skills now require the ability to read, write, and calculate. A person with a postsecondary diploma is less likely to be illiterate or innumerate than someone with only a high school degree.

What will it take to succeed in the job market of the future? For transitory and spiralling workers, the only constant will be change. In fact, the very notion of "jobs" will come to seem an anachronism during the working lives of many young Canadians. Jobs were developed during the 19th century, when factories required units of labour to do the same tasks over and over again. In the information age, workers will apply a wide range of skills to an

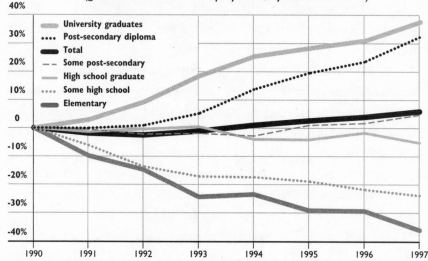

FIGURE 3: EMPLOYMENT AND EDUCATION
(growth or decline in employment, by education level)

Legend:
- University graduates
- Post-secondary diploma
- Total
- Some post-secondary
- High school graduate
- Some high school
- Elementary

Source: Calculations by David K. Foot based on Statistics Canada, *Labour Force Annual Averages, 1989-1994*, catalogue 71-529 (1995), with updates.

ever-changing series of tasks, rather than occupying a particular job. While routine tasks are being taken over by machines, non-routine ones still need people to do them. These people will need strong generic skills that can be applied to the many different challenges they will face during their careers.

One of the most important skills is communication, both oral and written. The decline in literacy has enhanced the value of those who can write clearly, concisely, and grammatically while also possessing the ability to make effective oral presentations. Interpersonal skills, including the ability to work effectively as part of a team, are also essential. So are computer skills, which have to be upgraded continually as technology advances. Finally, the successful worker of the future needs the kinds of skills that an old-fashioned liberal arts education provides: the ability to assemble information, analyze it, and think about it. People with these skills are what Robert Reich calls "symbolic analysts," workers who manipulate symbols such as mathematical data and words and who identify and solve problems. Many occupations fall into this category, from research scientists to movie directors.

But a continued demand will exist for skilled people who can work well with their hands as well as their brains. It is a paradox of Canada's labour market that with 9% of Canadian workers unemployed, many employers still can't find the workers they need. For example, many manufacturing firms in southern Ontario are having trouble finding skilled machinists and other tradespeople. Partly, this is because the demarcation line between white-collar and blue-collar work has faded as information technology has invaded the shop floor. The machinist at the millennium is a "symbolic analyst" with a vocational college degree, a knowledge of computers, and an ability to work in a team. Joe Repovs of Samco Machinery Ltd. in Toronto needs people like that to make the customized assembly lines he produces for manufacturing plants all over the world. "These machinists are doing a tremendous amount of brain work," Repovs says. "When you're a custom manufacturer, engineering gets it about 80% right; the rest of it has to be done by the guy on the shop floor. We engineer on the shop floor during production and post-production, debug the systems and make them work."

Repovs sends employees as far afield as Australia and Poland to supervise installations. And although the work is well paid (his top operators in 1998 were earning $90,000 a year), Repovs can't find all the skilled workers he needs and as a result has to turn down business. "We lack tool and die makers, fitters, and CNC [computer numerical control] machine operators. We are looking for the experienced hand but that person is virtually unavailable. If he is any good, he is fully employed."

In today's economy, continuing education is as important in blue-collar employment as in other sectors. The time is past when manufacturing companies could rely on the immigration program to deliver the skilled workers they needed, so companies have to develop their own skilled labour just as European companies, with well-developed apprenticeship systems, have traditionally done. Repovs runs classes for his workers and brings in outside experts to keep them up to date on new developments in metallurgy and metal fabrication. The education program "enables us to put out a superior product and enriches the lives of the employees," says Repovs.

Throughout this book, there are clues to where the jobs of the future will be found. The chapters on real estate, investing, retailing, leisure and recreation, cities, and health care all point to growth areas of the economy that will need trained people in the future. For example, the slower real estate market, resulting from the changed demographic structure of Canadian society, means that many people will find it difficult to sell their homes for enough money to trade up to the bigger houses they want as their kids get older. Instead, they renovate, and the renovation business is booming as a result. That means work for the architects, interior designers, carpenters, cabinetmakers, painters, electricians, and plumbers who are able to create the kitchens and bathrooms of their customers' dreams. Although the architect might practise his craft on a computer rather than a drafting board, most of what these skilled workers do will never be done by computers and will always be in demand. But the key word here is skilled. In an aging population, shoddy work will be neither tolerated nor rewarded.

Provincial governments are closing hospitals and putting a new emphasis on home health care just as the oldest boomers are on the verge of needing more health care services, especially for their aging parents. That means home health care will be a growth business in the years and decades to come, bringing with it employment for a wide range of health care and personal service workers. The expansion of health care into the home is already well underway (see Chapter 9) and, unfortunately, much of it is of inferior quality. Those private home care operators who are able to build reputations for quality and service will have a chance to grow rapidly in the years to come.

Some of these companies may originate with one individual operating on her own who understands that her best customers may be those who buy her services on behalf of their parents. A front-end boomer has parents in their 70s and 80s. These parents need health care services that, in some cases, are being managed by their children. But those children are not health care experts, are extremely busy, and may live far away from their parents. They might eagerly employ the services of an experienced individual – perhaps a nurse laid off from a management position in a hospital – to monitor their parents' health, arrange for care as required, and report to them on a regular basis. As the health care system is restructured, many opportunities like this will open up for health care workers ready to seize them. Many of these health care workers will be former employees in vertical organizations creating new transitory career paths for themselves.

Young people planning their careers need to determine which subspecialties of their areas of interest will be most in demand. Interested in medicine? Then consider that the echo ended in 1995 and the current crop of babies are those being born to the busters, a smaller generation. That means fewer babies and less demand for obstetricians and pediatricians. On the other hand, the services of many other specialists will enjoy stable or increasing demand. For example, cosmetic surgery is used by all generations but most especially by the huge boom generation, which is rapidly losing the youthful appearance many of its members value so highly. Research in this field, driven by demographics, is making rapid strides. New techniques of laser surgery, for example, have been successfully employed to remove wrinkles and other marks of aging from the faces of people as old as 86. About 1.5 million cosmetic surgery procedures a year are performed in North America, double the number of a decade earlier. Tracking the aging of the boom, cosmetic surgery will continue to grow rapidly in the years ahead. Another booming business will be cosmetic dentistry, to whiten and otherwise improve aging teeth.

The aging of the boomers also will sharply boost demand for the services of ophthalmologists and other professionals who treat eye problems. Ninety-eight per cent of people over 65 need some vision correction. Most problems can be corrected with lenses or laser surgery but more serious disorders, including cataracts, glaucoma, and macular degeneration, become increasingly common with age. In fact, cataract surgery is the most frequent operation for people over 60.

The demographic approach can be applied to a wide array of occupations. Perhaps accounting appeals to you. In that case, it's worth considering that, in an aging population, white-collar crime inevitably increases. Because of budget constraints, some police forces have had to cut back on the resources they are able to devote to this kind of crime, just when those resources should have been bolstered (see Chapter 7). RCMP Commissioner Philip Murray has admitted the inevitable result is a two-tier police system with forensic accountants being paid by private companies to track down fraud because the police can't afford to. This means that forensic accounting – a term that until recently was largely unknown – will be a growth industry. The services of forensic accountants will be increasingly required by all organizations, both public and private, profit and non-profit, to detect fraud.

A young person typically has more time than money, while a middle-aged person has more money than time (see Chapter 5). Increasingly, imaginative transitory workers are finding ways to sell some of that valuable commodity, time, to harried, hurried, front-end boomers. Jim Davidson of Toronto is a classic example of an entrepreneur exploiting the opportunities created by demographic change. In 1993, Davidson, a former car salesman, set up on his own as an agent for people wanting to buy a used car. He had two things to offer: knowledge and time. He knew which models made good used cars and which ones didn't, he could spot cars whose provenance was dubious and whose speedometers showed less mileage than the car actually had, and he knew what cars were worth and how not to get taken by a dealer. Even with that store of knowledge, finding a good late-model used car took him time. But he had the time, and his customers, most of them busy front-end boomers in their 40s, didn't. Davidson found the car, negotiated the deal, and arranged delivery.

Davidson's business has evolved with his customers. Good used cars are getting rarer, and his customers now want new cars anyway. So Davidson now buys only new cars, advising customers on which vehicles best suit their needs, arranging test drives, working out deals with the fleet managers of major dealerships, selling the customer's old car for him, and, finally, delivering the new one. The discount he negotiates is usually well above what the average person could get and more than his typical fee of about $500. This service has proved so popular with Davidson's clients – virtually all of them boomers – that he has gone from a one-man operation to a staff of four. And he has earned fees training people in nine other North American cities who have set up similar businesses.

Davidson operates the way life insurance agents have always operated: he visits his clients at their homes at their convenience. This mode of doing business will become increasingly common in the years to come as more people become more pressed for time. Successful service providers such as travel agents, lawyers, and accountants will find themselves making house calls. Even doctors will make house calls.

Japan, because it is a much older society than Canada, provides useful clues to our future. "In Japan, you don't go to a car dealer," says Davidson. "The Nissan, Honda, or Toyota representative comes over with his laptop and CD-ROM and shows you all the cars, and he has a printer so that he can leave you a printout with all the options and prices."

Davidson was born in 1967, immediately after the baby boom. Some people in his age group resent the relative success of the front-end boomers, but Davidson happily exploits that success as he builds his business. His own contemporaries have plenty of time to shop for a car on their own. "But if I get a lawyer who's off to the opera on Tuesday, and the baseball game on Wednesday, and he's having business guests over on Thursday, what's $500 to him? That's one billable hour of work." As Davidson points out, the boomers took most of the traditional jobs. Younger people like him "have to make our own."

Growth in demand for manufactured goods is slow today because the largest part of the population already has most of what it needs. As Canada becomes more of a service economy, resourceful young people will continue to invent new services to fill new needs created by demographic change. For example, there would have been little demand for the services of professional dog walkers in the 1950s when there were lots of young children and stay-at-home mothers to take care of family pets. In the late 1990s, however, dog-walking has come into its own as an occupation. Many boomers bought dogs when their children were born in the 1980s, but now the children are grown and not always around to take care of their pets and both parents are at work. Or the dog owner has no kids but because she's at the peak of her business career is so busy that she hasn't always got the quality time her canine friend requires.

That creates a business opportunity for professionals like Deena Cooper of Toronto who is hired to take dogs on one-hour walks. Deena's Dog Services employs four part-time walkers, provides day-care and training, and sells dog accessories. And because city dogs often don't get to run as much as they need, Wanda Squire started Leaps and Bounds on 20 hectares of land in Mount Albert, Ontario. The dogs are picked up at their city homes, get to run for a couple of hours, have lunch and a bath, and come home. Both businesses had annual revenues in 1998 in excess of $100,000.

However, dog-walking won't be a growing industry for long, again because of demographic change. Those canines acquired during the 1980s, are becoming seniors themselves. These dogs will soon die

Aging boomers, aging dogs

and many will not be replaced. The next generation of dog-buyers, the busters, eventually also will need the services of walkers but because there aren't as many busters as boomers, demand will start to wane during the next decade. The declining years of the boomers' pets will be lucrative ones for Canada's veterinarians, who not only treat expiring animals but also dispense drugs to them. But those making career decisions at the millennium should be aware that the demand for veterinary services, like that for professional walkers, is likely to decline. Pet ownership peaks between the ages of 45 and 54, an age group that is currently inflated because of the passage of the boom through middle age. But someone over 65 is one-third as likely to own a pet as someone in the 45-to-54 group. The pet industry, therefore, will peak early in the next decade but will decline once the boomers enter their senior years.

Dog walkers originally catered to a rich clientele that could afford such a frill, but they then found that a broader market existed for their service. Personal fitness training has followed a similar path. Once associated with movie stars and wealthy executives, this service has gained a growing clientele among busy people in mid-career who want to get a fitness program underway but need some advice and encouragement. "The baby boom generation can afford it and they're breaking down fast," trainer Karen Leslie told the *Edmonton Journal*. Although her expertise is in another field, Leslie is selling the same commodities as Jim Davidson – time and expertise. Having her come to the house is less time-consuming than joining a class at a fitness club. As for expertise, her Edmonton clients "want to make sure they're doing things properly so they don't hurt themselves."

Let's look at some other employment opportunities that, because of the demographic shift, look promising at the millennium:

Elder law: Specialists in this emerging field develop expertise in such areas as conflicts over property, decisions regarding mental competency, medical treatment, and elder abuse. The demand for elder law is being driven by the increasing longevity of the relatively large cohort born before World War I. Elder lawyers will truly come into their own in about 20 years when the large World War II generation, followed by the boomers, begins to need their services.

Tourism: This sector is a big winner in an aging population (see Chapter 6) because older people have the time, money, and inclination to travel. Tour guides, interpreters, airline personnel, and bed and breakfast operators are just some of the wide variety of jobs the tourist industry creates. As well, the growing interest in eco-tourism and other forms of educational travel creates new opportunities for people with training in botany, archaeology, and history.

Eyeglasses: This is one of the best opportunities in retailing because 80% of people over 40 need glasses and by 2006 the entire boom will be over 40. Making this field even more enticing is the emergence of glasses as a fashion accessory, so that many people want several pairs.

Education: Births have declined since 1990, so that demand for primary educators will be in decline. However, the echo generation will continue to push up high school enrolments for a decade to come. And adult education, for both boomers and pre-boomers, is a growth industry. Moreover, demographics hold out promise for aspiring teachers for another reason – many of those currently in teaching jobs will be retiring over the next decade. In Ontario, for example, 30,000 teachers were expected to retire between 1998 and 2003. This means that even school systems with flat enrolments will have to hire new teachers.

Financial services: The boom is passing en masse from its spending to its saving and investing years (see Chapter 3). This creates many opportunities for fund managers, financial analysts, financial planners, and accountants.

Biotechnology and pharmaceuticals: A race is on to find cures for a wide range of conditions that affect the health of millions of people (see Chapter 9). These rapidly growing industries require biologists, chemists, geneticists, and information technology experts.

TOWARDS A FLEXIBLE WORKFORCE

In Canada, we go to school full-time, work full-time, and then go into retirement full-time. In an aging society, characterized by job shortages, rapid technological change, a need for continuous upgrading of skills, and underfunded public pension plans, this system no longer makes any sense. Some people are working more hours a week than they would like, while many more can't find any work at all. Some people work full-time although they would prefer semi-retirement, while others, still full of health, energy, and talent, are forced to retire at 65.

The time has come to take seriously the need for a flexible workforce in Canada. A flexible workforce would not only be happier and healthier, it would be more productive because it would make better use of the talents of all Canadians. A flexible workforce is one whose participants, rather than staying in one occupation with one employer for life, move easily between jobs, employers, and industries. It's also a workforce that allows its participants both to begin and to end their working careers gradually, and that provides plentiful opportunities for retraining.

Elements of a flexible workforce already exist. Some high schools, colleges, and universities, for example, offer cooperative programs in which periods of study are interspersed with periods of employment in the student's field of interest. This is precisely as it should be. People should be able to ease into the workforce, combining work and study, at the start of their careers, and then gradually ease out of the workforce towards the end of their careers, by cutting down to four days a week, then three, and so on down to zero.

Senior managers don't like this idea much because they don't really want their workers to have flexibility. Management can't quite accept that a part-time worker is a committed worker. Then there are the complications of working out pension and other fringe benefits for part-timers. But these complications are minor compared with the benefits that a flexible workforce would bring. Many overworked people in their late 40s and 50s, who have paid off their mortgages and educated their children, would willingly work four days a week for 80% of their salary or nine months a year for 75%. This would save their employers large amounts of money because they are the highest-paid people on the payroll. And half a senior manager's salary pays the full salary of an entry-level employee.

Such a system should be voluntary. A mandatory flexible work arrangement puts an unfair burden on those who can least afford to work reduced hours, such as young people burdened by large mortgages or the most poorly paid workers. And those who volunteer have to be committed – for example, by signing a three-year contract promising to accept nine months, and nine months only, of work per year. That gives management a chance to plan and ensures that no one takes the program frivolously. This system benefits both the company and the employee. The company saves on the salary of a high-priced employee and, in many cases, gets a more productive employee; it also gets a chance to revitalize its workforce by hiring some younger workers. Part-time workers get time off for other things, such as establishing new businesses or careers and enjoying leisure and recreational pursuits. This system also allows workers to ease into retirement gradually. A final advantage is that the part-time senior worker is available to train and act as a mentor to the newcomer.

It's in the interest of all employees to become more versatile. If diversifying risk makes sense in personal financial planning, it makes just as much sense in career planning. Most of us would not put every penny we had into one type of investment. But we do just that when managing our own human capital: we become completely dependent on one occupation and one employer. We are therefore just as vulnerable as investors with all their money in real estate – if the market takes a tumble, they are in big trouble. The transitory worker, or free-lancer, is diversified and thus not dependent on the good will or good fortune of any one employer. A salaried worker can't duplicate the independence of a freelancer, but she can be alert to possibilities for expanding and improving her skills. A salaried worker could have two part-time jobs instead of one full-time job, each in a different occupation. In that situation, the disappearance of one job would be much less of a disaster.

THE FUTURE OF RETIREMENT

Like the idea of jobs, retirement was a 19th-century invention that is becoming outmoded as the 20th century draws to a close. It was invented in the 1880s by German chancellor Otto von Bismarck to help quell revolutionary fervour among German workers. Now it has become a system in which the state pays people not to work, including quite a few who don't need the money and would rather keep working.

Just as young workers should be able to ease their way into the workforce while being trained in their chosen occupations, so older workers should be able to ease their way out while retaining the dignity and sense of self-worth that comes with productive activity. A good worker doesn't suddenly lose his skill and knowledge at the age of 65. As challenges to mandatory retirement at 65 by doctors at the Vancouver General Hospital and others demonstrate, many older workers see no good reason to succumb to enforced idleness when they still have the energy and ability to work.

Moreover, older workers have qualities that make them more valuable in certain jobs than younger workers. Gilles Guérin, professor in the School of Industrial Relations at the University of Montreal, recounts an experiment in which two salesmen, an older retired person and a young person, were placed behind the counter of a hardware store. Which would the customers prefer? "All the customers went to the retired person," Guérin told the weekly news magazine *L'actualité*. "And it's perfectly understandable: in a hardware store, you are paying for advice and experience just as much as for a particular item." While young workers are the masters of high tech, older workers are masters at what has been called "high touch" – those fields of sales and service where human contact, empathy, and experience count most. These are valuable qualities in an aging population with a predominantly service economy. Of course, a hardware store also needs younger workers as well because they may have a better understanding of the needs of young customers and can do some heavy lifting when required. The most effective sales staff will include employees of different age groups.

Many older workers would probably be less tempted by early retirement if they could begin working part-time well before the age of 65. This would be highly beneficial, both to individuals and employers. Full early retirement damages organizations, in both private and public sectors, because priceless knowledge, gained over decades of experience, is lost forever. "The transfer of knowledge from one generation of workers to the next doesn't have time to take place," Guérin says.

There are signs, particularly in the United States, that the tide is turning in favour of older workers. Because of the low unemployment rate and shortage of skilled workers in certain fields, some companies have taken to recruiting among their own retired ex-employees. Since 1995 in the United States, more than 1 million people over 55 have un-retired, accounting for 22% of job growth.

Given longer life expectancy and the changing nature of work, it is not surprising that many people would choose to remain productive members of the workforce past the age of 65. In the past, when much work was physical, workers became less productive with age and were worn out by the age of 65. But in a knowledge economy, workers wear out much more slowly, and the older ones are among the most productive because they know the most. Moreover, many people simply don't have the means to take a 20-year vacation starting in their 60s. To ensure an annual income of $30,000 for 25 years beginning at 60 requires savings of $500,000. Yet, according to a poll by Deloitte and Touche, only 18% of Canadians expect to have that much.

Sooner or later, demographics will impose a system of gradual retirement as an integral part of a flexible workforce. In an increasingly competitive world, the most knowledgeable and experienced workers are too valuable to be put out to pasture before they are ready. Moreover, as has been well publicized, the ranks of Canadian seniors will begin a period of rapid growth in 2012 when the first boomers turn 65. At that time, compulsory retirement for 65-year-olds will come under increasing attack. In a period of rising life expectancies and in the context of a flexible workforce, it won't make much sense. The Canada Pension Plan already allows for flexible retirement. But it doesn't allow a partial pension to be paid to a person who is only partially retired. It should.

The western Europeans, it is worth noting, already have the older society we are going to get. They are supporting it through increased productivity. As has been explained above, demographics and technology are in the process of creating a more productive Canadian economy. Companies are adding machines because they are cheaper than workers, with the result that output per worker – productivity – is rising. But if we are to support our seniors through productivity gains, tax reform will be essential. It can't be done through payroll taxes alone because of the shortage of workers to pay the pensions of all the retired boomers. We have to tax capital income, which will mean higher taxes on corporate earnings and capital gains as well as the introduction of inheritance taxes.

The solution is not to do away with mandatory retirement, which is still necessary to open up room at the top for plateaued boomers and create new opportunities for younger workers. Instead, we should permit partial retirement in the context of a flexible workforce. Those in their late 50s could be working four days a week, after which they would gradually shorten their work week until they are working only one day a week by their early 70s. They could start drawing a partial pension at 55 but would not reach full pension eligibility until 75. In this way, they could remain productive members of the workforce into their 70s, gradually retire with dignity, be present to mentor younger workers, and help reduce the pressure on the Canada Pension Plan.

This idea was proposed in the first edition of *Boom, Bust & Echo*. In 1997, *L'actualité* put it to the test to see if workers would be interested in such a system. The response was overwhelmingly favourable. Of Quebeckers polled, 73.3% were in favour and only 26.7% against. However, they preferred a rapid form of gradual retirement, with the ideal formula being $3^1/_2$ days of work starting at age 55, $2^1/_2$ days after 60, $1^1/_2$ days after 65, and half a day after age 70. Not surprisingly, older people proved more responsive to the idea than younger ones – 64% of the 18-to-24 age group were in favour compared to 75% in the 45-to-54 age group.

Because of demographics, there is no better time to introduce wide-ranging reform to Canada's retirement system than at the millennium. The cohort entering retirement during this period is the Depression kids, the people born in the 1930s who are the wealthiest people in the country. They, more than any other group, have reaped the rewards of the rise in real estate values and stock prices in the later years of their adulthood. These seniors can afford to adapt to the changes that would be necessary as part of a move towards a more flexible workplace, including delaying full pensions until after age 65. The time for reform is now. The longer we wait, the harder it will be.

Chapter 5

The New Rules of Retail

B y 1995, most of the boomers had finished having babies. The echo had run its course, and a new bust was underway. Obviously, Canada would have a dwindling number of young children at the millennium. What does a company whose target market is located at the bottom of the population pyramid – a company in the doll business, for example – do in such a situation?

One strategy would be to do what the major Canadian beer companies did in the 1980s when the aging of the boomers resulted in a drop in demand for beer. Instead of altering their product, they stepped up their marketing efforts in an attempt to get a larger share of a shrinking market. However, a more promising approach might be to develop a related product that could attract the attention of an older, larger age cohort. That's what Mattel Inc., maker of the Barbie doll, decided to do.

Just because a boomer was too old to play with dolls, did that have to mean she would never buy a doll for herself again? The boomers were entering their investing years and collectibles (see Chapter 3) were being added to many investment portfolios. Moreover, the readiness of boomers to buy new versions of old cars or to listen endlessly to the music of their youth testified to the power of nostalgia. Why not, reasoned Mattel's strategists, produce an upmarket Barbie doll for collectors? And so was born a new line of dolls – the Barbie Collectibles, including such glamorous ladies as "Grecian Goddess Barbie Doll" and "Barbie as Eliza Doolittle at the Embassy Ball," aimed at affluent middle-aged women willing to spend as much as $1,300 to invest in childhood memories.

Mattel's was an imaginative response to an increasingly complex retail environment. The boomers, who will be 34 to 53 in 2000, have bought most of the things they need. The older boomers will have passed out of the spending stage of their lives and into the saving and investing stage. They will pay for quality when they want something, as sellers of $1,500 sets of golf clubs and $50,000 cars can attest, but they aren't likely to buy a lot of anything that stores have to offer. Meanwhile, the leading edge of the echo turns 20 in 2000, launching a period of growth for products whose major appeal is low price.

Because of the new demographic situation, the same beer companies that struggled during the 1980s will do well again at the millennium. The premium brands they developed during the 1990s to win back older drinkers will have continuing appeal to aging boomers well into the new century while the movement of the echo generation into its late teens and 20s will spark rising sales of lower-priced, mass-market brands.

The beer companies, mainly through luck, are in an ideal position to exploit the latest demographic shift. Others, like Mattel, have to work harder to succeed in the new environment. In general, retailers who do well at the millennium will deploy one of the following strategies:

1. Choose a market, focus on it, and don't pay attention to anything else. The boomers get so much attention as the biggest cohort that it's easy to forget they are only one-third of the population. Many retailers make profits selling products and services that appeal to the various cohorts that make up the majority of Canadians born before or after the boom. But because these cohorts are smaller, success is often harder to achieve.

2. Find a way to differentiate the same product, so that it can be sold with different levels of service into different markets at different prices. The airlines are masters of this strategy. They sell one product – a seat on a plane going from Point A to Point B. If you've got more money than time, you can pay full fare to go whenever you want while retaining the right to change your reservation at any time to suit the dictates of your hectic schedule. And if money is plentiful, you can pay still more for a bigger seat and better service. Others on the same flight will pay less but will lose control of their time – they will be locked into firm departures. And the youth travellers, for whom time is far more abundant than money, will show up at the airport on a standby basis, waiting for hours in hopes of getting a seat at the last minute at a cut-rate price. A furniture store that offers to put together unassembled products or a car service centre that does home pick-ups and deliveries uses the same principle of differentiating identical products for different customers with different needs and means.

3. Change, improve, or alter a product in some way to expand its demographic reach. If the new or altered product can attract the attention of the boomers, so much the better because where the boomers are is where the growth is. This is the route Mattel took. It's also the strategy of Callaway and other manufacturers of golf equipment who are able to persuade affluent boomer golfers to replace their existing clubs with new, technologically superior ones that may help their aging bodies to hit longer shots.

Let's take a step back and look at the fundamentals of demographics as they apply to the world of retailing. A young person has little money and lots of time. If she wants to buy a new stereo, she checks out every store in town because every dollar saved is important and, what's more, she has plenty of time to hunt for bargains. Once she's made the purchase, she takes the system home and puts it together. It doesn't matter how long it takes.

A middle-aged person has more money but less time. He's got heavy responsibilities at work and at home. He is not going to spend his precious leisure hours doing comparison shopping to try to save $50 on a pair of speakers. This person wants a top-quality stereo system from a store with a good reputation, and he wants it with a maximum of speed and a minimum of fuss. He may even pay extra to have it delivered and assembled, because the time saved is worth more than the additional cost.

During the 1990s, Canada began a major transformation from

a predominantly young to a predominantly middle-aged society. For that reason, retailing in Canada entered a new era of quality and service. In the years to come, stores that compete on the basis of quality and service will have a much better chance of success than stores that compete solely on the basis of price.

Although the environment for cheaper goods will improve in the first decade of the new century as the teenagers of the echo generation become young adults, the movement of the boomers into late middle age means that retailers offering quality and service will have an edge in the marketplace for many years to come. Since stores sell goods obtained from manufacturers, the makers of goods must also place renewed emphasis on quality if they wish to maintain their market share in an aging population.

As the average age of the population increases, not only do quality and service assume ever greater importance, but product preferences change. The shrewdest retailers know how to forecast these changes and prepare for new market demands. They know that the best way to predict which way the market is headed is to look at where the early boomers are now. These front-end boomers aren't a big group, but the massive boomer population of 9.9 million people always catches up with them. If you need to know which products and services will be in greatest demand in Canada in the future, take a close look at the products and services that the key group born in the last three years of the 1940s is buying today.

For example, the streets of Canada in the late 1990s are crowded with minivans. In the mid-1980s, minivans were comparatively rare. But who was driving them? Front-end boomers born in the late 1940s. They had young children and had to trade in their Volkswagen bugs and sports cars for something bigger. Detroit, in a rare example of timely marketing, came up with the minivan, and the rest is automotive history. As the younger boomers caught up with the front-enders, the minivan's share of the Canadian car market rose steadily, from less than 1% in 1983 to 20% in 1997. Next time you see a minivan coming down the street, see who's behind the wheel.

Chances are it won't be someone under 30 or much over 50. The minivan was the vehicle of the boom in the 1980s and 1990s.

A major market shift like that is propelled by demographics, not by marketing decisions. It was because Canada was a young country in the 1960s and 1970s that its streets were filled with cheap, small cars. This phenomenon occurred in spite of the Big Three automakers, not because of them. They would have preferred to continue selling the larger and more profitable vehicles that ruled the North American car market until the arrival of cheap European and Japanese cars forced them to deliver what most consumers wanted.

A country filled with young people is one whose retailers compete predominantly on price. In such a country, anything that can lower the average cost of production and reduce the price to the consumer is important. A young Canada during the 1960s and 1970s enabled the big retail mall to be born and to thrive, making it possible for stores to lower costs and pass the savings on to customers. While the emergence of the echo will mean that the malls won't disappear,

Quality coffee with service

their glory days are over. In the 20 years to come, the demographic shift will favour a revival of neighbourhood specialty stores supported by loyal customers for whom price is no longer the most important factor in a purchase decision.

Stores that can deliver good products and good service will dominate this new marketplace, while stores that waste customers' time and treat them rudely will disappear. The art of customer service is something at which Canadian retailers had been notoriously incompetent because, until the 1980s, they were operating in a marketplace that didn't require it. That is no longer true, and stores that fail to provide good service risk losing their most prosperous customers. An Angus Reid poll, based on interviews with shoppers during the 1997 Christmas shopping season, found that the more a person earned, the less likely that person was willing to wait for service. Only 46% of customers earning at least $60,000 a year would wait more than five minutes compared to 63% of those earning less than $30,000. The Canadian retailers that prosper in the changing marketplace of the coming years will be those that succeed in adopting customer service as a way of life.

To better comprehend what's in store in the years ahead, let's review the past quarter-century of Canadian retailing (see Figure 4). Between 1971 and 1981, the front end of the boom moved into adulthood. At the same time, business was slow for Canada's obstetricians because the baby bust reduced demand for their services. The result was a children's market that declined by 14% during the 1970s. Inevitably, the toy and baby food businesses suffered steep declines in sales. A toy company that was good enough to beat this declining market by five percentage points still suffered a whopping 9% plunge in sales; the marketers in such a company deserved a bonus but, unless their bosses were exceptionally sophisticated about demographics, they probably got fired instead. Meanwhile, the youth (15-to-24-year-old) market was growing by 17% over the 1970s. Someone selling a product that this age group wanted – recorded music, for example – and who increased sales by 10% probably thought he was hot stuff, and yet he wasn't even keeping up with the

FIGURE 4: CANADIAN POPULATION GROWTH BY AGE

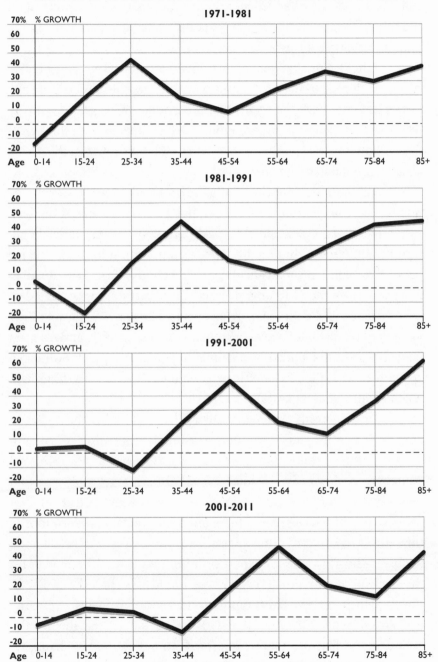

Source: Calculations by David K. Foot based on Statistics Canada, Revised Intercensal Population and Family Estimates, July 1, 1971-1991, catalogue 91-537 occasional (July 1994), and on Statistics Canada, Population Projections for Canada, Provinces and Territories, 1993-2016, catalogue 91-520 occasional (December 1994).

natural growth of the market. Meanwhile, the growth of the boomers into adulthood resulted in boom times for makers and sellers of all the things people need when they set up a new household: furniture, appliances, and cars, especially used cars.

The 1980s showed how dramatically markets can change from one decade to the next because of demographic shifts. The echo began in 1980, with the result that the under-15 age group grew by 5% over the 1980s – a turnaround of 19% compared with the 1970s. That's how toy companies on the verge of bankruptcy in the 1970s became profitable in the 1980s.

But entrants into the youth market (aged 15 to 24) during the 1980s were the products of the smaller baby-bust generation; as a result, that market declined by 17%. That's why the beer industry got into trouble. It couldn't blame foreign competition for its problems because foreign brewers were effectively excluded from the Canadian market by provincial listing, pricing, and distribution systems. But government could not protect the beer giants from a 17% drop in their key group of customers. Even a company whose sales team was good enough to beat the market by a couple of percentage points still had a 15% drop, which looked pretty awful compared with the 17% growth obtained almost automatically in the 1970s.

It wasn't only the beer industry that suffered in the 1980s, of course. Performers and producers of music appealing to a youth audience found their material pushed off the air as radio stations switched to oldies formats that appealed to a target audience that was swelling by 47% during the 1980s. The stations did this not because their managers were too staid to appreciate modern music; they did it to survive. Who, after all, would want to target a market declining by 17%? Some expert opinion had it that the reason for the decline of new music was that it was worse than the music of the 1960s and 1970s. This argument does not make sense. If young people couldn't fill Olympic Stadium or B.C. Place during the 1980s, it was because there were fewer young people. No band, no matter how talented, can continually fill stadiums when the size of its target audience is in steep decline.

The biggest growth during the 1980s was in the 25-to-34 age group. Industries that understood this and were able to exploit it did well. The pet food industry in the United States, for example, knew that people acquire their first dogs or cats at about age 28. This industry did a good job of targeting its market and enjoyed excellent growth throughout the decade. In the same years, the front-end boomers were moving out of rented apartments and into their first homes, with the result that demand for consumer durables such as appliances was strong. The consumer spent us out of the recession of the early 1980s. The arrival in the retail marketplace of this huge generation with wants greater than its cash flow triggered the growth of the credit card as a medium of payment for the masses. Annual spending charged on Visa and MasterCards grew from $4 billion in 1977 to $68 billion in 1995, when the boomers began leaving their prime spending years.

The advent of the echo into its spending years will add some healthy diversity to the Canadian retail marketplace in the first decade of the new century. Nevertheless, the boomers, because they are the largest group, will continue to be the dominant force. Suppose you are a successful 50-year-old executive or professional working 60 hours a week in a high-pressure job. Your spouse also has a job with important responsibilities. Your kids are into their teen years, going through the wrenching transition to adulthood that so often makes life trying for their parents. Your own parents are in their 70s or early 80s, and their declining health is increasingly a cause of concern. Meanwhile, you are running a house in the city and perhaps another in the country. You have an active social calendar. Moreover, you continue to value the leisure activities that are so important to a balanced life – recreation, travel, reading, and cultural events. A charitable organization that you've supported for many years has come to rely on your energy and expertise.

This is your life at the brink of the new millennium. Do you really have time to take a defective product back? Do you have time to make three telephone calls to find out if something you need is in stock? Of course you don't, and that's why you are no longer prepared to support merchants who waste your time. During the 1970s, when the front end of the boom was in its 20s, Consumers Distributing Inc. prospered by offering low prices in exchange for no service and long waits. The customer chose from a catalogue that had everything from wedding rings to air conditioners, filled out a form, handed it in at a counter, and then waited while an employee fetched the stuff from the warehouse. Because the waiting area was crowded with no seating and the waits were as long as 20 minutes, Consumers sometimes used the slogan "Suffer a little, save a lot."

That approach worked in a marketplace where people had time and little money, but by the 1990s, when the situation was the reverse, it was out of step with what the market demanded. The arrival of a powerful new competitor, Wal-Mart, offering low prices and a better shopping environment, compounded Consumers' problems. The company went bankrupt in 1996.

Busy middle-aged people with responsible jobs have always been demanding customers. What's new at the end of the 20th century is that, with the aging of the boom, a larger percentage of the population than before is in the age group that insists on quality and service. That means that some of the stores that seemed invincible in the early part of the 1990s – stores like Wal-Mart, Price Costco, and Home Depot – may be heading into turbulent waters. These American megastores entered Canada at a time when a large segment of the Canadian population was in its early to middle 30s. At that age, many families have two small kids and a pile of debt, including a mortgage on a recently acquired house. Price is extremely important to such people, so they are prepared to invest a large chunk of their spare time in the pursuit of bargains.

But as we approach the new century, these people are in their 40s and their financial situation is growing more secure. Will they still be willing to drive ten kilometres in search of a bargain? Will they be prepared to roam the aisles of a megastore to save a few dollars on products they could have found closer to home? Will they be prepared to drive to an Ikea or an Idomo, wander around looking for the new table they need, go to the warehouse section to find the right package, wait in line to pay for it, tie it to the roof of the car, and then take it home to assemble it themselves? Probably not.

One way the 40-year-old discovers he's well and truly grown up is that suddenly people he used to think of as authority figures – policemen and doctors, for example – are younger than he is. Another moment of truth comes when he walks into the Ikea store he avidly patronized as a student and young adult and realizes that he's in the wrong place. He says to himself, "Hold it. I'm a grownup now. I don't have to put up with this anymore." The management of Ikea understands that the demographic shift is changing the way they must do business. They know Ikea has to adapt to the changing needs of aging consumers while at the same time guarding its valuable franchise of price-conscious shoppers in their 20s and 30s. They are doing this by offering delivery and assembly for an extra charge. This is a way of appealing at the same time with the same products to younger shoppers for whom price is primary and to older ones who are prepared to pay for extra service.

As the millennium approached, the impact of the demographic shift was transforming the Canadian retail landscape. Eaton's stores were increasingly out of favour with both the quality-conscious and price-conscious segments of the market. T. Eaton Co. Ltd. had to file for bankruptcy protection in 1997 while it restructured its operations, closing some stores and upgrading others. While Eaton's managed to stay in business, the combination of unfavourable demographics and market saturation eliminated others. Consumers and K-Mart, which was bought by Hudson's Bay Co. and merged with Zellers, disappeared. So did 11 SportDepot stores in Canada that were closed by their owner, Illinois-based Sportmart Inc. Home Depot, a U.S.-based big-box home improvement store, absorbed a Canadian competitor, Aikenhead's. PetsMart, a U.S. pet supply warehouse store, announced plans for a Canadian invasion and then thought better of it.

It was in response to demographic change that the warehouse stores had first appeared in North America in the 1980s. That was the decade when the largest part of the boom generation was passing through its prime spending years. The boomers were buying their first homes and filling them with furniture, appliances, baby clothes, and toys. They were buying their first cars. And they were loaded with debt, including student loans, car loans, and mortgages. These consumers needed basic goods at the lowest possible prices.

The warehouse stores slashed prices by eliminating a costly step in the retail process – storing goods in a warehouse before putting them out for display on the shop floor. Instead, the warehouse was the shop floor. The new stores grew rapidly through the 1980s right up until the mid-1990s. Then the combination of too many competitors and too many boomers who had stopped buying put the brakes on expansion of the sector. Even the U.S. stores who pioneered the big-box concept in North America, Price Club and Costco, realized the market was not big enough for both of them and merged to become Price Costco.

Retailers are creative people who thrive by developing new concepts in response to changes in the market. Finding favour recently is the idea of combining size and wide selection with quality, a pleasant ambience, and prices that, if not lower than other stores', are competitive. In this way, merchants hope to attract more affluent customers, including many aging boomers, as well as value-conscious consumers from other cohorts. The best examples are the book superstores, including Chapters and Indigo in Canada and Borders and Barnes and Noble in the United States. These stores have attractive decor, cafés, and comfortable sofas to make browsers feel welcome. Some of them carry music and computer software as well as books. A recent twist on this concept is Summerhill Nursery and Floral in Toronto, a garden centre offering not only plants and garden supplies but also cut flowers, a gardening bookstore, and a cappuccino bar.

The success of Chapters proves the concept works. But the advent of superstores does not mean smaller competitors are doomed. The superstores have a flaw – lack of service in the form of knowledgeable personnel. Because of their size and need to keep costs low, they must rely on young workers who tend to be long on energy and enthusiasm but short on expertise. For many customers, a smaller bookstore that can offer expert advice has an edge over a superstore.

At the millennium, the retail environment in North America appears to be evolving towards the model previously developed in the older countries of western Europe. The warehouse store was not invented in North America. The French *hypermarchés* – vast shopping surfaces containing everything from groceries to, in some cases, cars – predated it by a decade. *Hypermarchés* in the suburbs of French cities coexist with tiny specialty stores in the city centres offering the high quality and personalized service that appeal to an older, affluent clientele. The southern French city of Aix-en-Provence, for example, has large stores on the modern outskirts. But in its central pedestrian precinct, it supports open-air markets and hundreds of tiny specialty shops. These stores take specialization to a level rarely seen in Canada – one, for example, sells only clothes for little girls while another stocks only garments that are blue and white.

Stores whose only attraction is cheap prices have faced a challenging time in Canada because of changes in the age composition of the population. These stores survived by upgrading the quality of their service, their products, or both. Significantly, Chapters and Indigo realized this even before they opened their doors, which is why they made large investments in decor and other amenities. Wal-Mart, with its excellent distribution system and huge buying power, has been able to dominate the discount sector by taking market share away from the competition – including many discounters, both large and small, that have gone out of business in its wake. But even Wal-Mart recognizes the appeal of smaller stores to an important segment of the market. That's why it announced plans to try out a new store format in several U.S. cities in 1998. Half the size of the format of existing stores, it's been christened "Small-Mart" by the business media.

Jean-Pierre Boyer, chairman of Métro-Richelieu Inc., the Quebec grocery chain, is a respected retailer who thinks small store formats have a bright future because of the impact of population aging. He told the company's annual meeting in 1997 that as people get busier and older they will want to avoid steering their grocery carts down miles of aisles. "Stores that offer selection and service, that's what consumers are looking for – not necessarily inhuman size," he said.

The older consumer might continue shopping at a big-box store for commodity items such as paper towels and brand-name breakfast cereals. After all, these things are the same no matter where you get them, so quality is not an issue. Price is the main concern with such products, and the megastores win on price. But service, more specifically convenience, is also an important consideration. The busy 50-year-old will shop for basic household supplies at Wal-Mart only if the inconvenience is not so great that it cancels out the price advantage. She might, for example, like to call the store from her office and place an order that she can pick up on her way home from work. She might also eagerly patronize the first hardware store in her area that offers to assemble unassembled products at a small extra charge. Retailers are going to have to work hard to come up with ways like these to adapt to the changing marketplace if they wish to make the transition successfully.

Let's take a closer look at the needs of the different cohorts in the retail marketplace at the dawn of the new millennium.

ECHO KIDS

In June of 1998, the departure of a member of the Spice Girls, a British band popular with teens and pre-teens, was page-one news in many Canadian newspapers. Had the same event taken place during the 1980s, it would not have broken out of the entertainment pages because not enough Canadians would have been interested. By the end of the 1990s, however, the echo generation, born between 1980 and 1995, was deeply involved in music and movies. Because the echo kids buy Spice Girls CDs and tapes, their boomer parents know about the Spice Girls. And if society's two biggest cohorts, the boom and the echo, are interested in the Spice Girls, then the Spice Girls are page-one news.

The arrival of the echo kids, the largest group of teens since the boomers themselves, is an important new factor in the retail marketplace of the late 1990s. Because of the echo kids, frozen pizza,

metallic nail polish, and name-brand sweatshirts were growth industries in North America. Because of the echo kids, Eaton's hired
Courtney Love in 1998 to advertise its clothes. Companies that just a
few years ago were focussed solely on figuring out what the boomers
wanted now had to ask themselves a second question: "What do the
boomers' kids want?"

The answer, of course, was that they wanted the same things
teenagers have always wanted – music and clothing their parents dis-
approved of and lots of unhealthy food. But there was a significant
difference from the last time teens were plentiful: these kids had more
money to spend. Demographics were the reason. When the boomers
were young, they had to compete for their parents' money with two or
three siblings because, at the peak of the boom, the average Canadian
woman was producing four children. The boomers themselves, however, produced only 1.7 children per family; that meant that two-
income boomer households had more money to lavish on each
offspring. And what some marketers called the "six-pocket" phenomenon – kids getting cash from two parents and four grandparents –
explained why many echo boomers could afford to spend $50 for a
Nike sweatshirt when a similar garment without the trademark could
be had for only $15.

The brand name is increasingly important – echo kids have
been saturated in television since birth and, as a result, they are the
most brand-conscious cohort in the history of the planet. "Since tweens
(children aged 9 to 14) are highly peer-oriented, a brand that gets it right
can quickly become a must-have for almost every tween," Lynne
DeCew of Imagination Youth Marketing told *Canadian Business* magazine. While getting it right can be lucrative, getting it wrong because of
poor market research can be costly even for a company as powerful as
Levi Strauss & Co. When the managers of its Levi's brand were late in
noticing that wide legs had become cool, the company's share of U.S.
blue jeans sales plunged from 31% in 1990 to 20% in 1997.

For the apparel industry in general, the arrival of the echo in
its teens is excellent news. "The recession is over in clothing,"
announced Herschel Segal, president of Château Stores of Canada, at

the company's 1997 annual meeting. "There are more teens with more influence and buying power than at any other time since the 1960s."

One other characteristic has marked the echo kids as different from previous groups to occupy the teen market. They are the first generation raised with computers, and, as a result, Web surfing comes naturally to them. This means that the Internet is an increasingly important medium for companies selling to the echo kids, but it is also significant for those targeting their parents. Because of their mastery of the Internet, echo kids play an important information retrieval role for many parents who don't feel at home in cyberspace. In fact, teenagers know more than their parents about computer technology in general. Kids have always had something to say about important family purchases, such as a car. But when it comes to the purchase of a computer or related equipment, an echo kid's opinion in many cases will be decisive.

Young consumers are also having an impact on the food industry. Just as today's young people don't remember a time when there were no computers, they also don't remember a world of meat and potatoes. Foods once considered "ethnic" or exotic are normal daily fare for today's urban youth. Jim White, a consultant to North American supermarkets and food manufacturers, says this trend will grow more marked well into the new millennium. The popularity of the wrap – a flavoured, coloured tortilla made out of wheat flour – is largely due to its appeal to young eaters, White says. "The wrap starts as a Mexican food and you put Chinese leftovers in it and heat it up in a microwave and you've got lunch," says White. That's an example of how foreign cuisines will continue to change North American eating habits as the echo kids reach maturity. "These kids grew up eating Chinese and Mexican," observes White. "It's in their DNA."

Nostalgia, an increasingly important tool for marketers targeting the boomers, has its place in the food industry. Many shops have opened in recent years specializing in the classic candies of the past – licorice, jelly beans, jawbreakers, and Tootsie Rolls. Echo kids, who are important customers for these stores, are delighted to find they share at least some tastes with their parents.

BUSTERS

In May of 1998, Gap Inc., a U.S.-based clothing chain, took out full-page newspaper ads to announce a grand event – the opening of its new babyGap store in Toronto. Gap is one company that can be expected to know something of demographics. After all, the company's name comes from the expression "generation gap," which was on founder Donald S. Fisher's mind when he opened the first Gap in San Francisco in 1969 in the belief that he could do a better job of selling blue jeans than existing stores could. As the company's success has proved, he was right.

Gap's timing was also good when it opened its first babyGap in 1990 in the United States. The echo, which had started in 1980, was at its peak then. There were lots of babies and their boomer parents were eager to dress them in stylish casual clothes.

But was Gap's timing as good when it decided to try the baby-Gap concept in Canada in 1998? By then, the reproductive careers of the boomers, aged 32 to 51, were winding down, which was why births in Canada had declined every year after 1990. The baby-busters, aged 19 to 31 in 1998, were replacing the boomers in the prime child-bearing years. And because the busters are 14% fewer in number in each year than the boomers, they won't be making as many babies.

Demographics, then, are not favourable at the end of the century for babyGap or any other seller of products for babies. This doesn't mean the babyGap store won't succeed. There will still be babies who need to be dressed, probably enough in the large Toronto market to support a new store sporting a trendy brand name. But there won't be enough babies to support a lot of new entrants to the baby clothes market and some stores may go out of business.

Caution is the watchword for anyone selling the kinds of products mainly bought by those in their late 20s and early 30s because markets that rely on the busters are shrinking markets. So sales of baby carriages and car seats are heading down. And because the advent of the busters on the real estate market (see Chapter 2) will dampen demand for housing, it will also restrain demand for the appliances first-time householders buy to equip their homes.

Smart retailers look for ways to extend their demographic reach beyond the small twenty-something group. Gap, whose products appealed to Gen-Xers and busters, decided it needed the echo boom as well. So it opened GapKids in 1986, followed by babyGap, to encompass all of that large population cohort. Ikea, sensing a decline in growth in demand for starter furniture that appealed to young buyers, expanded its business by emphasizing furniture for home offices, which older buyers were more likely to need.

Because of the impact of the baby bust, a video store is one business it would be wise not to open at the millennium. Renting a video appeals to housebound folks with kids and a mortgage, a state of affairs the boom has been in for the past two decades. When the kids no longer need a babysitter, boomers are liberated from the "cocoon" (see Chapter 10) and can seek entertainment outside the house again. After 2000, the cocooning cohort will be the busters. Because there are fewer of them, the video rental business will have fewer customers.

Paradoxically, however, the decline of cocooning will help to extend the video business's lifespan. That's because, with fewer people seeking entertainment at home, less incentive exists for telecommunications companies to install technology that would make video obsolete. This technology, which already exists, can deliver movies digitally to individual homes, thus freeing consumers from having to pick up and return videocassettes. It's better than movie channels on cable TV because viewers can screen films at a time of their own choosing. But installing the technology would be extremely expensive – probably too expensive, given the declining market for home entertainment at the millennium.

BOOMERS

Changes in retail patterns often reveal underlying social changes. How we choose to spend our money says much about who we are and where we are in our journey through life. The *Wall Street Journal*, in an analysis of spending patterns during the 1990s, found significant changes. While total spending in the United States rose 15% during the first seven years of the decade, spending on new cars dropped by 28%. Meanwhile, spending on casino gambling doubled, and spending on alternative medicine jumped 69%. Spending on tobacco was down 19%, while spending on alcohol increased by only 1.7%. The same survey also noted a sharp increase in spending on sports and fitness and on volunteer activities such as community organizations and political groups. In general, these changes indicated that an aging population was changing its priorities – people were becoming more interested in staying healthy, having fun, and doing good – and less interested in conspicuous consumption. Here's how these changing priorities are affecting some of the most important segments of the boomer marketplace.

Food

As they get older, people eat less and they eat better. People in their 40s and 50s don't need as many calories as people in their 20s and 30s, and they have less of a sweet tooth. Because they are older, they are more aware of mortality and thus more likely to consider the health implications of what they eat. Moreover, they usually have more money than they did when they were young. These inevitable repercussions of aging have profound significance for Canada's $89-billion-a-year food industry.

The food industry is being transformed by the demographics-driven trends described in the first edition of *Boom, Bust & Echo*. These trends have intensified since that edition was published in 1996. They can be summed up in two words – healthy and fast. People are increasingly conscious of the relationship between their health and their diets and, at the same time, the food industry keeps finding new ways to make preparation easier and swifter.

Jim White, who was a driving force behind the President's Choice brand of quality food products that has been a big winner for the Loblaw supermarket chain, says the brand succeeded because it satisfied consumer demands for better food. Satisfying these needs was a complex process. In some cases, better meant more exotic. In others, it meant healthier foods low in calories and fat. In still others, it meant more indulgent foods, such as the Decadent chocolate-chip cookie, which was higher in calories than an ordinary cookie. Different people with different tastes responded to these various offerings, but what they had in common was a willingness to spend more for better. "It's all driven by age," says White. "The market has gone from bulk products of inferior quality to products of better quality, either real or perceived. These products have fewer chemicals in them and they cost more. But the baby boom is willing to pay."

At the approach to the new millennium, the boomers are in the busiest years of their lives. With both partners working, most evenings there isn't much time or energy left over for cooking. They want something better than a frozen dinner and yet less time-consuming than a meal in a restaurant. The food industry is zeroing in on this need. Some supermarkets and upmarket grocery stores are becoming "grocerants" – competing with restaurants to sell full-course, ready-to-eat meals that can be enjoyed in the privacy of the home at lower cost than the same meal in a good restaurant. Some U.S. chains have hired their own chefs to prepare these meals. In Ontario, Loblaw has brought in the Mövenpick restaurant chain to cook for its customers in some of its stores. Oshawa Group Ltd.'s IGA has an open-kitchen concept called Marketplace Meals offering a wide array of ready-to-eat dishes. Restaurants are fighting back by placing a new emphasis on take-out. In the United States, take-out is the fastest-growing part of the food business, so much so that in 1996, for the first time ever, more restaurant meals were eaten away from restaurants than in them.

This attempt to cater to people with gourmet appetites but fast-food schedules will continue through the next decade as supermarkets find new ways to produce "home-meal replacements," also known as HMRs. "All the supermarkets are looking for the same thing," says White. "They are trying to find something for the customer who doesn't want to go out and spend $50 to $75 on dinner for two but wants something better than a $14 take-out pizza." The big winners, White believes, will be the stores that can provide high-quality, non-frozen meals on a much larger scale than is currently possible using on-site cooking. The original edition of *Boom, Bust & Echo* described the ready-to-eat salad in a bag introduced by the grocery industry in the mid-1990s. The salad remains fresh for 14 days, and some come complete with dressing. The same concept is being extended to other foods. One shopper might need some side dishes to go with a chicken he cooks himself. Another might buy seven slices of prime rib in a bag as a main course. White is working with an Australian manufacturer to develop a way of packaging refrigerated products to give them a one-year shelf life.

"This is the golden ring," says White. "Whoever gets there first will make a lot of money. And it will be wonderful for the consumer. This food will be restaurant quality, home-cooked quality. It's not going to be cheap, but it's a lot cheaper than going to a restaurant. The same quality in a restaurant could cost you five times as much, depending on the restaurant and how white the tablecloths are."

Convenience, it seems, is something many people can never get enough of. American housewives spent 44 hours a week cooking and cleaning in 1900; by 1996, they were spending 17 hours a week. And since many housewives are also members of the general workforce, that number will probably keep declining, at least until the boomers start retiring. Environmental concerns over the copious amounts of energy used to refrigerate and freeze foods have all but disappeared in the rush to convenience. "Freezer sections are bigger than ever, and refrigerated sections are going to be bigger than ever," says White. "Refrigerated is for the boomers. The echo generation is going to hit the freezer sections because frozen is still cheaper."

For several decades, natural or organic foods have had a small presence in the food industry, catering to the needs of a health-conscious minority. At the millennium, they are becoming big business. "When you get to be a certain age, you realize you are not going to be here forever and you'd better do something to sustain the quality of life that you have," says White. "That involves a reversal of your diet. And so you drop the butter and cream – or save them for special occasions – and eat more healthily."

Whole Foods Market, which operates 75 natural-foods super-markets under several names across the United States, had sales of $1.1 billion in 1997, representing an estimated 12% of the total nat-ural-foods retailing industry. The company is so confident of continu-ing growth in demand for natural foods that it has announced a target of 140 stores by 2003. The interest in natural foods does not mean that people will be lining up at conventional health food stores with their sombre collections of whole grains and overpriced vitamin supple-ments. But they will shop at a modern, well-laid-out Whole Foods store or an attractive store like Capers in Vancouver that combines natural foods with gourmet items.

The healthy eating trend is not confined to patrons of natural-foods stores. Statistics Canada reported in 1996 that Canadians were eating an average of 31 kilograms more fruit a year and 22 kilograms more vegetables than 20 years previously. Consumption of fish, recom-mended as a lower fat source of protein than meat, had risen to 8 kilo-grams per person. Meat consumption, at 59.1 kilograms in 1997, remains much higher than fish but is down 8.1 kilograms since 1987.

Coca-Cola is a good example of a company making a success-ful, if occasionally painful, accommodation to marketplace transi-tions caused by demographics. Soft drinks are traditionally a young person's drink, so Coke seemed to be headed for trouble when the baby bust reduced the supply of its traditional consumers during the 1980s. Coca-Cola thought it was responding to changing tastes when it invented "new Coke." It didn't fully appreciate that it already had what an aging marketplace wanted: Diet Coke. This product, which is consumed by females of all ages and men over 30, is the third most popular soft drink in the United States after regular Coke and Pepsi.

Meanwhile, Coke has rediscovered its pop-swilling youth market – in the developing world, which has a much younger popu-lation than the industrialized world (see Chapter 11). Coca-Cola, a truly global company, now earns most of its revenues outside the United States. Back in North America, it is busy unveiling new brands for the growing teen market of the echo. If it misses, as it did with an unsuccessful introduction of Cherry Coke in the 1980s, it keeps working until it gets the formula right. A new version of Cherry Coke appeared headed for success in 1998. "It's got the right kind of counter-culture appeal, particularly if it's a product [teens] know their parents won't be drinking," observed retail analyst Len Kubas. "They might say, 'We can drink this stuff and our folks can't because it has all this sugar.'"

To maintain the loyalty of the boomers, Coke continues to expand its various lines of juices and bottled waters. These drinks, besides being healthier, have an advantage over soft drinks that all players in the food industry are going to need as the population ages: higher margins. "When people start to eat less, the industry has to get as many dollars from less food," observes White. "We have to move people up from hot dogs at 99 cents a pound, because they are not going to be eating hot dogs. So how does a sausage maker stay in business? By inventing chicken or rabbit sausage and figuring out how to bead olive oil into it so it has the right kind of fat. You will have chicken sausages stuffed with dried tomato or something that's healthy. You will still be eating things that look like breakfast sausages, but they will have healthy ingredients so that you will want to eat them."

That's how demographics drives technological advances in the food industry, and that's how Coca-Cola and the sausage companies can beat the demographic odds and stay in business.

Alcohol

Population aging is both bad and good news for the booze industry. It's bad because, as people get older, they drink less. But it's good because, as people get older, they drink better. The movement of drinkers towards quality was evident in the 1997–98 fiscal year results of Canada's largest liquor retailer, the Liquor Control Board of Ontario (LCBO). Sales of premium wines sold in the LCBO'S Vintages stores increased by 19%, single malt scotch was up 25%, cognac rose 10%, and champagne was up 15%. Significantly, all of these beverages are expensive, are normally consumed in small quantities, and appeal to sophisticated palates.

On balance, however, population aging is not positive for alcohol. Nor is it good news for tobacco, another legal drug that is a major industry in our society. People start using both as teenagers. Usage then begins to flatten during the 20s, stays flat during the 30s, and drops sharply during the 40s and 50s. Moderate use of alcohol is, according to many studies, good for the health, whereas tobacco is always hazardous. Canadians, in their collective wisdom, understand this. That is why alcohol is used by 80% of the population in their 20s and 30s while tobacco captures only 40%. Men drink more than women. Their use of alcohol declines a bit in the 30s and flattens in the 40s, while female use drops dramatically in the 40s.

The last of the boomers turned 30 in 1996. That meant the entire generation was past its prime alcohol and tobacco consumption years, with only 18% of Canadians left in the age groups associated with increasing consumption. The good news for the beverage industry was that the eldest members of the echo generation reached 18, the legal drinking age, in 1998. That signalled the start of a period of rising sales volumes, especially for mass-market beer brands and cheap wine.

Growing awareness of the health implications of excessive use of tobacco and alcohol coupled with high taxation accounts for some of the drop in consumption, but even with less negative publicity and lower taxes, population aging alone would result in a substantial decline. In Ontario, for example, sales of beer by the Brewers' Retail monopoly were 2% lower in 1997 than in 1993. Sales of wine, which is preferred by older people, rose 10% during the same period, while those of spirits, which are preferred by still older people, finally moved up a bit in 1997, after years of decline. One reason was the return of the martini – 50-year-old boomers behaving at the end of the century as their parents had back in the 1950s.

Through the 1980s and 1990s, in an attempt to counteract declining sales and in response to the demands of an aging population for a decent shopping environment, provincial liquor monopolies across Canada made major improvements to the level of quality and service they provided. The LCBO did well enough that Premier Mike

Harris praised its newfound efficiency and friendly service and dropped a plan to privatize liquor sales.

Cigarette smokers tend to be loyal to one brand, so tobacco companies have little opportunity to boost profit margins by winning older, more affluent customers over to better and more expensive versions of the same product. But taste in alcohol varies widely depending on age, and people do tend to move up to more expensive products. Over their lifetimes, people who enjoy alcohol proceed from beer to wine to spirits. But of course, this is not an all-or-nothing proposition. The person who casually consumed a six-pack of beer at a party in his late teens might sip one bottle a week as a 40-year-old on the night the family sends out for pizza. And the 50-year-old who has come to enjoy a shot of whiskey before dinner doesn't stop drinking a glass or two of wine with dinner. But he drinks less wine because he is now drinking spirits as well.

The Canadian wine industry, centred in Ontario and British Columbia, moved from plonk to quality wines during the 1980s. The industry's timing was perfect, because these were the years when the boom was switching from beer to wine and gradually learning to tell good wine from bad. By 1997, Canadian wines had shed their plonky image and knowledgeable consumers were ready to part with $10 or, in some cases, much more for a bottle of local wine. As part of this coming of age, Niagara wines were beginning to dominate the local marketplace just as local wines dominate the local marketplace in other wine-growing regions. Ontario wines had 46% of sales by volume in the province, almost three times as much as French wines, which were the second most popular.

If the Ontario wine industry had deliberately based its strategy on demographic analysis it probably would have followed the same path. In the 1970s, when the boomers were young, the industry produced and sold large volumes of inferior, low-priced wine made with Labrusca grapes. Back then, if it had switched to higher quality and more expensive vinifera grapes, it would have had difficulty selling its products because the Canadian market was not ready to pay high prices for wine. Interestingly, although Australia's vineyards started producing good wine about a decade before Canada's, its industry's sales didn't take off until the Australian boomers, like their Canadian counterparts, were in their late 20s and 30s and ready to appreciate wine. Even if Ontario icewine had existed in 1970, there weren't enough consumers ready and able to part with $40 for a half-bottle to make developing so expensive a product worthwhile. Icewine appeared on the market just when a growing number of boomers had both the knowledge to appreciate good wine and the money to afford it.

Clothing

"I used to take an 8, then I took a 6, now I take a 4, pretty soon I'll take a 2, and then I'm going to be 0. But I'm not shrinking. I'm the same size." That comment was from Bernadette Morra, fashion editor of the *Toronto Star*, in the first edition of *Boom, Bust & Echo*, voicing a common complaint of the minority of the Canadian population who have grown older and wiser instead of older and wider. Morra was joking but in the fashion industry nothing is too absurd to be unthinkable. In fact, two major designers are now offering size 0 dresses for slim women so that others can continue to wear the same sizes they wore before their bodies expanded. In all likelihood, the next edition of *Boom, Bust & Echo* will record the introduction of the first negative sizes in women's clothes. Meanwhile, not only have dress sizes been redefined to accommodate boom bulge, even men's waist sizes have been relaxed by some manufacturers who are putting 32-inch labels on pants that fit comfortably around spongy 34-inch waists.

This kind of fantasy marketing is the industry's response to population aging. The fashion industry has no problem dealing with the arrival of the echo generation into their fashion-conscious teens. The industry understands a 15-year-old who wants blue nail polish and platform running shoes. But it doesn't quite know what to make of a 50-year-old who wants to be comfortable and fashionable at the same time, who knows she's older but isn't quite ready to admit it.

"Certain people in the industry are beginning to wake up to the fact that there is a size issue here," says Morra. "One designer offers the same outfit in three different cuts – one with wide shoulders and narrow hips, one with narrow shoulders and wide hips, and the other thick all the way through the middle. This is aimed at the changing, spreading boomer figure. But while the size issue is being addressed, the industry is not really marketing to older people. You pick up a magazine and it's still got Kate Moss on the cover."

It is probable that a relationship exists between the befuddlement of the industry in the face of the aging of the boom and the slow rate of growth in sales. But there may be little the industry can do to alter the reality that a middle-aged person is preoccupied by many things other than the pursuit of the perfect outfit – children, for example, and travel and gardening and aging parents.

The problem for the apparel industry is that the people who most increase their spending on clothes are 25-to-30-year-olds, and that age range is occupied in the late 1990s by a relatively small cohort, the baby-busters. Retailers should be aware of such demographic shifts and be prepared for them. When the boomers passed out of their prime buying years, many retailers weren't prepared and suffered the consequences. Dylex Ltd., the clothing retailer whose empire included Fairweather, Big Steel Man, and Town & Country, made large profits dressing clothes-hungry young boomers in the 1970s. But Dylex failed to adapt its business strategy to the demographic reality that, because of population aging, the market for many of its products had shrunk. That was a major reason why, in the 1990s, Dylex became insolvent and had to seek court protection from its creditors.

Boomers may not be shopping as much as they used to, but they still need clothes and in middle age they are putting increased emphasis on comfort. "Elastic-waist pants used to be the lowest end of fashion but now there are high-priced designers making them," says Morra. "It's not being offered as something for a spreading waistline but as a great pair of pants, very chic and stylish. I have a pair by Canadian designer Lida Baday. I feel like I'm wearing pyjamas when I have them on.

"We're also starting to see a lot of drawstring waists on the designer runways. Calvin Klein's spring '98 collection was full of drawstring waists. Again, that is something that is going to fit a much broader group of people than the standard pant waistband." To accommodate boomer expansion, textile manufacturers are combining Lycra with many other fabrics and developing new ways of weaving wool and other fabrics so that they give.

One manufacturer who knows how to prosper in an older marketplace is Armani, whose clothes for both men and women feature a loose silhouette that is kind to aging figures. Armani understands that the magic words quality and service apply just as much to clothes as to any other product in the retail world of the 1990s. His knowledge of the changing needs of his customers may be why, in a 1996 interview in *New York Magazine*, he declared that fashion was finished. Fashion will, however, revive towards the end of the first decade of the new century when the echo generation moves into its prime clothes-buying years.

More immediate good news for the industry is that spending on clothes by women rebounds after the age of 50. Just as they do in the supermarket, these knowledgeable shoppers will buy less but better. "It's easier to manipulate a younger market into buying what's fashionable because they're insecure," explains John Winter, one of Canada's top retail consultants. "By the time you're in your 50s you've seen trends come and go for 30 years. You know what looks good on you, and that's what you buy. Women will spend more on a single item of clothing, but it's likely to be a classic like a Chanel jacket. They'll shop at stores they couldn't afford when they were younger."

One last fashion item, the running shoe, deserves a mention. The case of running shoes illustrates the danger of an overly simplistic approach to using demographics to forecast behaviour. It might have been logical to assume that companies that rose to prominence during the aerobics boom of the 1970s would be in trouble in the 1990s, when some older boomers started slowing down. Such a prediction would have been wrong. The sports shoe business is doing fine, as a sophisticated use of demographics would have predicted. First of all, companies that started out making shoes for runners have expanded their product lines to include shoes for walkers and golfers.

They also produce the basketball shoes that are so popular with the large echo generation. Moreover, just because somebody decides to give up running doesn't mean she gives up running shoes. As people get older, they need and can afford better shoes. After they have trod many thousands of kilometres over the years, feet tend to flatten and widen. The older shoe buyer is more interested in comfort than the younger buyer and pays more attention to arch and ankle support. A well-made running or walking shoe offers these qualities better than most other kinds of shoes. Because of demographics, it was predictable in the 1970s that a large market for shoes offering support and comfort would exist in the 1990s, as would a growing market for orthotics designed to fit the individual foot. And it should not be surprising that companies that learned how to make comfortable shoes for young runners in the 1970s would be able to adapt that know-how to the needs of older consumers in the 1990s.

Cars

As the millennium approached, something strange was happening on the streets of North American cities. The invasion of the sport-utility vehicle (SUV) was underway. Middle-aged boomers were driving Jeeps and Jeep imitations to work and to the shopping mall. These cars were a peculiar choice. They were not designed for city use but for rough off-road conditions that most of their owners never encountered. They guzzled gas, handled like trucks (which, in fact, is what they were), and were harder to park and less manoeuvrable than cars designed for use on crowded city streets. Moreover, SUVs carried the highest profit margins in the industry. What was going on? It was understandable that boomers would eventually outgrow their minivans. But why would they switch to one of these overpriced, clunky things when they could drive a zippy new sedan instead?

Marketers and industry analysts had lots of answers for the steadily increasing market share of light trucks, a classification that includes pickups, SUVs, and vans. J. Walker Smith, managing partner of Yankelovich Partners Inc., believes that whereas prosperous people in their 40s and 50s used to move up to the biggest, plushest car they could afford, the boomers don't want the same cars their parents had. "They're looking for adventure, which I think is the appeal of sport-utility vehicles. You never drive them off road, but you have an adventure as you go from your driveway to the grocery store and back home."

The boomers may think they are being adventurous but, in their middle-aged car-buying habits, they are essentially behaving just as their parents did before them. Their parents drove big cars. When the boomers were in their teens and 20s, they drove cheap small cars, the obvious choice for a young person with little money and no family. Because there were so many young boomers, small cars dominated the North American roads during the 1960s and 1970s. Now that the boomers are older, they want big vehicles, and the auto industry has come full circle. Big cars dominate the roads again.

For Canadian auto industry analyst Dennis DesRosiers, the SUV is a natural progression from the minivan. "A typical boomer bought his first minivan in 1983, his second in 1988, and his third in 1993. Meanwhile, he acquired two kids, a dog, a cat, and a cottage. Now, about 15 years after he bought the first van, the kids have completely different interests and do not want to be spending time with their parents, nor do their parents want to be driving them around. The cat and the dog are dead, and our boomer wants an alternative look. He doesn't like the image of a minivan, it smacks too much of the 30-year-old. But he likes the utility. So he buys a sport-utility vehicle. The boomers are doing that en masse."

While some ex-minivan drivers opt for luxury four-door sedans, many are addicted to having a vehicle that makes it easy to transport unwieldy objects from the store to the home or from the home to the cottage or boat. The SUV isn't as good in this respect as a minivan but it beats a sedan.

Probably the most important appeal of the SUV is safety. Young people think they're immortal, which is why Ralph Nader was ahead of his time in the 1960s with his warnings to a youthful North American population about unsafe cars. But as people get older, they naturally become more conscious of their mortality and this awareness is reflected in many consumer decisions. Some people change their eating habits in quest of better health and greater longevity. Others rebel against consumerism and try to build simpler, more meaningful lives. And car buyers start to ask questions about safety. They want a vehicle designed to minimize chances of an accident and maximize chances of survival should an accident occur.

The industry has been responding to this need for more than a decade with the result that many cars now have antilock brakes, airbags, and other safety features as standard equipment. But bigness is the ultimate safety feature. If a truck is going to collide with a car, it's better to be a passenger in the truck than in the car. As a result, a lot of people are buying SUVs, not because they are feeling adventurous, but simply to defend themselves from other trucks, including vans, SUVs, and the convoys of giant freighters roaring down North America's highways.

For a growing number of drivers, even the bulk of a standard SUV is no longer enough. They are opting instead for bigger SUVs such as the GMC Suburban or pickup trucks like the Dodge Ram. These kinds of vehicles, originally invented for practical, utilitarian purposes, are being decked out with the sort of luxurious touches, like wood-grain consoles and six-disc CD changers, once reserved for Cadillac and Mercedes sedans. In fact, by 1997 most of the luxury car brands, including Mercedes, Lincoln, Lexus, and Infiniti, had rolled out their own versions of the SUV.

GM's Cadillac division was an exception, with its Escalade SUV not due to appear until the fall of 1998. Although Cadillac dealers had been pleading for a luxury SUV to sell, GM's brain trust was of the opinion, until 1997, that few luxury SUVs would ever be sold. That was the sort of thinking that contributed to the steady decline in GM's North American market share. In the first two months of 1998, Daimler-Benz, helped by its popular Mercedes SUV, sold almost as many cars as Cadillac in the United States. And Ford's Expedition and Navigator SUVs, vehicles in the same price class as Cadillac, were outselling Cadillac by a wide margin.

Cadillac missed out on the luxury SUV craze while it focussed its efforts on giving its cars a more youthful image that would attract affluent boomer buyers. The attempt was not working well. "Cadillac's and Buick's shares have been declining quite radically now for about a decade," says DesRosiers. "They have not been able to move down to a younger age class. They still are primarily in that 55 or older category. Those people are dying, and the ones behind them aren't going to be interested in that style of vehicle. That's why Cadillac introduced the Catera. It's sportier, and targeted to the needs of a 45-to-55-year-old. But it still has the Cadillac badge on it and they're having trouble with it. Those buyers are going to a Mercedes, BMW, or a Lexus. If they stay domestic, they go to a monster truck. That's much more hip than a Cadillac."

Even their high susceptibility to theft (see Chapter 7) does not seem to deter eager buyers of SUVs. Not surprisingly, this boomer-led lunge back to oversized vehicles was beginning to spark a negative reaction as the millennium approached. Studies showed that people in cars were far more likely to be killed if they were struck by an SUV

Bigger boomers, bigger cars

or other light truck than if hit by another car. Size was not the only reason. The higher frames and bumpers on the SUVs were another factor, and some safety advocates wanted the vehicles redesigned.

Because of their poor fuel economy, SUVs were also attacked as harmful to the environment and inconsistent with attempts to curb emissions and reduce global warming. The California Air Resources Board was considering making SUVs meet tighter emission standards. The problem was that improving fuel efficiency might mean reducing the size of the vehicles and their size was their main appeal.

The automakers' response to the emissions issue was to step up research on clean-burning vehicles. All the major players are developing non-gasoline-powered cars or gas-powered cars that use advanced catalytic converters to eliminate most emissions. A major beneficiary of the movement towards non-polluting cars was Ballard Power Systems, of Vancouver, whose hydrogen fuel cells can power buses and cars with no exhaust except water vapour. Although by the summer of 1998 it had not yet made a cent of profit, Ballard's stock soared on the future promise of its technology.

On balance, the demographic shift seemed positive for the auto industry. The boomers were moving into vehicles that were highly profitable for manufacturers. Meanwhile, members of the echo generation would buy their first cars in the decade after 2000, giving the small car sector a boost. But there was an ominous cloud on the horizon – boomer retirement. Many boomer families have two cars. When they retire, they won't need two cars. What will that do to the car market?

"We know quite definitively that when consumers retire, they shed vehicles," says DesRosiers. "They maintain two cars for the first year or two, but they use their vehicles about a third as much because a third of driving is related to work. Ultimately, the insurance costs and the bother of having two vehicles start to add up and people get rid of the second one. Sometime around 2010, and certainly by 2015 to 2020, the industry is going to go through an unprecedented downturn as the boomers retire and shed vehicles.

"Where do those vehicles go? Into the used-car market.

There's going to be a whole whack of relatively new cars out there that will be dirt cheap because there will be too many of them. Consumers, for five to ten years, may move away from buying new vehicles. [At the millennium] we're in an unprecedented upside of the industry in North America. But if you are an executive in the industry when the boomer retires, you've got to make sure you're retiring with him."

In the meantime, those executives were working hard at finding ways to tap the boomer market. In 1998, Toyota released the Solara, a two-door coupe designed, according to the company's advertising, "for baby boomers who are ready to move from vans and sports utility vehicles to something that's sportier and more stylish." But middle-aged consumers usually prefer four-door cars. Whether enough boomers would buy a new two-door to make the Solara a success remained to be seen.

However, a retro two-door, the Plymouth Prowler, is very definitely a popular hit. The Prowler is one of the most imaginative and audacious cars Detroit has ever produced. It's a replica of an old-fashioned hot rod and deliberately impractical, with no room for groceries or anything else except two passengers who enjoy rumbling down the road with the top down in a $50,000 jalopy one reviewer described as "a bit like driving a go-kart – fun, exciting, but somewhat painful too."

Nostalgia is an important weapon for marketers targeting the boomers. The Prowler was followed in 1998 by a new version of the Volkswagen Beetle that has also been an instant success; other companies had their own retro cars in the works. These cars will never account for more than a small portion of sales but manufacturers understand that they are a good way to call attention to themselves. Most of the cars on the road – sedans, minivans, and SUVs – are indistinguishable. The new Beetle, on the other hand, is unique. Even if most buyers won't indulge in one, they might pay more attention to Volkswagen the next time they're car shopping.

The original edition of *Boom, Bust & Echo* pointed out that most consumers don't enjoy the shopping process. Many resent the time-wasting haggling over price, while others complain of being treated in a condescending manner or subjected to high-pressure sales tactics. These methods are ineffective with an aging population because older, experienced consumers won't put up with them. In the United States, car superstores with salaried salespeople and car brokers are taking a growing share of the market. The same trends will occur in Canada. Meanwhile, there are signs that dealers are improving, if only a bit. A survey by Maritz Canada Inc., a market survey company, found that 56% of Canadian women and 50% of men in 1997 were satisfied with their car purchase experience compared to 52% and 45%, respectively, in 1994. In the United States, Mazda set a new standard of service when it offered to go to customers' homes or offices to repair faulty wiring in some of its 1999 model cars. When car dealers are ready to make house calls, a new era of service truly has arrived.

Consumer Electronics

One of the premises on which *Boom, Bust & Echo* is based is that participation rates in a wide variety of activities – such as buying certain goods, participating in certain sports, or succumbing to certain diseases – are stable over time. In other words, people act their age, which means that a 40-year-old in 2000 is as likely to play tennis as a 40-year-old was in 1990 or 1980.

But what happens when we try to forecast the future of products that are in a rapid state of evolution? Prediction then becomes more difficult. What percentage of 60-year-olds will use computers in 2010? That's hard to say because technology changes so quickly. Currently, boomers are less likely to use computers than busters or echo kids. But boomers use television and telephones as much as other cohorts. What if computer, telephone, and television are the same machine? What if advances in speech recognition eliminate the need for computer users to learn to type? Such changes could dramatically affect participation rates in unpredictable ways. Technology, therefore, is one area where the predictive power of demographics is circumscribed. What can be stated with certainty, however, is that the easier a technology is to use, the more likely an older person, including a boomer, is to use it. This is not because older consumers are incapable of figuring out a complicated piece of technology but because most of them lack the time to become adept at using it. In its early days, the Internet was the preserve of expert computer users. But with ever more powerful hardware making possible much simpler software, the Internet is not a great deal harder to use than the telephone. That's why the over-51 customers of Internet Direct, an Internet service provider, went from 13% of the total in 1997 to 18% in 1998.

The more transparent a technology, the greater its penetration of the boomer market is likely to be. A refrigerator is a good example of transparent technology. To use it, one need know nothing of the scientific principles underlying its design and manufacture. There are no operating instructions to study and no technical vocabulary to master. The fridge user comes to any fridge for the first time with all the skills needed to operate it – the ability to open a door and shut it.

Back in the mid-1990s, a major electronics manufacturer brought out a line of VCRs with the stripped-down model going for the lowest price and the full-featured model going for the highest. These VCRs didn't sell very well. Then an executive had the bright idea of reversing course, redesigning the best-built and most expensive model to reduce the number of features on it and make it the simplest of all to operate. Sales turned around immediately.

The lesson was that transparency resulting in time-saving sells, and the good news is that we are likely to see more and more of it in the years ahead. Speech recognition is the most promising new development. Because of it, computers and related technologies will finally be accessible to the many older people for whom the keyboard has been a significant barrier. The industry has been working on speech recognition for many years but until recently, the systems were slow and unreliable. The latest systems allow users to speak at a normal pace while dictating documents, without pausing between words. Good systems can understand even strong accents and will accept such commands as "bold."

The millennium era will see rapid development in this technology. Users will be able to issue voice commands, telling their computer to go to a particular Web site or to locate a file containing certain data. Intelligent voice word processors will be able to distinguish "where" from "wear" or suggest alternative words. Speech e-mail systems already exist – users can listen and reply over the phone, issuing all commands by voice.

The advent of speech recognition has importance beyond the world of computers. It greatly enhances the possibilities of automation in a wide range of retail areas, including fast-food restaurants and gas stations. Older boomers who felt unsure of themselves when asked to follow instructions on a screen and enter information on a keyboard will adjust to this technology with ease.

PRE-BOOMERS

As we leave the 20th century, we have both an aging population and a slower-growing seniors' market. The reasons for this apparent paradox are simple – and important for retailers to understand. The seniors' market is growing slowly because the new entrants at the millennium are those born during the 1930s, a decade when few people were born in Canada. Yet we have an aging population because members of the largest single group, the 9.9 million boomers, are entering the sixth decade of their lives.

An aging population and an old population are two different things, however, and when we use such phrases as "the greying of society," we have to be careful what we mean. It's true that boomers are exhibiting grey hair and other signs of age. But the peak of the boom, those born in 1961, won't be 65 years old until 2026. That's a long way off, and the boomers as a group are a long way from being old. As for the World War II generation, they too aren't yet old, although some have already taken early retirement. Marketers should take care not to annoy people in their 50s and early 60s by portraying them as senior citizens before their time – unless they are offering discounts.

For the first time in our history (see Figure 4), the over-65 population is bifurcating into two very different marketplaces: the slow-growing, affluent group of young seniors, and the rapidly growing, much less prosperous market composed of people over 75. As a result, a single marketing strategy no longer works for all seniors. Because of the wide variations in the taste, needs, and circumstances of the senior population, it's more useful to break them down into young seniors (65 to 74), mid-seniors (75 to 84), and senior seniors (85 and up). These three groups have three distinct lifestyles. The young seniors are still healthy and spend a lot of time and money travelling. The mid-seniors are still at home but health problems are rendering them less mobile. Many senior seniors are in nursing homes.

The young seniors' market grew by 37% in the 1970s and by 29% in the 1980s, then slowed to growth of 13% in the 1990s. The recent seniors have done far better than they ever imagined they would when they formed their expectations in the grim days of the Depression of the 1930s. Because they did so well, they went out and acquired more of everything, including kids. That, along with immigration, is what triggered the baby boom. Today, the parents of the boomers are the richest group in Canada. They are part of the reason the cruise ship industry is expanding at a rapid rate (see Chapter 6). Quality and service are the only way to sell to these people. They don't need much, but they can afford what they need. That's the good news for retailers. The bad news is that when young seniors have to replace refrigerators or cars, they are very tough customers because they have had plenty of experience buying refrigerators and cars.

Many young seniors will be ready to move out of empty nests with more rooms than they need. This group is not a market for retirement homes, although many of them will be interested in new real estate developments that feature luxurious smaller houses fronting a golf course. Seniors with different lifestyle preferences are helping to fuel a boom in luxury condo construction in the downtown areas of some major cities.

However, most seniors will stay in the same houses in which they raised their children and spent their working lives (see Chapter 2). They will want to stay there as long as they can, until they are mid- or senior seniors. Important opportunities exist for retailers whose products can help seniors live in dignity in their own homes despite the increasing frailty that comes with age. Home security systems will continue to be in demand, especially in urban areas where the elderly have been targets of home invasions and are increasingly concerned about safety. Home automation, currently in its early stages, will tap into a huge market in the new century. As the "home plug-and-play" standard is adopted, it will become easy to link appliances and other electronics in the home. In this way, for example, when occupants leave, the home security system can be armed, lights shut off, and temperature lowered automatically. Speech recognition systems will play an important part; physically challenged people will be able to turn on lights and open doors merely by issuing voice commands.

In recent years, the food industry has begun to discover the potential of older consumers. Big companies like Campbell Soup and smaller ones like Dinner Date Inc. of Toronto have developed lines of quality frozen meals that are delivered to customers' homes.

Towards the end of the next decade, the affluent Depression cohort will be entering its mid-senior years. The arrival of a wealthy group of retirees will mean an expanded market for upscale retirement homes that have more in common with luxury hotels than with the typical old folks' home. This trend is already well underway. An example is Le Wellesley in Pointe-Claire, Quebec, which has a licensed dining room, afternoon tea served daily in a lounge, a variety of recreation facilities, and a beauty salon. Most luxury retirement homes charge from $1,500 to $4,000 a month.

The fastest-growing segment of the seniors' market at the approach of the new millennium is the over-85 group. It is mainly female because women live six years longer than men, on average. It is also poor because the husbands of these women did not have transferable pensions. Few of the women had careers of their own and so they were unable to accumulate much savings. These people don't buy much. What they do buy tends to be merchandise such as incontinence pads and other health and personal care needs. Their major need is affordable nursing homes.

The Revival of Main Street
At the end of the 20th century, the resurgence of the small local specialty store is underway. An older, affluent consumer wants to shop at the neighbourhood bakery, butcher shop, or clothing boutique where

the staff knows her name, her likes, and her dislikes. She may also enjoy stopping at her favourite coffee bar before heading home – gourmet coffee bars have proliferated across North America in recent years as part of the movement towards quality. Research shows the main consumer of gourmet coffees is a boomer earning over $40,000.

The revival of the local shopping strip is good news for the quality of urban life. After two decades in which malls and mega-stores dominated the retail marketplace, the idiosyncratic specialty retailer is poised to make a comeback. Because of favourable demographics, Canada's retail landscape is going to become more interesting.

There are a couple of qualifications to this happy prospect. Many people would never think of going shopping without a car, and so neighbourhood shopping districts that make parking available have the best chance of success. Initiatives to improve traffic flow by restricting on-street parking are therefore a threat to local shops. The other qualification is that only neighbourhoods with a substantial population of people over 40, who have more money than time, will be able to support these stores. Small towns and younger communities can't do it. For example, the oldest city in Canada historically, St. John's, Newfoundland, is one of the youngest demographically, with a higher proportion of people in the 20-to-24 age group than most other urban areas. That makes St. John's more fertile ground for suburban malls than for small neighbourhood shops.

The revival of Main Street Canada won't be the only throwback to the past as retailing embraces quality and service. Home delivery could also make a comeback. Dairyworld Foods, which operates under the Dairyland trademark, has 42 franchised home delivery routes in the Vancouver area, offering free-range eggs and baked goods as well as dairy products. "We never take a person away from the supermarket," says David Somerset, manager of home service operations. "We only make their life more convenient between trips." This kind of service is attractive not only to seniors but also to stay-at-home parents and the growing ranks of professionals in their 40s and 50s working in home offices. It's a good example of how demographic change can take us back to the future.

* * *

At the millennium, the older members of the echo generation are young adults. During the first decade of the new century, they will be entering the labour market for the first time, setting up a household for the first time, buying used cars and the cheapest fridges and stoves they can find. If they want some salad, they'll make their own rather than blow $3 on fancy greens in a bag. Retailing based on low prices is heading for a comeback in Canada. Businesses based on low prices that manage to survive the 1990s will have a new lease on life after 2000. But at the same time as the young echo generation is entering the marketplace, the 45-to-54 age group will grow by 20%, while the 55-to-64 group explodes by 49% (see Figure 4).

This will be a confusing marketplace for many retailers. One strategy will be to address both the young and older segments at the same time. This can be done successfully if the merchant remembers that the younger consumer is interested primarily in price while the older shopper places a high value on quality and service. Car mufflers are a good example. A muffler is a muffler no matter who buys it; the difference is in the service. Offer the busy middle-aged customer pick-up and delivery and a guaranteed work schedule. Offer the younger one – or the older, retired one – a 20% discount if she is willing to show up at a less busy time and wait for service. That way you satisfy the needs of both customers and keep them both happy.

Other retailers will decide to specialize in one market or the other and some will succeed. As we enter the new millennium, an increasing number of retailers will find success at the lower-price part of the marketplace because of the impact of the echo kids entering their 20s. The boom is the largest single demographic cohort but it is only one-third of the population, and the other two-thirds also has needs to fill and money to spend. However, it's always easier to succeed in a growing market than in a smaller one, and in Canada the most growth is where the boom is. Canada will have more older consumers than young ones for many years to come. The age of quality and service has a long future ahead of it.

Chapter 6

Tennis, Anyone?

"Jackrabbit" Johannsen, the legendary pioneer of cross-country skiing in Canada, was still skiing five kilometres during a weekend on the trails of Quebec's Laurentian Mountains at the age of 104. The heart-attack patients of Toronto's Dr. Terry Kavanagh, many in their 50s and 60s, recuperate by taking up vigorous exercise, and some of them go on to compete in marathons. Countless other feats of strength and endurance by older folks in Canada and all over the world attest to the truth that aging and decrepitude need not go together. In fact, experts say it's never too late to get fit, and that a fit person of 70 has the same oxygen-carrying capacity as an unfit person of 30.

But what people could do and what they actually do are different things. If Jackrabbit Johannsen were typical, he wouldn't have become famous. Most people, as they get older, become less active and less inclined to engage in strenuous activities. As a result, their leisure and recreation habits change. The impacts of these changes, on every recreational pursuit from badminton to birding, are dramatic. Moreover, these impacts are predictable.

Anyone involved in leisure and recreation can be prepared for these changes well in advance. There is no excuse for a community to spend money on hockey rinks at the millennium that are likely to be empty in 2005, while neglecting to provide the parks and walking trails that an aging population needs. Canada can't afford mistakes like those; if we pay attention to demographics, we can avoid them.

Spectator Sports

People who earn their living as sports commentators are remarkably obtuse when it comes to the impact of demographics. In the 1970s, when all the boomers were young, it was often hard to get a ticket to a Canadian Football League game. In the 1990s, when the boomers are 20 years older and therefore less likely to attend a football game, it can be hard to give one away. Yet the impact of demographics on sports attendance is rarely if ever mentioned on the sports pages of Canada's newspapers. Sportswriters would prefer to find other explanations for falling attendance such as, in the case of the Canadian Football League, increased interest in the American brand of football as played in the National Football League. Yet NFL attendance has shown signs of weakness as well, even including an increase in the number of no-shows at sold-out games.

The basic demographic fact of spectator sports is that younger people go to more games than older people. For example, 50% of the 18-to-24 age group attend sports events while only 30% of the 45-to-64 age group attend. This means that the aging of the boom puts downward pressure on sports attendance. At the same time, however, other factors are operating to boost attendance. For one, the Canadian population as a whole has increased, thereby increasing the market for everything, including professional sports. Moreover, the large echo generation is entering its prime sports attendance years. And every once in a while an exciting player, a tight pennant race, or an especially important game will bring boomer fans back to the sports stadiums. But these factors are not enough to offset the negative impact of the aging of the boom; invisible it may be to sportswriters but it is real nonetheless and very powerful.

In the latter years of the 1990s, baseball, the leading spectator sport in North America, was suffering at the box office. The sad state of the baseball business was evident when the 1997 World Series had the worst television ratings ever. In March of the following year, spring training games in Florida, games that during the 1970s and 1980s would have attracted packed houses, were played in front of rows of empty seats. Things weren't much better once the season started. Baltimore and Cleveland, which both had beautiful new downtown stadiums, were drawing lots of fans as were a handful of other teams, but most were playing in front of crowds far smaller than those of the glory days of the 1970s and 1980s. Even the New York Yankees, with one of the best teams in recent baseball history and playing in the largest market on the continent, could not attract many sellout crowds to fabled Yankee Stadium.

It was in this environment that the Montreal Expos were pushing for a new downtown stadium to be financed with $100 million of private money and $150 million from the federal and provincial governments. The rationale was that only by moving away from unattractive Olympic Stadium could the Expos improve their abysmal fan support. To win approval of its plan, the team offered a carrot and a stick. The carrot was that a new stadium would boost business in downtown Montreal and provide tax revenues. The stick was that without a new stadium, the team would be sold and moved to some other city.

This was the same line being pitched by owners of several U.S.-based teams that were also demanding public funds for new stadiums and it was beginning to wear thin. For one thing, once the novelty of a new stadium is gone, attendance returns to normal, as the Toronto Blue Jays have found. Second, because of expansion, baseball is running out of markets large enough to support a major league team, so the threat of moving is becoming less credible. Finally, the lukewarm interest Montrealers have shown in baseball for most of the past two decades, in combination with the erosion of the potential fan base due to aging, raises the question of whether the city can support big-league baseball regardless of the quality of its stadium. It's hard, therefore, to imagine a less worthy use for $150 million of public money than a stadium for professional baseball.

Uninviting stadiums were only one of the reasons the experts offered for declining attendance at various sports. Others were labour unrest, obnoxious behaviour by overpaid players, declining quality of play, ineptitude on the part of some teams, and increased competition from other forms of entertainment. These factors are undoubtedly relevant. But even in their absence, attendance was going to drop because of the demographic shift. An important reason is that once the kids are old enough to go to a ballgame on their own, Dad no longer has to take them. That doesn't mean he will never again set foot in Olympic Stadium or SkyDome, but instead of a dozen or more games a season, he might take in only two or three.

This doesn't mean all of Canada's professional franchises are in danger of imminent demise. Professional franchises are located in major cities, which have a younger population than the country as a whole (see Chapter 7). As well, a franchise in a major centre like Toronto draws on a vast market, including residents of cities and towns within a two-hour drive who make the trip to one or two games a year. This means that the future of the Blue Jays, Canadiens, Grizzlies, and most – although certainly not all – of the other professional franchises in Canada is reasonably secure. But professional sports in North America at the millennium are a mature industry. The days of rapid growth and sold-out seasons are over.

Participatory Sports and Recreation

A nation of young people is a society of hockey and tennis players. A nation of older people is a society of gardeners and walkers. These gentler, more individualistic pursuits replace the more vigorous activities of youth partly because the human body (even the well-trained human body) becomes less flexible and less responsive as the years take their toll. Another important reason is that middle-aged people have busier schedules, both at the office and at home, than young ones and naturally gravitate away from activities that require more time and more than one participant. If it's tough to get two time-pressed 40-year-olds together for a tennis match, it's that much tougher to get a dozen of them in the same place at the same time to play hockey. It may be possible only once a week instead of every day, as when they were younger.

The data on the impact of aging on leisure pursuits is clear and remarkably stable over time. As with all human behaviour, two key factors determine the growth of various leisure activities: the size of the population and the rate of participation. The latter undergoes dramatic changes as the population ages. For example, 16% of Canadians between the ages of 18 and 24 are waterskiers. But members of the 45-to-64 age group restrict their waterskiing activities to piloting the boat; only 2% actually put on skis and take to the water.

Of course, aging isn't the only demographic variable. Immigration is another, and high levels of immigration mean more younger people, which in turn means faster growth for active sports. An upward movement in the fertility rate would also boost participation in active sports 10 to 15 years later. But neither of these variables is powerful enough to offset the impact of the aging of the boom.

As a result, projections show that resting will be one of Canada's most popular leisure "activities" in the years to come. So will reading, hobbies, and attendance at museums, theatres, and places of worship. In contrast, participation in sports as well as attendance at sports events will become less popular. These facts have important public policy implications. Even with the impact of the youthful echo generation, Canada probably has all the football fields, squash courts, and volleyball courts it needs. If funds are available for new facilities, they should be devoted to walking trails, curling rinks, and swimming pools for recreational swimming, because an older population continues to engage in these activities.

The impact of demographics on leisure and recreation has significance for the labour market as well. If your daughter wants a career in recreation, she would be better off teaching dancing than teaching tennis, because aging boomers are more likely to take up the rumba than pick up a racquet.

This sort of analysis rubs a lot of boomers the wrong way. "We're different," they say. "We're fitter than our parents were, and we're going to stay young a lot longer." To an extent, that prediction may be accurate. The most fundamental indicator of fitness is whether one is dead or alive, and older people are changing their behaviour in that regard dramatically – life expectancy has soared from 61 in 1931 to almost 79 in 1997 and continues to rise (see Chapter 11). It would be bizarre if the enhanced vigour and durability that makes increased life expectancy possible were not also reflected in an increased level

FIGURE 5: GROWTH IN SPORTS PARTICIPATION, 1996-2001

	AT CURRENT RATES		UNDER "YOUTHFUL" RATES	
	Growth	**Rank**	Growth	**Rank**
Hockey	2.36	8	3.88	7
Downhill Skiing	5.05	5	4.99	5
Swimming	5.55	3	6.33	3
Golf	7.01	2	7.56	1
Baseball	2.67	7	4.34	6
Cross-Country	7.34	1	7.35	2
Volleyball	3.33	6	3.62	8
Tennis	5.21	4	5.39	4

Source: Calculations by David K. Foot based on Statistics Canada's 1992 General Social Survey and on Statistics Canada, *Population Projections for Canada, Provinces and Territories, 1993-2016*, catalogue 91-520 occasional (December 1994).

of physical activity among the various age cohorts. And in fact a 1997 study by the Canadian Fitness and Lifestyle Research Institute found that all cohorts were more active in 1995 than would have been expected based on projections of 1981 activity levels. For example, in the 56-to-65 age group, 28% were physically active in 1995 compared to only 18% of those who were in that age range in 1981.

Nevertheless, the study also confirms that a declining level of activity still accompanies the aging process. As was to be expected, a comparison of pre-boomers, boomers, and busters found that the youngest group, the busters, was the most active and the pre-boomers the least active. Figure 5 looks at the impact of increased activity levels among older cohorts for the eight most popular sports in Canada as identified by Statistics Canada's 1992 General Social Survey, which was the latest available as this book went to press. These sports are hockey (a participation rate of 6.4%), downhill skiing (6.3%), swimming (6.2%), golf (5.9%), baseball (5.6%), cross-country skiing (4%), volleyball (3.8%), and tennis (3.5%). In the chart, the first two columns show the projected growth in participation from 1996 to

2001, based on historical behaviour of different age groups. Under this scenario, six of the eight sports grew more slowly than the over-15 population.

The second two columns in the chart show a participation pattern that has been altered on the assumption that in future people might behave in a more youthful manner than their predecessors. As you can see, it doesn't much change the outlook for active sports; it just slows down their decline a bit. Whether or not the boomers prove to be more robust than their parents as they get older, making or selling binoculars for birdwatchers and concertgoers will be a faster-growing business in the years to come than making or selling most kinds of sporting equipment.

Let's take a more detailed look at what the future holds for some of Canada's favourite leisure activities.

Hockey

In the last Statistics Canada survey on sports participation, this was the most popular sport in Canada, played by 1.4 million people over the age of 15. By comparison, the second most popular sport is downhill skiing, with 1.3 million adherents, closely followed by swimming, golf, and baseball. Hockey is also one of the most popular activities among boys under 15. Minor hockey boomed right through the 1960s and into the 1970s, until the impact of the baby bust caused growth to subside in the late 1970s. One impact of the decline was that suddenly older players could get rink time at convenient hours. Some suggested that this showed hockey was gaining popularity among older players. In fact, more older people were playing, but only because there were more older people and because rink time was available.

Today the echo kids are in their prime hockey-playing years, so the rinks have filled up again. But the echo peaked in 1990, which means that demand on hockey facilities will peak around 2002 and decline thereafter. Because of the impact of the echo as well as ongoing demand from busters and boomers still playing hockey, Canada did need some new hockey rinks in the 1990s. But this need is diminishing, and it is important that communities not overbuild. Just as no community can afford to build enough roads to ensure that rush-hour traffic moves as quickly as midnight traffic, so Canadian communities can't afford to build enough rinks to easily accommodate a decade-long hockey "rush hour." New rinks should be built sparingly and selectively, and they should be easily adaptable to curling, which increases in popularity among those over 40, a group that includes a growing number of boomers.

Skiing

More than 58% of downhill skiers are under 35. Forty-four per cent of skiers take up the sport when they are under 17; only 12% start skiing when they are over 35. Skiers 24 years old and younger ski 12.3 days a season, while skiers aged 35 to 44 get to the slopes only 8.5 days per season.

Statistics like these paint a picture of a sport that declines in popularity in an aging society. The 1990s have been a reasonably good decade for skiing because the sizeable echo generation is moving through its pre-teen and teenage skiing and snowboarding years. That's why skiing was projected to grow 5% from the mid-1990s through to 2001. But skiing doesn't have the growth potential of activities that appeal to older age groups – activities like birdwatching, which will grow two and a half times as much as skiing over that same period.

Some say you can't judge the future by the past. New equipment has revolutionized the sport, they point out, making it more attractive to older skiers. It's true that improvements in boot technology and the invention of parabolic skis have made skiing both easier and safer. Instruction techniques have been improved and standardized. And the new detachable, high-speed chair lifts are a major advance – they are much easier to board and dismount from than the old lifts, and they allow skiers to spend more time skiing down the mountain and less time riding up. Yet another argument in favour of a bright future for downhill skiing in an aging society is that, except in deep powder snow, it isn't a particularly strenuous activity. If it were, fewer overweight, unfit people would be seen cruising expertly down the trails of Canada's ski resorts.

But the best that skiing can hope for is that all of these positive factors will add up to a small increase in the skiing participation rate for middle-aged and older people. That won't be enough to offset the abrupt decline that historically takes place in skiing with age. In 1982, for example, the participation rate for the 45-to-64 age group was a measly 3%, compared with 15% for the 18-to-24 group. In 1982, that ski-happy 18-to-24 group included a large part of the huge boom generation. By 2000, most of the boomers will be past their prime skiing years and beginning to enter the 3% marketplace.

That was why, in the winter of 1998, various American and European companies making ski equipment experienced sagging sales and slumping stock prices. This happened at a time when most stocks were up and when the Winter Olympics in Nagano, Japan, had sparked interest in winter sports. The manufacturers were stuck with an oversupply of their products because they underestimated the demographic shift away from skiing.

Obviously, participation varies depending on the availability

Virtual skiing

and quality of skiing. Statistics Canada reports that the overall skiing participation rate in British Columbia, Alberta, and Quebec, the provinces that have the biggest mountains, is as much as three times as high as in the provinces that don't have big mountains. Montreal and Vancouver both have good skiing close to the city centre. As an alternative to taking in a movie for an evening's entertainment, a Vancouverite can spend a couple of hours under the lights on one of the North Shore mountains. Toronto is not so blessed. And because Ontario has no mountains and therefore no skiing comparable to what can be found in British Columbia, Alberta, and Quebec, fewer Torontonians would be attracted to the sport in the first place. As a result, a higher percentage of older Vancouverites will continue skiing than older Torontonians. But more younger Vancouverites will also be skiing. The percentage fall-off in participation remains the same. Older people, wherever they live, just don't ski as much as young people.

In order to maintain the loyalty of their customers, ski operators have to provide quality and service. The managers of such ski resorts as Blue Mountain in Ontario and Mont Tremblant in Quebec understand that. Their product, from the quality of food to availability of babysitting, is markedly improved from the days when they were in a seller's market.

Local ski operations that depend on day-trippers from nearby urban areas face an uncertain future. Only the very best operators among these businesses will survive into the next century. Some local hills, competing for market share among young customers, are seeing snowboarding replace skiing as their main attraction. Those resorts that have sufficient land and snow will be able to expand their market by laying out new cross-country trails. Cross-country appeals to older skiers more than downhill.

The handful of elite destination resorts that attract holidayers from afar have better prospects than the local resorts, because they have a much bigger market to draw on. Whistler-Blackcomb, in the Coast Mountains north of Vancouver, has a secure future because it is a magnet for affluent skiers from all over North America and has long been a favourite of Japanese skiers. As well, in the latter years of the

1990s, it began attracting a growing number of customers from Europe; in the spring of 1998, bookings from Britain went up 200% after Princes William and Harry accompanied their father, Prince Charles, on a Whistler ski vacation.

Both Whistler and Blackcomb are operated by Intrawest Corp., of Vancouver, whose success is based on an understanding that affluent, mature skiers want to do more than ski when they go on a ski holiday. All of Intrawest's ski operations in various parts of North America have at their base pedestrian villages offering shopping, entertainment, and a variety of accommodation. These resorts also have golf courses and hiking and cycling trails to attract summer visitors. "Leisure time is a much more comprehensive experience than simply skiing or having dinner in a restaurant," says Joe Houssian, Intrawest's chief executive.

His formula has been so successful that proposals are under discussion for competing destination resorts near Whistler. These are risky propositions because there may not be enough North American skiers to support them all, which would leave the new resorts excessively vulnerable to economic problems in key foreign markets like Japan.

Tennis

In the mid-1970s, 30 million Americans were playing tennis. By the mid-1990s, only 16 million Americans were playing tennis. Why? The *Wall Street Journal* declared that people had been turned off tennis because "unshaven brats and grungewear fashion plates" are dominating the pro tennis tour. It apparently didn't occur to this serious, fact-filled newspaper to acknowledge the powerful demographic factor at work: the average age of Americans is increasing, and in general, older people don't play tennis as much as younger ones do.

Tennis has been much improved in recent years by technological advances. The modern graphite frames absorb all the shock of hitting the ball so that it is not transferred to the arm and elbow, as was the case with wooden and older metal frames. Because of the new equipment, tennis players are less susceptible to tennis elbow and tennis shoulder, and the sport is more accessible to older people. But they still don't do it. Tennis participation falls from 33% in the 18-to-24 age group down to 7% in the 45-to-64 age group. That's why tennis clubs that had waiting lists in the 1980s needed new members in the 1990s.

The good news at the millennium is that the echo generation is moving into its tennis years; that will revive participation, although not to the same levels as the 1970s. The revival was already evident in the summer of 1998, according to Mary Lynne Boursella, recreation director of the Algonquin Resort in St. Andrews, New Brunswick. "We have new tennis courts and didn't want to see them idle, so we organized a tennis camp for 6-to-15-year-olds. We had a huge turnout."

As for the older people who still play, tennis clubs should adopt the new credo of all product and service providers: quality and service. Many tennis clubs have done just that. One reason tennis participation falls off is that older people are pressed for time and it's difficult to get two people, or four for doubles, on the same tennis court at the same time. That's why many clubs now arrange matches for their players.

Golf

Golf is one of the most time-consuming of all sports. A round of 18 holes typically takes four hours or more to play. In addition, golfers need to warm up at the practice tee and green before a round, place and record their bets, and replay the day's events in the clubhouse lounge afterwards. Throw in travel time to and from the course, and you've extracted six hours from a day. This is what makes golf the perfect sport for retired people; it gives a focus and purpose to their day as well as the companionship of friends and some beneficial yet not strenuous exercise. For those who aren't up to a four-hour walk in the park, electric golf carts are available. The presence of paunchy golfers on the professional tour attests that one can play this game at the highest level even without a high level of fitness.

Given all that, it's not surprising that golf is one sport in which participation increases with age, from 5% in the 19-to-24 age group to 10.2% in the 35-to-54 group, before dropping off to 8.7% in the over-55 group. And while the total percentage of older Canadians playing golf is not high, those who do play spend a large part of their lives on the course. Golf's growing popularity made it the strongest segment of the sporting goods industry. And it enabled ClubLink Corp., a King City, Ontario-based company that owns 23 courses, to increase its profits by 158% in 1997 over the previous year. Meanwhile, in Prince Edward Island, golf is giving a boost to an already healthy tourist industry. Players from all over North America are discovering the beauty of the island's seaside courses, reminiscent of the famous links courses of Britain and Ireland. In 1997, 14% of visitors came to play golf, up from 8% five years before.

Evidence of golf's powerful appeal to older people is that golfers play more as they get older. According to a 1996 survey conducted for the Royal Canadian Golf Association, while the average golfer gets in 14 rounds a year, over-65 male and female golfers play 37 and 21 rounds respectively. The outstanding example of the enthusiasm of older golfers is Paul Stelmaschuk of Kelowna who, in 1997 at the age of 74, played 388 rounds, a new Canadian record. What makes this feat particularly impressive is that Stelmaschuk, retired director of the school of agriculture at the University of Manitoba, played all his rounds in Canada – in Kelowna during the summer and on rainy Vancouver Island during the winter. Only on 46 days that year did he not play golf; he played two rounds on 69 days. "I love the game," he explains. "And I keep getting better at it."

Golf is growing, but that doesn't mean any investment in golf will automatically succeed. Both the product and the timing have to be right. During the economic boom times of the 1980s, for example, many new courses opened in Canada, including some offering equity memberships for amounts as large as $50,000. Some of these courses did not attract enough members to survive as private clubs and were forced to open up to the general public. These clubs failed for two reasons. One was that, with the economic recession, many companies could no longer afford corporate memberships for their executives. But more important, the front-end boomers who were increasingly taking up golf weren't yet ready to part with a big chunk of cash for a club membership. In the late 1980s, they were just beginning to turn 40. At that age, people still have kids at home and a mortgage. As the new century draws near, the successive waves of boomers turning 50 are discovering they have more discretionary income at their disposal because their kids have moved out and their mortgage is history. The result is that some of the courses built in the 1980s will be able to go private as originally planned. Because their developers did not pay enough attention to demographics, these courses were ten years ahead of their time.

Performing Arts

In the 1980s, the future seemed grim for high culture in Canada. Audiences were dwindling, younger people weren't coming, and the financial picture was shaky. The Vancouver Symphony almost folded and other arts companies faced an uncertain future. But music aficionados were more pessimistic than they needed to be. They fretted that, as the oldest members of the audience died, no younger people would come along to replace them because the boomers, raised on the Beatles and the Rolling Stones, would never tune in to Bach and Rachmaninoff.

Culture lovers should relax and enjoy the music. Boomers are human beings, not a new species. Previous generations also had their own popular music, and they too eventually learned to appreciate classical music. Middle-aged and older people have always been more interested in the classics than young people, and the ranks of the middle-aged and seniors will grow explosively in the decades ahead. The future of classical music in Canada has never been brighter.

When a new hockey rink was constructed in 1994 at Acadia University in Wolfville, Nova Scotia, the old one was remodelled into a centre for Shakespearean theatre. That transformation perfectly symbolizes what will happen in Canada because of population aging: attendance at hockey and other spectator sports is likely to grow at rates well below population growth, while growth in attendance at plays and other cultural events will probably exceed population growth. As a result, we will need more theatres and fewer arenas.

By the mid-1990s, the turnaround was already becoming evident. The Toronto Symphony, the Canadian Opera Company, and the Vancouver Opera Association all reported growing audiences after years of falling attendance. In 1997, the Shaw Festival at Niagara-on-the-Lake, Ontario, enjoyed record sales and box office receipts were up again in the summer of 1998.

Other theatre companies as well as art galleries are also savouring new-found popularity. Where have the new recruits to the arts come from? From the same people who caused sales of recorded classical music to double in the first part of the 1990s. These front-end boomers are in their 40s, the age when most people start paying attention to serious music and theatre. (It's also the age when their children are old enough to be left home alone, so that parents, liberated from dependence on babysitters, start going out again.) It was because of the front-end boomers that the Vancouver Opera Association was able to report in 1995 that 64% of its new subscribers were under 50. As the boomers age into their 50s and 60s, audiences for serious live entertainment will continue to grow. At the Neptune Theatre in Halifax, for example, 20% of the audience is between 55 and 64, although that is currently a relatively small population cohort. When the boomers are in the 55-to-64 age group, attendance at the Neptune will set new records.

These trends illustrate that the notion of "cocooning" as a permanent new lifestyle has been greatly exaggerated. Cocooning (see Chapter 10) never was a new value system; it was merely the normal behaviour of people in their 30s with a couple of kids and a mortgage. Because so many people found themselves in that state at the same time, people unacquainted with demographics mistook cocooning for a new mode of behaviour rather than the passing phase that it was. In 1992, the Canadian Arts Consumer Profile, a national survey of arts consumption in Canada, rediscovered the obvious: most people love going out. A large majority of respondents – 66% – said they wanted to attend concerts more often. Moreover, the report dispelled the idea that fans of popular and serious culture occupy two solitudes.

In fact, 25% of rock audiences reported also attending the ballet, and 25% of opera-goers paid to see stand-up comedians at work.

As further indication of a decline in cocooning, Statistics Canada reported that the long-term, gradual decline in television watching resumed in 1996, after being temporarily stalled in 1995 by the introduction of several new specialty cable channels. Despite having more choice on television than ever before, Canadians watched an average of 22.8 hours a week in 1996, almost an hour less than the 23.7 hours a week they watched in 1987.

One other art form deserves mention: the musical. In the 1990s, with the front of the boom generation in its 40s, musicals have become a multimillion-dollar business. Audiences flock to new shows such as *The Phantom of the Opera* and to old ones like *Show Boat*. People in their 20s generally don't like this kind of entertainment. They would much prefer to see a movie, a form of entertainment that appeals most strongly to people in the 17-to-24 age group. People in their 40s are much more receptive to live musicals, and they can afford the extravagant ticket prices. Andrew Lloyd Webber's timing, therefore, has been demographically perfect. He started in Britain, which has an older population, and moved to North America when North America's demographics were ready for him. Had Webber come on the scene with the same music a decade earlier, he would probably not have had the same degree of success.

Birdwatching and Walking

Fans of *The Beverly Hillbillies* loved to laugh at prissy Miss Hathaway, the birdwatcher. Now many of the same people who considered Miss Hathaway's pastime so absurd can be found stomping rural trails on chilly mornings, with guidebooks, binoculars, and birding scopes in hand. At Point Pelee, a southern Ontario park renowned for its bird show during the spring migration, watchers often appear to outnumber birds.

We don't read much about this activity. That's why it comes as a shock to learn that in the United States, 65 million birdwatchers spend more than $5 billion annually on bird-related products. That's almost as much as Americans spend to attend all professional sports. The 65 million includes anyone who has a birdfeeder and watches birds out the kitchen window. About half that many people in the United States and Canada are serious enough to take excursions specifically to view birds.

It's not surprising that birdwatching has become big business. It combines gentle exercise, travel, and intellectual challenge (identifying birds) with the joy of collecting: serious birders keep detailed accounts of their sightings and compete to add rare species to their records. These factors help explain why, in a projection of growth rates of outdoor activities between 1996 and 2011, birdwatching was predicted to be the fastest-growing of all: 6% growth, compared with 3% for golf and 4.5% for fishing. Birdwatching, gardening, and walking are among the few activities that people do more of as they get older. That's why Canada will have some of the world's most closely watched birds over the coming decades.

Although birdwatching is the most peaceful and innocuous of activities, it is capable of provoking intergenerational conflict between the boomers and the busters. In Toronto and elsewhere, naturalists, including birders, have clashed with mountain bikers and in-line skaters in their teens and 20s, accusing them of severely damaging the few bits of nature that have escaped urbanization. "Recently my wife and I went birding on Toronto's Lower Don Trail," recounted a correspondent in the *Globe and Mail*'s letters column in 1995. "[We] were subjected to continual verbal abuse from both the skaters and bicyclists who considered that they and they alone had the right of passage." Another correspondent promptly replied on behalf of bikers and skaters. "The real source of danger in our parks is pedestrians who walk two or three abreast ... deaf to oncoming bikers and skaters who need to pass if they are to enjoy the parks," he wrote.

In Ontario, the Bruce Trail Association has had to set up a committee to mediate the conflict between bikers and walkers. "We're hoping for a resolution, but it may be like the conflict between cross-country skiers and snowmobilers. Eventually they set up their own separate trails," says Jacqueline Winters, executive director of the organization responsible for the 775-kilometre Bruce Trail, the longest continuous footpath in Canada. "Mountain biking is more a sport of the young. Walkers tend to be over 35, very many of them professional people. The conflict will be between these two groups."

As a majority of the population moves from activities like tennis and spectator sports to ones like walking and birding, the movement to make the countryside more accessible will intensify. The most spectacular example is the Trans-Canada Trail, which is scheduled to open on July 1, 2000, as the longest recreational trail in the world. It will cover 14,000 kilometres from the east coast of Newfoundland all the way to the west coast of Vancouver Island, with a branch stretching north from Calgary to Tuktoyaktuk on the Beaufort Sea. It will be suitable for hiking, cycling, horseback riding, skiing, and snowmobiling. Another example of the demographics-driven movement to make use of the great Canadian outdoors is the Canadian Rails to Greenways Network, which promotes the rehabilitation

Cohort conflict

of abandoned rail corridors for recreational purposes. Similar movements exist in the United Kingdom, the United States, Australia, and New Zealand, where population aging is also occurring.

Travel

The upmarket travel business recruits its customers from affluent individuals in their late 40s and older. As this group expands in the years to come, the travel industry will reap the benefits. These front-end boomers have paid off their houses, their kids are starting to leave home, and they are at the peak of their earning power. This adds up to more discretionary income than they have ever had before. They are ready for something a bit more adventurous and unusual than the standard package tour to Mexico, Hawaii, or the Caribbean – perhaps a walking tour of Nepal or an excursion to view birds in Costa Rica or a trip to Irkutsk on the Trans-Siberian Railway.

Largely for demographic reasons, the next two decades will be a golden age for the travel and tourism industries. In Canada, tourism spending grew by 26% from 1986 to 1996 in 1986 dollars – a rate 2% higher than the increase in gross domestic product. Total employment was up 22%, almost twice the rate as in the economy as a whole, to 384,000 jobs. It was no coincidence that in the midst of this growth, airports were becoming what the great train stations of the 19th century had been – imposing gateways to great cities. Vancouver opened an impressive new terminal whose focal point was a magnificent Haida totem pole. In 1998, New York's Kennedy and Toronto's Pearson airports were both about to undergo major overhauls. And the new terminal at Washington's National Airport was so appealing that even people who weren't travelling were going there for lunch.

Sam Blyth, whose Blyth and Co. travel agency in Toronto specializes in upmarket and exotic travel, cites three trends that explain why travel, especially adventurous travel, is a booming business at the transition from one millennium to the next. All three trends, as it happens, are discussed elsewhere in this book:

- More people are taking early retirement. In some cases they have been involuntarily retired from management positions, with handsome severance packages (see Chapter 4).
- The rise in the stock markets has made some people richer than they expected to be and that new money, says Blyth, "has become fun money to be used for luxuries. Travel is the number one luxury that people like to buy." (See Chapter 3.)
- "People are arriving at an older age in a healthier state, so they are able to embark on more travel and more exotic travel. When my mother and father got to 60, they couldn't do anything terribly active but these people can." (See Chapter 11.)

Demographics help explain the apparent increase in vigour in older people. A growing body of research (see Chapter 9) demonstrates a close relationship between economic status and health status. Blyth's customers in their 60s are the Depression babies, who are the wealthiest cohort in Canadian society because they were always in the right place at the right time with respect to jobs and investments (see Chapter 1). So it's not surprising that this group would arrive at retirement in fighting trim and ready for action.

Blyth's older customers are increasingly attracted to what the industry calls "soft adventure holidays," which are easygoing walking or cycling holidays in Europe or the United States. But the hottest segment of the travel industry is eco-tourism, which was growing in the late 1990s at a rate of 20% a year, six times the growth rate of the rest of the industry. Eco-tourists want to see spectacular scenery while learning new things from qualified experts. An example was a two-week trip organized by Adventure Canada of Mississauga, Ontario, in the fall of 1997 that went from Greenland across the Davis Strait and down the Labrador and Newfoundland coasts to St. John's. On board the Russian exploratory vessel were a marine biologist, an archaeologist, and an ecologist. The 73 passengers, whose average age was in the mid-60s, transferred to Zodiac rubber boats for excursions from the ship to places of interest on the coast and, once on land, hiked five to six kilometres a day, often over rocky terrain.

Some eco-tours are even more rigorous – hiking in the mountains, for example, or ocean kayaking, or rafting down fast-flowing rivers. Most customers for this kind of travel are affluent boomers in their 30s and 40s. That is the same market driving the growth of quickie vacations based on the notion that a day or two in a completely different environment can be a pause that refreshes. Weekend vacations by Americans increased by 70% between 1986 and 1996 and now account for more than half of all travel in the United States.

The other big growth area is cruising, which for years has been trying to appeal to a younger market and has finally succeeded. In 1998, the average age for North American cruisers was 44, fully 12 years younger than just 10 years before. This success was achieved by making cruising a family affair for boomers and their echo kids. That's why giant vessels like the *Sun Princess* now have splash pools and play areas for toddlers, ice-cream kiosks, and plenty of kids' entertainment.

At the end of the 1990s, several companies were launching ships displacing in excess of 100,000 tons, even bigger than such

Have empty nest, will travel

giants of the glory days of transatlantic voyages as the *Queen Mary* and the *Queen Elizabeth*. The difference was that the new ships carry 3,000 people, whereas the great transatlantic liners carried 1,200 in more spacious accommodation. These new giants of the seas offer gambling, a variety of restaurants, and lots of action for people of all ages. This sort of holiday is less a relaxing ocean getaway than a Las Vegas-style package tour transferred to the sea.

While the big ships have their appeal, especially to families with kids and buster couples, many older boomers as well as pre-boomers balk at being part of a crowd. Smaller vessels offering trips to unusual destinations for more intimate groups of travellers will have greater appeal to this group. High-quality tours to such places as the Galapagos and Antarctica will continue to attract a steady stream of discriminating travellers in the new century.

Gambling

An Italian politician once argued that lotteries were bad public policy because they encouraged people to gamble away money that was needed to feed, house, and clothe their families. Nonsense, replied Amintore Fanfani, the Italian prime minister at the time. Lotteries, he declared, were perfectly justifiable because they were a "tax on idiots." What he meant was that, because the odds of winning a major lottery prize are infinitesimal, only an idiot would waste money in the attempt.

Canada, it seems, has a plentiful supply of apparent idiots. Quebec launched the first provincial lottery in 1970 and the rest of the country soon followed. By 1996, lottery sales nationwide were $3.4 billion. And lotteries, of course, are only one of many ways available for people to lose – and occasionally win – money in games of chance. Horse racing is well-established in Canada, although its monopoly as the only public venue for legal gambling has been wiped out by the rapid growth of video lottery terminals and casinos – numbering 55 across Canada by 1998 – raking in $2.5 billion.

Still more is spent on illegal gambling in its many forms, including betting on professional sports. Finally, large sums of money change hands in private gambling, whether on the golf course or at kitchen-table card games. The latter, from a consumer standpoint, is the best kind of gambling. Unlike a lottery, which returns less than half the money wagered to bettors, all of the money bet in a private poker game winds up in the hands of the winners. But lotteries have one big attraction that a poker game doesn't: the chance, however remote, of winning a huge, life-changing prize worth millions of dollars.

Who gambles? Theory suggests that young people would have a big incentive to try to win a lottery, because if you can obtain a lot of money early in your life you won't have to work for the rest of it. Furthermore, theory also suggests that people between the ages of 25 and 50 are too busy raising children to participate in gambling. But the actual demographic profile of gamblers is different from what economic and sociological theory would predict.

Fanfani was wrong: most lottery players aren't idiots. To them, a lottery ticket is less an investment for financial return than an investment in fun and risk. Gambling, in other words, is recreation or entertainment, which is why it is discussed in this chapter rather than the one on investment. People are most likely to afford recreation in their 40s and 50s. And that is when they start buying lottery tickets and visiting casinos.

Several factors account for the dramatic growth in gambling in Canada over the past two decades. These include a growing population; the arrival of Asian immigrants with an above-average interest in gambling; mass travel, which introduced many Canadians to the world of casinos in Las Vegas and elsewhere; and the eagerness of cash-strapped governments to exploit gambling as a revenue source.

But gambling's biggest asset is the aging of the boomers into their gambling years. When lottery sales rose over the 1980s, marketers credited better games and better distribution systems. Actually, it happened because the front half of the boom reached 40, the beginning of its gambling years. Gambling will continue to pick up steam into the new century as the front end of the boom moves through its 50s while the back end enters its gambling 40s.

This demographic development doesn't mean all forms of

gambling will prosper. The retail credo of the 1990s, quality and service, applies as much to gambling as to any other product. The 50-year-old is a knowledgeable consumer. If she is going to buy a lottery ticket, it has to be readily available, and the game has to be sophisticated enough to interest her.

Amid growing competition for the gambling dollar, will lotteries continue to get away with offering the poorest odds of any form of gambling? Maybe not, if horse racing can make itself more accessible through off-track betting and if casino gambling continues to expand. Both pay back a much higher percentage of money wagered than lotteries do. On the other hand, public lotteries target their profits for worthy causes such as hospitals and recreation facilities; the consumer is thus prepared to be short-changed as a gambler, knowing that his losses are being used for the common good. In the face of growing competition, however, lottery marketers will have to make the social case for their product more strongly than ever before.

In the 1990s, casinos, previously allowed only in the state of Nevada and Atlantic City, began to appear in other parts of North America. Some viewed this as a sign of declining moral standards. At the same time, and in complete contradiction, arguments were voiced that the increasing acceptance of "family values," the decline in popularity of pot smoking, and increased interest in spirituality were signs of resurgent moral conservatism.

In fact, these changes had little to do with morality and much to do with demographics. Interest in spirituality increased because middle-aged boomers started to become aware of the fact of their own mortality, while pot smoking declined because it is most popular among people in their teens and 20s, and the numbers of such people fell during the 1990s. Family values came to the fore because the number of people in their 30s and 40s raising families increased. And casino gambling is booming because a massive wave of 50-year-olds is washing over North America and 50-year-olds enjoy gambling. Thus, the arrival of casinos in localities that once shunned them is largely a normal market response to surging demand.

But the concerns of those who regret the spread of gambling

should not be dismissed lightly. Gambling is often associated with criminal activity, which may be why the crime rate in Niagara Falls, site of Canada's most successful casino, has risen by 10% since the casino opened. And just as gambling's opponents had predicted, the social consequences were proving to be pernicious. *Maclean's*, after interviewing economists, police, and social workers for an investigative report on gambling, concluded that "casinos destroy at least one job for every one they create, they cause bankruptcies that bleed communities dry, they breed crime and corrode families."

Video lottery terminals were proving to be particularly destructive because they are one of the most addictive forms of gambling. Of course, most players lose, leading some to commit suicide and others to steal to get more money to lose. A 1996 study in Nova Scotia showed that 74% of the government's $78 million in revenues from the terminals came from problem gamblers.

Just as an aging population is more interested than a younger population in gambling, so it has more criminals adept at money-laundering and other forms of fraud (see Chapter 7). One kind of fraud, passing counterfeit money, increases in the vicinity of casinos. If governments are going to encourage the spread of gambling, they should also ensure that law enforcement agencies have the resources and expertise they need to combat gambling-related crime. Yet rather than increasing these resources, they are cutting back on them at the same time as their gambling revenues swell. This is the height of irresponsibility.

Volunteering

A huge difference exists between leisure activities such as listening to music, rolling dice, or playing basketball and philanthropic ones such as raising money for cancer research or being a Big Brother to a child in need of adult companionship. But both are done outside the hours reserved for gainful employment, which is why the future of volunteering is in this chapter. It's not really inappropriate: leisure and recreation pursuits are fun, and volunteering is one of the most richly satisfying activities one can undertake.

Registered charities spent $90.5 billion in 1994, an indication of the importance of the volunteer sector to the Canadian economy. And it is about to become even more important. Volunteering is one of those rare activities that people do more of as they get older. Young people do it too, but for many of them we call it parenting. As their kids grow up and leave home, older people have more time to offer free to worthy causes other than their immediate family. Because of population aging, volunteering, like classical music, is a pastime that will grow in the years to come.

This augurs well for the future of non-profit organizations. Non-profits deliver a variety of services – low-cost housing and rehabilitation of criminals are just a couple of examples – for which there is not always an open market. They also have lobbying and educational functions. All these activities are performed by a staff that is a mix of paid employees and volunteers. This sets non-profits such as the John Howard Society or the Heart and Stroke Foundation apart from both for-profit companies, which have only paid workers, and community groups – local residents' associations, for example – that have only volunteers. A non-profit also has a mixture of funding: it is paid, either by the recipients or the government, to deliver some programs but it also relies on grants and donations. Its management is forever trying to bolster the funding to pursue the vision of the organization.

These are complicated organizations to run, and they are likely to become more complicated as governments back out of the delivery of services, leaving us all more dependent than ever on non-profit organizations for many of these services. The result will be rapid growth in the non-profit sector and tremendous pressure on these organizations to respond to society's new demands. Intensifying this pressure is the fact that some governments have cut their financial support for non-profit organizations just when we need these organizations more than ever. There is no demographic justification for withdrawing public funds from non-profit organizations. The peak of the boom is still in its 30s; these boomers are at least ten years away from having time and money to donate to volunteer organizations.

FIGURE 6: CHARITABLE CONTRIBUTIONS BY AGE

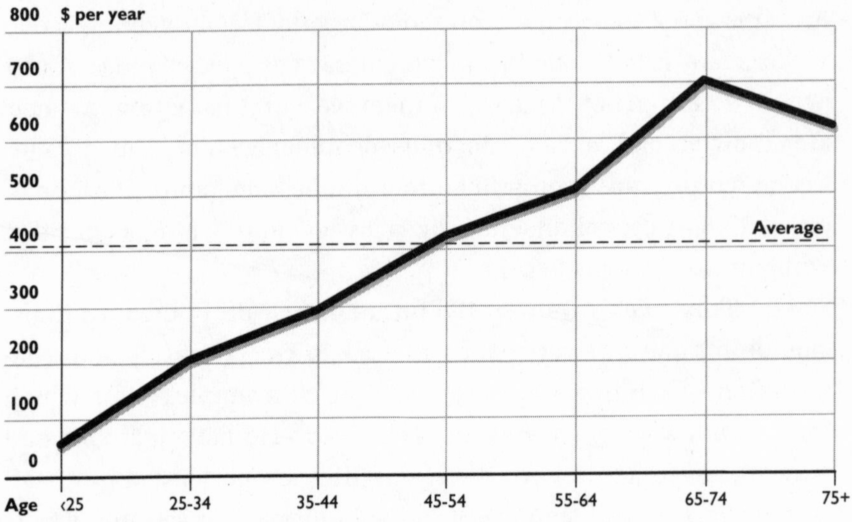

Data are for 1996. Source: Based on unpublished data from Statistics Canada's Family Expenditure Survey.

These organizations needed continued government support to get them through the transition period of the 1990s to an era when the demographic shift will result in increased financial support from non-government sources.

Fortunately, because of population aging, a new source of highly skilled professional managers is becoming available to guide these organizations through this difficult and challenging period. The front half of the boom is in its mid-to-late 40s and early 50s. That's mid-life crisis time, when you ask what you are going to do with the rest of your life. If you are a junior vice-president in a large corporation, you realize you are never going to be president because too many other people are in the way. You're also fed up with working for someone else. This is when you seek career counselling, start your own company, and discover spirituality. This is also when, after years in the corporate world, you rediscover the idealistic side of your personality.

As the 1990s progressed, more and more older members of the boom generation discovered they had plateaued in their careers. They also wanted a more meaningful life, even if it cost them a big drop in salary. As a result, some talented and able executives, stalled and bored in the corporate world, have became available to non-profit organizations. Some quit their jobs while others were downsized. But their compensation for accepting a lower salary is huge: the satisfaction of working for a worthy, perhaps even urgent, social cause along with more responsibility and more authority than they ever enjoyed before. In the United States, consultants have emerged to help executives in the transition to the non-profit sector. And 75 U.S. universities were offering degrees in philanthropy in 1998, five times more than in 1990.

The new professionalism that these people will bring with them may require a difficult adjustment for the old guard who have been running these organizations, and who may lack MBAs and corporate experience. But the old guard has a wealth of knowledge that the non-profit sector is going to need, and part of the challenge for the new managers will be to avoid alienating them.

Population aging means more than just a new source of paid talent for the non-profit organizations. It also means a boost to fundraising efforts, as the ranks of people in their 40s and 50s swell. These front-end boomers will be in their prime savings years; they will have more discretionary income and therefore be more likely to support organizations that serve society and that they themselves may one day have to draw on. As Figure 6 shows clearly, donating money to charity increases steadily with age until retirement, from an average of $184 by taxpayers under 35 to $669 by taxpayers over 65.

With their children grown, boomers will be able to donate more of their time on an unpaid basis. But many will still be working and, as a result, will still be under severe time constraints. They may be available for volunteer work, say, Tuesday nights for three hours. The organizations that are most adept at accommodating this valuable talent when it's available will reap the rewards. Since the boom, because of its size, is such a powerful element in our society, we will see renewed pressure for the Canadian government to do what the American government has done for more than 60 years: allow expenses incurred in the course of doing charitable work to be deducted from income taxes. It is up to government to find innovative ways to encourage people to get involved in volunteer organizations. If it does, all the ingredients are in place for a renaissance in the non-profit sector in the new millennium.

Chapter 7

Urban Renewal

P eople get emotional about the cities they live in. That's why debates about urban planning, architecture, and transportation are often so heated. More than just a difference of opinion is involved in these discussions. Those who consider themselves on the right side of controversial urban issues often assume that those on the other side are not only misguided but also guilty of bad taste, selfishness, or some other moral failing.

The emotionalism is understandable because a lot of poor planning and bad city-building took place during the 20-year growth spurt triggered by the entry of the boom into the labour and housing markets. Historic buildings were lost, scenic views were blocked, rapid transit lines were built in the wrong places, and the needs of pedestrians and cyclists were neglected. Almost everyone agrees that cities with lively downtowns that are welcoming to pedestrians are better places to live than cities given over entirely to the car. And good planners and developers know that, while the growth of suburbs is inevitable, sprawl isn't. But debates on urban issues too often neglect a crucial element: demographics. Planning and development decisions have less impact on the way our cities develop than changes in the composition and needs of the population.

The 20-year-old single person who lives downtown and rides the bus or subway is not morally superior to the 40-year-old parent who drives a car. The young person rides the subway because, living downtown, he doesn't need a car and, being young, he can't afford one. The parent, on the other hand, needs to deliver her son to the hockey rink, her daughter to skating class, and the dog to the vet, and she'll pick up a few bags of groceries on the way back. Whether she lives in the inner city or the suburbs, she can't easily accomplish this trip by public transit. Twenty years in the future, the same young person who today happily zips around town by bike, bus, or subway will be at the wheel of a minivan or something similar, hauling kids, dog, and groceries. It won't happen because he has changed his views on urban planning. It will happen because he is 20 years older.

The last two decades have witnessed growth of the suburbs and decline in transit ridership. These things happened not because of planning mistakes but because Canada has an aging population. The boom generation, one-third of the population, got older and bought bigger houses and bigger cars. They got busier. They moved to the suburbs. They had longer trips to make because they were living farther from work, and more people to carry because they were raising families. The suburbs and the automobile suited their needs more than the inner city and public transit.

DOWNTOWN AND SUBURBS

Canada is among the most urbanized of countries, and cities play a crucial role in our national life. Canada has every right to be proud of its cities. When Corporate Resources Group, an international personnel consulting company based in Geneva, issues its annual rankings of 192 cities around the world according to their quality of life, Canadian cities are prominent at the top of the list. In the 1997 ranking, Vancouver ranked first, Toronto was third, and Montreal was 15th. Other international rankings of cities have come to similar conclusions.

Why do Canadian cities rank so high? Because they are small big cities rather than big big cities. All the cities near the top of the liveability list are small big cities like Vancouver, Geneva, and Auckland. Big big cities like New York, Tokyo, and Mexico City are ranked much lower. The main reason Canada's major cities do so well, and their great strength, is that they are big enough to be lively and interesting and yet small enough to avoid the severe congestion, pollution, and general unmanageability associated with the world's biggest urban centres. A second reason is that Canada's biggest cities still have healthy downtowns. It is not the suburbs that distinguish Toronto from Detroit, a once-great American city that became a symbol of urban decay. Detroit's suburbs are as handsome and liveable as those of Toronto or any other Canadian city. But, despite recent improvements, Detroit lacks a central core that is pleasant and safe to live in and walk in, that is home to residents of a variety of income levels, and that has a good transportation system as well as a full array of entertainment, cultural, educational, and shopping facilities. Canada's best cities have all these things.

How have we done it? Through a combination of luck, good planning, and demographics. Perhaps the best example of pure good luck was Vancouver's failure to implement various schemes to slice up its downtown with freeways during the 1960s. Local politicians were eager to build, but Vancouver was saved from their folly by the Social Credit premier of British Columbia, W.A.C. Bennett, who refused to contribute any money. Bennett's power base was in the interior of the province, so he didn't need to support megaprojects in Vancouver to get re-elected. Had Toronto been blessed with similar benign neglect by the Ontario government, its downtown would not have been permanently disfigured by the Gardiner Expressway, built between 1955 and 1966, which walls off the lakefront from the city.

Toronto's great success has been in protecting vast tracts of single-family housing in and around downtown from highrise redevelopment. These neighbourhoods of red-brick houses on quiet, leafy streets have given Toronto one of the healthiest central cores of the major cities of the world. Wise political decisions to protect the stability of old established neighbourhoods were the basis for this success but demographics played a big part. During the 1970s, the front end of the boom flooded the market for rental accommodation (see Chapter 2). Like all young people, they wanted to be in the centre of the action: downtown. In Toronto, the policy of protecting old neighbourhoods encouraged renovation of existing structures rather than tearing them down and developing new ones. In the 1980s, when they were ready to own homes of their own, the front-end boomers supported this policy enthusiastically and spent millions of dollars to restore and modernize old houses, ensuring the long-term viability of the downtown neighbourhoods.

Meanwhile, in all major Canadian cities, billions of dollars were invested in new commercial and residential buildings to meet the demands of the huge generation flooding the labour and housing markets. Although many uninspired developments were built, there were also good ones, including two of the most innovative and attractive new inner-city housing projects anywhere: the south side of False Creek in Vancouver, and the St. Lawrence project in Toronto. Immigration was another demographic factor that added lustre to Canada's cities. Immigrants tend to be in their 20s, an age when people find downtown living attractive. Their talents, particularly in the field of gastronomy, further enhanced the attractiveness of Canada's major cities.

Downtown Canada is alive and well, and about to get even better as the echo generation moves in, but there is no reason for complacency. Canada's two largest cities, Toronto and Montreal, exhibited signs of decline throughout most of the 1990s. Both cities had an unusual number of empty storefronts as well as many homeless people and panhandlers. A lingering recession through much of the decade had a lot to do with both cities' problems, while political instability caused by separatism exacerbated the situation in Montreal. But powerful demographic trends had been working against downtown and in favour of the suburbs since the beginning of the 1980s. In fact, it is a measure of just how strong Canada's downtowns are that they remained comparatively healthy after almost two decades during which demographics have favoured the suburbs. In contrast, the cores of many large U.S. cities have suffered much more severely from the flight of affluent boomers to the suburbs.

The early boomers pushed house prices in the inner city so high that many late boomers couldn't afford to live there. Many of those who could afford it preferred to switch to a suburban lifestyle when the kids came along. As a result, the arrival of the boom in its childbearing years coincided with a massive growth spurt in the suburbs. In Toronto, for example, the population of the central city increased only slightly between 1981 and 1996, going from 599,000 to 656,000, while that of the Greater Toronto Area (GTA) grew from 3.4 million to just over 4.6 million. Almost all the population growth occurred in new suburbs of new houses in new subdivisions. These houses lacked the charm of the Victorian residences of the central city but they were affordable, they were big, they had yards, and they had garages big enough for two cars or even three.

Canadians are now coming to the realization that they cannot afford this type of development any longer. In a 1995 report called *Economics of the Urban Form*, Pamela Blais, a Toronto economist, said roads, utilities, and other public services used in suburbs are paid for with billions of dollars in subsidies from provincial governments and urban taxpayers. Developers take advantage of these invisible subsidies to build inefficient communities, raising taxes and service costs throughout the area and driving away businesses. Blais's study concluded that huge savings would be available if a more compact form of development were adopted in future. In the Toronto area, taxpayers could save up to $4 billion in operating and maintenance costs over the next 25 years if more compact neighbourhoods were built, while the capital costs for roads, transit, and utilities would be as much as $16 billion less. On the west coast, the Greater Vancouver Regional District has concluded that $2.2 billion could be saved on transportation costs if new growth were more concentrated. A study showed that private cars in the Vancouver area enjoy public subsidies of $2,700 a year each, seven times the subsidy for public transit. As a result, Vancouver has developed a growth management strategy, including zoning changes and new charges for utilities such as sewers, aimed at discouraging sprawl.

Because of the demographic shift, the pressure for suburban growth should subside in the years to come, which may make such reforms easier to implement. With all the boomers past their prime childbearing years and the baby-bust generation 44% smaller, new family formation will continue to slow down as will births and the pace of growth of bedroom suburbs. Moreover, an aging society with more discretionary income will be prepared to pay the user fees that analysts such as Blais are recommending, providing they get good service in return. For example, with most of the boom driving cars, the 1990s were an excellent time to build new roads paid for by user tolls. "I am having a passionate love affair with Highway 407!" Sandra Frost, a resident of the Toronto suburb of Mississauga, wrote to the *Toronto Star*, referring to a new toll highway north of the city that opened in 1997. "My usual 45-minute trips across the top of Mississauga are reduced to 5 or 10 minutes at the most." Saving more than 30 minutes per trip is extremely valuable to a busy commuter and well worth the cost of the tolls.

Meanwhile, as the front-end boomers move through their 50s and 60s in the two decades ahead, the demographic shift will lead to strong growth in the ranks of "penturbanists" in Canada. That's a term invented by Jack Lessinger of the University of Washington, who believes increasing numbers of people will flee the big cities in search of a quieter and less expensive way of life. The suburbs aren't far enough from the big cities for these people – they will want to settle in small towns and small cities (see Chapter 2). This tendency will be particularly pronounced in Canada, because many urban Canadians grew up in small towns and rural districts and may want to move back home, or to a place that reminds them of home, when they retire.

TRANSPORTATION

Buses, streetcars, and subways were invented to serve densely populated inner cities. They were not invented to serve sparsely populated suburbs. Public transit makes money in the core; it loses money in the suburbs. Unfortunately for public transit, the aging of the boom generation triggered the growth of sprawling suburbs and stagnation in the inner cities. The aging of the boom was a disaster for many of Canada's public transit systems.

Canada's largest public transit system, the Toronto Transit Commission (TTC), which serves the amalgamated city of Toronto, recorded 432 million passenger trips in 1985. In 1997, despite an improving economy, the system was used for only 380 million trips. Montreal's transit system also lost riders, but not as many. The Société de Transport de la Communauté Urbaine de Montréal carried 337 million passengers in 1997, down from 350 million in 1985.

Economic recession had a lot to do with the decline in ridership, as did bad decisions about transit service. As the suburbs grew, transit systems expanded to serve them. This involved shifting resources from the centre, where transit is viable, to the suburbs, where it isn't. Transit needs 4,000 people per square kilometre to pay for itself. In Toronto, the inner city has 6,540 people per square kilometre; the suburban district of Etobicoke has only 2,500. Richard Gilbert, a Toronto urban consultant, says the TTC's policy of reducing inner-city service to pay for suburban service is crazy because it involves "taking away services where there is ridership to put on service where there is no ridership."

It makes no sense to build expensive subway systems or even to run conventional buses in most suburban areas because, no matter how good the service, not enough people will use it. This fact can be seen by anyone who drives down a suburban Toronto freeway unofficially called the Spadina Expressway, which connects a northern district to the inner city. The expressway has a subway line running above ground down its centre median. Except for brief periods during the weekday rush hours, these subway cars are almost empty. The people who are supposed to be riding in them are sitting in traffic jams on the expressway, watching the empty trains roll by.

Obviously, this was no place to put a subway, because the population density along its route is insufficient to support it. Demographics made such an unwise decision possible. The rapid growth of the suburbs, triggered by the movement of the boomers out to the new subdivisions, gave the suburban politicians the power to impose their wishes on the inner city. In the case of the Spadina subway, they outvoted the inner-city councillors who wanted to tunnel a subway under a densely developed street instead.

Subways should be built where riders are, not where one hopes they might be at some time in the future. Yet even the experience of the Spadina subway has not taught the Toronto politicians this simple lesson. That explains why, in 1996, they approved yet another suburban expansion of the subway. They decided to spend $875 million on a 6.4-kilometre line running underneath a street called Sheppard Avenue in a sparsely populated residential district. This was a decision of awesome stupidity because the population required to support the subway was not present anywhere in its vicinity and the same councillors who voted for it were against the sort of high-density developments that might some day make the subway line anything but a perpetual money-loser. The project's chief supporter, Mel Lastman, who went on to become the first mayor of the amalgamated Toronto, promised that development fees on the route of the new line would help defray its cost but by 1998 none had materialized, although by then the cost had ballooned to $920 million.

Another decision that badly weakened the TTC in the early 1970s was to equalize all fares regardless of the length of the trip; going one stop on the subway downtown costs the same as a 40-kilometre trip from one side of the metropolitan area to the other. This was a way to make the profitable inner-city routes subsidize the suburban routes, in a futile effort to get suburbanites to ride the transit system. The only result of such policies is to reduce service on the successful routes, which then lose riders, a loss that is not compensated by a corresponding gain in the suburbs.

Let's take a closer look at the demographics of public transit. A person's use of the transit system rises over the teenage years and peaks at the age of 19 (see Figure 7). The 19-year-old has little money and plenty of time to wait at bus stops. Transit therefore suits his needs perfectly. The front-end boomers were in their teens during the 1960s, with the first boomers turning 20 in 1967. That's why Canada's major transit systems enjoyed booming growth during the 1960s and 1970s. In those heady days of ever-increasing demand, the TTC paid its bus drivers a $50 bonus to recruit new drivers.

But the peak of the boom turned 20 in 1981. It was predictable that average transit use would decline after that date. A more dense form of development in the suburbs and better management of the

FIGURE 7: AVERAGE DAILY TRIPS PER PERSON, GREATER TORONTO AREA

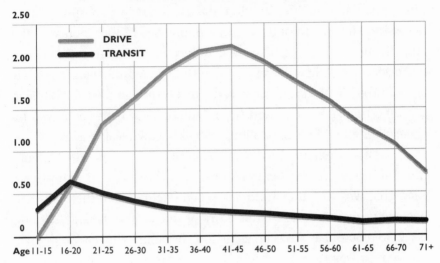

Data are for 1996. Source: Based on data from Transportation Tomorrow Survey, Joint Program in Transportation, University of Toronto.

transit system could have reduced the decline, but some decline was inevitable, as Figure 7 makes clear. Even in a hypothetical scenario in which no suburban development has been allowed, with a growing population housed instead in a much more intensively developed inner city, transit use would decline because of aging. The decline in transit use that starts at 20 continues for 45 years, right up until retirement age. By age 51, a person is almost one-third as likely to ride the bus as at 15. After retirement, most people have less money and more time. Predictably, they then begin to use the transit system more, but they don't make nearly as many trips as young transit riders do.

Car use starts when a teenager reaches the legal driving age and peaks in the early 40s. This is the typical middle-aged consumer described in Chapter 5, for whom time is valuable because it is scarce. The car costs him more than a transit pass would, but it saves so much time that it's more than worth it. This is especially so for the person who lives in the suburbs. In most cases, he has no subway or other rapid transit near his home, the nearest bus stop is several blocks away, and once he gets there, the wait is often long. His workplace may well be located in some other suburb, also not well served by transit. And then there are the kids to be picked up and the shopping to be done. In this situation, the car is not just an option, it's a necessity. The advent of the cellular phone has further increased the attractiveness of the car, because it allows the suburban commuter to make good use of his time even when stuck in a traffic jam. The average suburbanite needs his car so badly that he gets in the habit of using it all the time, even for short trips that could be better achieved by some other form of transportation, such as his own feet or a bicycle.

This is where all of North America was as the new millennium approached. The boom had moved off transit and into private cars. That was why transit ridership had declined and the roads had become crowded. In the latter years of the 1990s, transit ridership began to rebound as the echo generation began moving about town on bus and subway.

Demographics explain two-thirds of everything. This does not mean that the other one-third isn't important. In the case of transit, the

The echo in transit

other one-third is extremely important, because if ways could be found to move more people back to transit, the quality of life in our cities would benefit greatly. Older consumers are motivated more by quality and service and less by price in making product choices. Quality is a matter of taste that varies from individual to individual. For some, riding a well-made bicycle while enjoying exercise and open air is an experience of far greater quality than sitting behind the wheel of a car. But for most, the private car is the most comfortable and convenient means of transportation. The only way to get some of these people out of their cars is to shift the balance of quality and service towards transit.

It is possible to increase both the convenience and the comfort of transit. While roads must not be neglected, government should not be over-solicitous in meeting the demands of drivers if the goal is to make transit a more attractive alternative. The huge advantage of the automobile is its ability to provide quick door-to-door transportation. But when quick turns into slow because roads are congested, and when the trip isn't door to door because parking is either not available, too expensive, or not conveniently located, the private car loses some of its comparative advantage. In this respect, the example of Toronto's SkyDome is instructive. The builders of the stadium wisely put it close to both the subway and the central train station, which is the hub of a commuter rail network. Meanwhile the roads near the stadium are congested and, while parking is plentiful, most of it is several blocks from the stadium entrance. The result? Some 36% of people attending Toronto Blue Jays games travel by public transit, compared with only 14% using transit for all trips in Toronto.

U.S. experience indicates that if you build a road, cars will come, and if you take the road away, cars will go away. Where they go is unclear. In 1973, a New York City freeway, the West Side Highway, collapsed and was not replaced. A comparison of traffic counts taken with and without it showed that only 7% of the lost traffic was diverted onto parallel roads. Most of the trips disappeared. The same thing happened in San Francisco after the Embarcadero Freeway along the waterfront was destroyed in the 1989 earthquake. It was not rebuilt and traffic engineers' warnings of massive congestion proved unfounded. On the contrary, traffic moves smoothly without the freeway, and its removal has triggered new private investment that is revitalizing the waterfront.

Of Canada's three major cities, only Vancouver does not have freeways emptying traffic into its downtown core and has no plans to build any. Moreover, a decision in 1998, after decades of debate, not to increase the number of lanes on the Lions Gate Bridge that connects the downtown core to the North Shore suburbs indicated that Vancouver has accepted the value of putting constraints on the movement of cars. Limiting cars does not necessarily limit growth. A 1996 report showed that the number of vehicles entering the central business area had declined for four years in a row. Yet during that period, downtown Vancouver was thriving and construction of new office and residential buildings continued at a rapid pace.

Where did the vanished drivers go? Some of them may have stopped coming downtown because they got jobs in one of Vancouver's fast-growing suburbs. Others may have moved downtown into apartments that were walking or cycling distance from work. Perhaps others car-pooled or switched to transit, which improved somewhat over the 1990s; by 1998, the elevated SkyTrain system was carrying 100,000 people a day and was about to be expanded.

But nobody knows for sure where all the drivers went just as nobody knows where the people who used to drive on the fallen New York and San Francisco freeways went. Traffic planning is not an exact science. One thing most Vancouverites do know, however, is that there are too many cars in their city, causing daily traffic jams on the Oak, Lions Gate, and other bridges as well as on suburban freeways. Is the answer to add lanes to the existing freeways and build new ones? That's the direction Toronto has taken, and yet traffic on the 16-lane Highway 401 often moves more slowly than the horse and buggy of the pre-auto age. The number of cars and trucks, it would appear, expands to fill the roads made available to them. The only way to circumvent this law may be to build toll roads, such as Toronto's Highway 407, described above.

As for transit, it's time to introduce some new ideas, especially in suburbs designed for cars that can go anywhere and not for large transit vehicles running on fixed routes. Since conventional large buses don't work in suburbs because the population densities are insufficient to support them, why not use more cost-efficient smaller buses? Since many people won't walk several blocks to a major street to find a bus stop, why not let small buses circulate into the side streets to get them? And why not let customers hail a bus instead of having to walk to a stop? These kinds of transit alternatives have met with success in Britain and elsewhere. They are particularly appropriate for a time-conscious, aging population. Such a population is prepared to pay for better service, so some suburban routes could charge a fare between that of a regular bus and that of a taxi.

Innovation will happen only if politicians allow the public transit systems to stop subsidizing hopelessly unprofitable routes with revenues from profitable ones. It's time for politicians and transit managers to recognize the demographic changes that have taken place in our cities over the past two decades and design transit systems to accommodate those changes. Municipal transit systems should be allowed to concentrate on what they do best: operating subways, streetcars, and buses along densely populated corridors. Let private entrepreneurs develop new kinds of small-scale services suitable to the suburbs. The result would be better service in both the central city and suburbs, and profits for both private and public transit companies.

Public transit is not a frill. It is an essential part of the urban infrastructure that allows a modern economy to function. An extreme example is Bangkok, whose economy has suffered because traffic jams make it difficult for anyone to get to more than two meetings in a day. In Hong Kong, by contrast, an excellent subway system and other public transit allow the busy deal-maker to attend six meetings in a day. In North America, the large echo generation is now moving through its prime transit-using years. For its benefit, and that of society as a whole, we must maintain safe, convenient public transit systems.

CRIME IN THE CITY

At first glance, the North American crime data for 1997 seemed puzzling. Car theft was up and so was fraud. But violent crime, including homicides, was down. Did this make sense? Was there any pattern here?

Yes, there was. These trends were the predictable result of change in the age structure of the population. Just as the likelihood that an individual will buy a certain make of car or play a certain sport goes up or down depending on that person's age, so does the likelihood that a criminal will commit a certain type of crime. Teenage criminals prefer non-violent theft. People in their 20s are the most likely to commit violent crime and use guns. Older criminals, who would rather avoid dangerous situations, turn to credit card scams and other kinds of fraud.

Viewed in this demographic light, the 1997 crime statistics were not surprising. Because of the aging of the echo generation, the teenage population was growing, which explained the rise in property theft. The bust, a smaller cohort, had replaced the boom in the violent crime age group, causing a decrease in murders and other violent crimes. Meanwhile, the large cohort of boomer criminals had moved into their fraud years, which was why forensic accounting was becoming a growth industry (see Chapter 4).

Statistics sometimes confuse and mislead, and this is especially so when they relate to crime. For much of the 1990s, overall crime rates have been in decline, and yet that statistical reality did not jibe with what many people knew, or thought they knew, of real life on the streets of our cities. Anyone who reads newspapers learns about gruesome, violent crimes. Most city dwellers know of someone whose house has been burglarized or whose car has been stolen. Many parents are reluctant to allow their children to wander about the neighbourhood, even if the neighbourhood is generally considered safe. Those who ride bicycles in the big city would not dream of leaving them unlocked.

Demographics coupled with a bit of historical perspective can help explain the apparent contradiction between statistics and real life. While many fluctuations occur in the data from year to year and place to place, and while some kinds of crime are up and other kinds down, overall crime rates tended to fall during the 1990s because the largest cohort in society, the boom, was past its prime crime years. When the peak of the boom turned 30 in 1990, it was inevitable that crime rates would decline.

But factors other than the age structure of the population also influence crime patterns. These include economic and social conditions, changes in family life, and law enforcement practices. The impact of these other factors was such that Canada's overall crime rate in 1995 was four times higher than it had been three decades previously, and violent crime was more than twice as high. It's easy for people who live in safe neighbourhoods and pass through the world in the sealed bubble of their automobiles to dismiss the concerns of those who think crime is getting worse. An older woman who walks to the grocery store in a low-income neighbourhood where sidewalk purse-snatchings are frequent occurrences knows the streets are more dangerous than they used to be.

Not only are they more dangerous in fact but, to her, they seem more dangerous than they really are because she is older and perceives the world differently. Older people generally are less agile and thus more fearful than younger people. An aging population also has more potential crime victims because it has more people who own something worth stealing. Moreover, as people get older, the likelihood increases that they, or someone they know, will have been on the receiving end of crime. And of course some older people, because they are frail, really are more vulnerable to muggers and other criminals.

At the same time, an apparent increase in violent crime by young people points to the possibility of a new trend developing that would not have been predicted by past demographic patterns. Some analysts have drawn a connection between increasing violence by youth and the disintegration of the family (see Chapter 10). "As a clinician, clearly I'm seeing that adolescents now are a lot more violent than they were," Dr. Louis Morisette, a Montreal psychiatrist, told the *Globe and Mail*. "They don't see people as whole persons – they see only a wallet that they can steal. . . . That makes them a lot more dangerous." If youth are getting more violent, we are in for a lot of trouble early in the new millennium as the echo generation enters its crime-prone youth years.

Let's look more closely at the demographics of crime. Historically, the 13-to-24 age group has been less violent than the group just ahead of it in age. The typical teenager's crime is one in which he doesn't come into contact with his victim. He knocks on the front door, and if no one answers, he goes around to the back, levers off the sliding glass door, goes upstairs to the bedroom, checks out the drawers, grabs any jewellery and money he can find, and picks up the VCR on his way out. This is your basic teenage break-and-enter.

But just as a person can expect to get promoted in the regular workforce once he accumulates some experience, so there are "promotions" in the crime workforce. A person in his late 20s, if he stays in the crime field, will move into bigger and better things. He'll graduate from breaking into homes to robbing banks. The 29-year-old's crime is more violent than the 19-year-old's. He may have a gun, and the chances that he will hurt people as well as property are greater.

Demographics explain the different growth rates in types of crime over the past three decades. We saw major growth in property crime during the 1960s and 1970s, when large numbers of boomers were passing through their break-and-enter years. A shift in growth from property crime to violent crime occurred over the 1980s and into the 1990s, as the last of the boomers moved out of their teen years into their 20s and early 30s. And at the threshold of the new millennium, those boomers still engaged in crime are switching to fraud.

Occasionally, a huge scam like the Bre-X stock fraud captures the public's attention but, for the most part, Canadians do not appreciate the extent of fraud or the damage it does to the economy. The estimated annual loss, to individuals, companies, and governments, is $12 billion a year – about 1 $^{1}/_{2}$% of Canada's gross domestic product.

The situation is bound to get worse because budget cutbacks have reduced the ability of the Royal Canadian Mounted Police and other police forces to combat fraud. This is an example of how failure by government to take demographic change into account results in misguided public policy. Cutting the police budget for fraud just when boomer criminals are gravitating towards it is like closing hospitals just before the largest part of the population is about to start needing them (see Chapter 9).

Budget cutbacks and low pay have driven some of the RCMP's top investigators into the private sector. The result, as RCMP Commissioner Philip Murray told *Maclean's*, is that "we're going to end up with two-tier policing with forensic accounting firms dealing with those kinds of [white-collar] crimes because the public purse simply will not be able to accommodate it."

The situation was so bad as the millennium approached that Canada was becoming known internationally as a haven for white-collar criminals. "There's so much fraud that the police can't keep up," according to Pat McKernan, a former Mountie who quit to work in the private sector. Many of the biggest frauds in Canada originate in the country's financial centre, Toronto. But because of budget cuts and a decentralization policy, the RCMP has closed its Toronto office, dispersing the staff to small towns in southern Ontario. Of the 60 commercial crime investigators who had been based in Toronto, half quit the force. Meanwhile, as of 1997, the Toronto police force had a two-year backlog of fraud investigations and was reportedly not even looking at cases involving less than $1 million.

This was the environment in which Statistics Canada reported in 1998 that fraud had dropped to its lowest level in 20 years, an egregious example of misleading statistics. In fact, all that had happened was that fewer bad cheques were being reported, partly because fewer cheques were being written in the age of plastic credit and partly because of changes in policing. Fraud rates "haven't dropped at all," Calgary detective Ernie Robson said in a Canadian Press story about the Statistics Canada data. "It's just that the police agencies, because of the amount of time and the manpower shortage, have had to adopt a policy that they only investigate bad cheques in higher dollar quantities."

While bad cheques were down, credit card fraud was rising

steadily. It cost Canadian banks (and ultimately the banks' customers) $88 million in 1997, about twice what the Mounties had to investigate all types of commercial crime in all parts of the country. Credit card fraud was becoming more sophisticated at the same time as it was becoming more prevalent. Whereas it used to involve stolen cards, crooks were now more likely to use counterfeit or altered cards. Another area of fraud that increased sharply during the 1990s was telemarketing, scams that cost Canadians $4 billion a year, according to federal estimates. Bogus investment schemes sold over the phone often targeted seniors. Phonebusters, an Ontario Provincial Police task force on telemarketing fraud, reported in 1998 that 80% of losses in telephone scams were suffered by people over 60.

One of the biggest and least-publicized areas of fraud is theft by employees from their employers. It's hard to detect because most of it is done in small amounts. For example, a manager in one Toronto organization investigated by forensic accountants at Peat Marwick Thorne had control over large amounts of cash received as payments. She regularly stole small sums of money. Over five years, these petty thefts added up to $500,000.

Companies engaged in downsizing are particularly vulnerable to this type of theft, because they have fewer managers in place to watch for it and because their efforts at restructuring may have left them with demoralized and disloyal employees. White-collar crime was going to increase dramatically anyway because of population aging. That the aging phenomenon coincided with a wave of corporate downsizing has exacerbated the situation. Canada is facing an epidemic of fraud as we move into the new century. Our vulnerability to this kind of crime will be all the greater if our police forces let down their guards when the danger is greatest.

Just as the entry of the echo into its teens and early adult years presents Canada's retailers with a more complex marketing challenge than just a few years ago (see Chapter 5), so it also complicates life for law enforcement agencies. A teenager is much more likely to take part in car theft, breaking and entering and other property crimes than a pre-teen. And when the echo generation begins entering its 20s after 2000, replacing the smaller bust generation in the violence-prone age group, chances are that the downward trend in violent crime will be reversed. The impact of the echo has already been experienced in rising rates of car theft, which doubled between 1987 and 1997. Particularly hard hit were Winnipeg, where thefts increased 234% between 1991 and 1996, and Regina, which recorded a 155% increase over the same period. Youths aged 15 to 19 accounted for 45% of those accused.

Most worrisome of all is the possibility, noted above, that teenagers are becoming more violent. One of North America's leading criminologists, James Allen Fox, dean of the College of Criminal Justice at Northeastern University in Boston, discerns an alarming absence of morality among some echo children in the United States, which he fears could lead to a plague of serious teenage crime by members of the echo generation. A Canadian example was the murder in 1995 of a retired couple in Montreal; they were beaten to death with a baseball bat. Three echo kids were charged. One police officer said it was the first murder he had seen in 31 years that was done just for the pleasure of killing.

We don't know whether this sort of crime will become more common or will remain an aberration. But Paul Steinhauer, a Toronto child psychiatrist, reports that school teachers "are almost unanimous in saying that there is a different quality to the violence going on in schools." Group attacks are more common than in the past, as is the use of weapons, he told the *Toronto Star*. Constable Chris Horsley of the Saanich Police Department, near Victoria, who found the body of murdered 14-year-old Reena Virk in 1997, echoes that concern. "Ten years ago you'd have a couple of kids punching it out in the schoolyard," he told journalist Sandra Martin in *Chatelaine*. "Now you have ten people jumping on one – swarming them – in the schoolyard or out in the community."

These trends, happening at the same time as the echo moves into its crime-prone years, offer no reason for anyone to feel complacent about crime in Canada. Our police forces are going to be busy at the millennium. But are they prepared?

THE URBAN – NON-URBAN DIVIDE

Look at Figure 8. One population pyramid shows the population by age in 1996 for Halifax-Dartmouth; the other shows the rest of Nova Scotia. The differences between the two are startling. Halifax's population is typical of large Canadian cities – it has a sharply defined boom, bust, and echo. The boom is smaller in non-urban Nova Scotia; that's because some boomers moved to Halifax or to cities in other provinces. Meanwhile, preschoolers are a bigger percentage of the population in urban Halifax, while those over 65 are a much bigger percentage of the population in non-urban Nova Scotia.

In general, urban Canada and non-urban Canada are two different countries. Urban Canada is younger than non-urban Canada. That's because the boomers and their children make up a larger part of the overall urban population. And while the total number of seniors is greater in the cities, they are more important as a percentage of the population in the non-urban areas. (It should be noted, however, that regional variations exist. For example, the echo is more pronounced in Ontario, Saskatchewan, and Alberta than it is in British Columbia.)

The urban–non-urban divide has important implications for both public and private sectors. Halifax has a smaller percentage of old people than the national average, but Nova Scotia as a whole has a larger percentage. This means that a marketing strategy that works in Halifax won't necessarily work in the rest of the province. And although a toy store might be profitable in Halifax, the demographics of non-urban Nova Scotia aren't promising for products aimed at the youngest segment of the population.

The urban and non-urban areas also have different needs when it comes to public goods. Non-urban Nova Scotia needs health care facilities while urban Nova Scotia needs daycare and schools. A Nova Scotia government that cuts health care to pay for schools should not be surprised when its non-urban vote erodes in the next election. The practice of off-loading responsibility for services to the municipalities is especially troublesome for non-urban and small-town Canada. These local governments have a smaller tax base

FIGURE 8: NOVA SCOTIA'S POPULATION, 1996

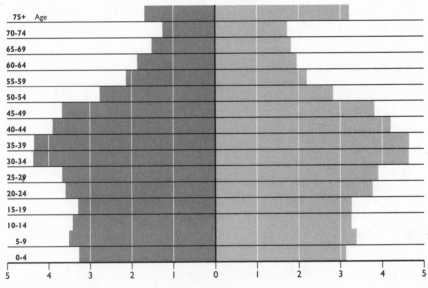

URBAN
MALE   FEMALE

Percentage of population

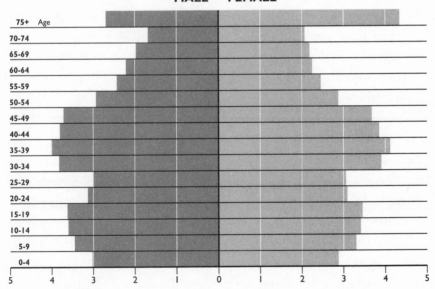

NON-URBAN
MALE   FEMALE

Percentage of population

Source: Based on data from Strategic Projections, Inc.

because the boomers in their prime working years have left and yet they have increased responsibilities for their large senior populations and the echo kids, especially where there are a lot of them. Inevitably, off-loading may mean declining federal and provincial taxes, but at the same time it will also mean rapidly rising local taxes.

THE FUTURE OF CANADA'S CITIES

Canada was a rural country that became a predominantly urban country over the course of the 20th century. Our population was only 20% urban in 1871. But by 1931, city-dwellers were a majority of 53% and by 1996, they made up 78% of the population. Yet, until recently, Canadians were never really comfortable with city life. In fact, until the 1970s, Canadian cities, except for Montreal and Quebec City, were dismal places. Zoning rules robbed the streets of colour and life by rigidly separating residential, commercial, and retail uses. Sidewalk cafés were forbidden. Because of puritanical liquor laws, there were few bars and nightclubs and hardly any decent restaurants.

The cities and the baby boom grew up at the same time. By happy coincidence, the influx of millions of youthful boomers into the cities coincided with the dawn of the age of mass travel. The boomers thus became the first generation in which large numbers actually saw Paris, Rome, and New York for themselves. If Parisians could have sidewalk cafés and New Yorkers could live in lofts in industrial areas, they wondered, why can't we?

As part of this maturing process, city-dwellers at the end of the 1990s were starting to appreciate aspects of their cities that had been neglected and abused. And they were starting to repair some of the damage done during the postwar decades of rapid growth. For example, Winnipeg's main intersection of Portage and Main had been a colourful landmark, famous as the widest and windiest corner in Canada. Then the city, as part of a redevelopment, put barriers up so that it became impossible for pedestrians to cross it except by tunnel. In 1998, plans were underway to undo the damage. By then, it had also dawned on Winnipeggers that the Exchange District, an area of warehouses that contains some of North America's best Edwardian architecture, is a priceless asset. Some of these warehouses were being converted into apartments. A similar phenomenon of old industrial buildings being reborn as places to live was occurring in the Yaletown district of Vancouver and in various parts of central Toronto.

These areas will continue to have commercial as well as residential uses. One of the most important lessons the boomers learned on their trips to Europe was that mixing uses is what brings a city to life. The best streets in the best cities were ones where people lived, worked, shopped, and played. And at the millennium, playing was an increasingly important industry in major North American cities. The demographics were favourable because the largest cohort, the boomers, could go out again now that their kids were old enough to be left alone. And the second largest cohort, the boomers' kids, were becoming big consumers of movies and other entertainment.

To appeal to the boomers, abandoned theatres in New York, Chicago, Toronto, and other cities were restored and rededicated to live entertainment. For the echo, elaborate entertainment complexes, including movies, virtual reality arcades, waterparks, and even indoor ski hills, were under construction. Some of these facilities were downtown while others were in the mini-downtowns of the suburbs. In this way, the arrival of the echo into its spending years was already giving a shot in the arm to the big cities just as their parents had done in the 1960s and 1970s. It won't be as powerful a shot because the echo kids are fewer than the boomers, and it will be partially offset by the movement of some boomers from the large cities to smaller ones (see Chapter 2). Nevertheless, there will be more riders for Canada's beleaguered transit systems, more people in the clubs and bars, and more renters for apartments.

Meanwhile, because of demographic change, the real estate market is less turbulent than it was, and that has its positive side. Many homeowners are settling for renovating and adding on to existing homes rather than moving up to bigger, more expensive ones. Renovation is always healthy for cities because it stabilizes and improves neighbourhoods. Another result of demographic change is the advent of the age of quality and service. An aging population is more likely to support small neighbourhood stores offering good products and friendly service, and less likely to drive long distances looking for bargains at discount megastores in the suburbs. The result is increased business for local shopping areas that maintain adequate parking.

The reason that small stores offer a more pleasant shopping experience is personal contact between the shopper and a merchant who understands the shopper's needs and might even know him by name. Personal contact is a fundamental human need, and it is the reason we will continue to have large cities even after technology has made it at least theoretically possible to dispense with them. We have lived with phone, fax, and e-mail long enough to realize that they can't replace face-to-face contact. That is why the computer industry itself, which created the technology that some people claimed would enable us to do without personal contact, operates in clusters of companies in close geographical proximity. So do companies in such other high-tech industries as financial services, telecommunications, and biotechnology. It is no accident that many financial services companies are clustered around Bay and King streets in central Toronto, or that many companies in the computer industry are clustered in the Ottawa suburb of Kanata. In the new economy, ideas are the generators of growth and wealth creation. The best way to produce new ideas is to have like-minded people working close to one another. The best place to do that is in large urban areas, and that's an important reason Canada's big cities have a bright future.

Chapter 8

Rethinking Education

M ost Canadians think Canada has a first-rate health care system and a second-rate education system. Although both the excellence of the health care system and the problems of the education system are often overstated, this piece of popular wisdom is essentially true. Health care standards in Canada are the equal of those in other advanced countries. On the other hand, Canada is usually somewhere in the middle of the pack in international rankings of scholastic achievement. The Third International Mathematics and Science Study, published in 1996, compared the performance of students in 41 countries. Canada finished 15th in science and 16th in mathematics.

Employers and university teachers complain that a Canadian high school diploma no longer certifies literacy and numeracy. As a new university year was starting in the fall of 1996, 22 professors from seven Ontario universities signed a newspaper article in which they bemoaned "a steady and alarming long-term decline" in the preparedness of first-year students. These students were "unable to understand articles and books their peers once regarded as standard work." They were less able than previous new arrivals to listen to a lecture and take notes that made sense, to prepare for an exam, or to research a subject in the library. "It isn't just a few, or even a large minority, we are talking about: it is the majority of students who are having trouble keeping up, and so are being cheated of the university education they ought to have been prepared to take advantage of."

And while high school graduates were having trouble reading and writing, others were even worse off: the 28% of Canadian students who didn't finish high school, one of the highest dropout rates in the industrialized world.

However, the Canadian health care and education systems do have one important thing in common: both are expensive by international standards. The health care system is the fourth costliest per capita in the world. And our spending on education is the highest per capita among the G-7 leading industrialized countries, according to the Organization for Economic Co-operation and Development.

We are spending more on education than other countries but not getting more in return. In a world economy in which success is based more on knowledge than on natural resources, Canada's relatively poor performance in education threatens our international competitiveness. Our social cohesion is also at risk. As more middle-class parents give up on the public system and enrol their children in private schools in search of academic excellence, society becomes fragmented. The high dropout rate increases that fragmentation, creating an underclass of unskilled workers, widening the gap between rich and poor, and increasing the demands on the social safety net just when the net has been shredded in the name of fiscal prudence.

The failure of those responsible for managing the education system to pay attention to demographics is the root cause of the system's inflated cost. Because Canada had the world's loudest baby boom, we experienced dramatic increases in school enrolments during the 1950s and 1960s. We had to expand the elementary schools, then the high schools, and finally the colleges and universities to accommodate hordes of new arrivals. As the population bulge passed through the different levels, to be replaced by a smaller demographic cohort, one school board after another made the same disastrous blunder: they failed to remove funds from the level with shrinking enrolment and pass the funds on to the next level, where enrolment was expanding. As a result, permanent inefficiencies were built into the system.

Today school boards continue to make the same mistakes and

Canadian taxpayers continue to pay for them. Let's look at the impact of demographic change on the four educational levels – preschool, elementary, secondary, and postsecondary.

DAYCARE AND PRESCHOOL

The Canadian fertility rate tumbled during the 1960s, with the result that the demand for kindergarten places declined shortly thereafter. In the late 1970s, the number of births started to increase, rising still more in the 1980s with the arrival of the echo. Preschool education was once again much in demand and, with the entry of large numbers of women into the workforce, so was daycare for the youngest Canadians. The demand was so strong that a proposal for a national daycare plan was an important issue in the federal election of 1988. Daycare had its time in the political sun only because of passing demographic conditions. In the first half of the 1980s, the combination of large numbers of preschool children, growing numbers of working women, and an active women's movement made daycare an issue the political parties had to contend with. But by the mid-1990s, with most of the echo generation beyond preschool, the politicians were able to put it on the back burner again. Given the importance of early childhood education and nutrition to the intellectual and physical development of all human beings, providing high-quality daycare for every child who needs it would be one of the wisest investments Canada could make in its future. Quebec, to its credit, seems to be the only province that understands this. While other provinces were freezing or cutting back spending on daycare, Quebec announced that it would create 7,800 new spaces in 1998 with further increases scheduled for 1999 as part of an integrated preschool program.

As the new century approached, the boomers were passing out of their child-producing years. That was why daycare was no longer a growth industry in most parts of Canada. Because of demographic variations from place to place, some towns and cities will be short of daycare places while others might have too many (see Figure 9). But in general, the outlook across Canada over the next decade is for a gradual decline in demand for daycare. That means a national daycare

FIGURE 9: PRESCHOOL-AGE CHILDREN IN 25 CITIES, 1996

	% of population	Rank
St. John's	5.8	23
Halifax	6.6	15
Saint John	6.6	13
Chicoutimi-Jonquière	5.9	21
Quebec City	5.8	22
Sherbrooke	6.2	19
Trois-Rivières	5.7	24
Montreal	6.6	12
Ottawa-Hull	6.9	9
Oshawa	8.2	1
Toronto	7.0	4
Hamilton	6.6	13
St. Catharines-Niagara	6.2	18
Kitchener	7.3	3
London	6.9	8
Windsor	6.7	11
Sudbury	6.3	16
Thunder Bay	6.3	16
Winnipeg	6.8	10
Regina	7.0	6
Saskatoon	7.5	2
Calgary	7.0	5
Edmonton	6.9	7
Vancouver	6.1	20
Victoria	5.2	25

Data are for children aged four years and under. Cities listed are the largest Census Metropolitan Areas. Source: Statistics Canada.

program, which should be considered a necessity in an advanced industrialized economy, is now much more affordable than it was.

ELEMENTARY AND SECONDARY SCHOOL

Going to elementary school is the only activity that is compulsory in Canada. For that reason, elementary school enrolments are the one area where demographics can predict the future with tremendous accuracy. If 1,000 children are born in a school district in 1994, it's certain that around 1,000 kids will enter Grade 1 in that school district in 2000. The only impediment to perfect predictability is the movement of children into and out of school districts.

The big growth in elementary schools began in 1953, when the first boomers turned their attention to the adventures of Dick and Jane. Increasing demands on the elementary school system, and steady expansion, continued through the 1950s and 1960s. In 1960, the first boomers reached 13 and entered junior high. That was the beginning of the expansion of high school enrolments. With constantly rising numbers of students at both the elementary and secondary school levels, the 1960s were the golden age for the growth of education in Canada.

To measure the total demand for elementary education by a particular cohort, a demographer looks at the midpoint between age 6, when children start school, and age 13, when they go on to Grade 7. That midpoint is age 9. When the peak of a cohort turns 9, demand for elementary education has peaked. After that, enrolment has only one place to go – down. The peak of the baby boom, which at that point consisted of those born in 1960, was 9 in 1969. After that, elementary school enrolments started to drop.

Until students are age 16, high school, like elementary school, is compulsory in most provinces, which means that, once again, demographics can predict enrolments – although with slightly less accuracy because those over 16 can drop out if they wish. The midpoint of high school attendance is age 16. Predictably, therefore, by the mid-1970s – seven years after the elementary school peak – high school enrolments started to go down.

When this happened in Ontario, the provincial government was surprised. After 30 years of school expansion, growth seemed the natural state of affairs. Neither school boards nor provincial officials were prepared for a downturn, and they weren't sure how to respond. The reason for the decline was simple: because fewer children had been born, fewer children were signing up for school. But the government decided it needed a group of experts to study the matter, so it set up the Commission on Declining School Enrolments in Ontario. Its job was to try to figure out why enrolments were down and what to do about it. The government was especially worried about what to do with excess elementary teachers and new ones fresh out of the province's education faculties who couldn't find jobs. What it should have done was send them back to university to learn how to be high school teachers over the 1970s. It also should have cut elementary school budgets in proportion to the declining enrolments and passed the savings on to the junior and high school levels, where enrolments would continue growing for some time. Instead, following the advice of the commission, the Ontario government ignored demographics and left the elementary budgets largely intact. Rather than recognizing the need to push funding forward in tandem with the largest cohort of the school population, the commission urged that declining enrolments be seen as an opportunity to improve education by reducing class sizes, introducing special education classes, and otherwise enriching the school system. That's how overspending gets permanently built into an education system: by leaving the same resources in the schools at a time when enrolment is dropping by up to 20%. This experience was repeated all over Canada during the 1970s and 1980s. Only the handful of school districts that experienced high immigration had full classrooms.

A Statistics Canada study in 1994 confirmed that our failure to adapt to demographic change is the reason we have one of the world's most expensive education systems. The study found that the education workforce, comprising teachers and administrators, grew by 20% between 1971 and 1991, while the school-age population was dropping by nearly that much, from 5.9 million to 4.9 million. In

1991, Canada spent $33.6 billion on elementary and high school education, a staggering $7.4 billion more than would have been spent had the ratio of students to teachers and administrators stayed at the 1971 level. In 1960, when the elementary schools were bulging with boomers and the eldest boomers were starting junior high school, real per-student spending was $2,000; by 1990, when the entire boom had passed through the school system, it was about $5,000.

The echo began in 1980. Inevitably, Grade 1 enrolment increased in 1986 for the first time in 20 years, then increased again in 1987. Yet the managers of our school systems were caught by surprise, proving once again that, while demographic facts are obvious once pointed out, they often go unnoticed until it's too late. Statistics Canada publishes annual reports showing how many people are born each year. Thus, school boards should have known that, births having increased in 1980 and elementary school being compulsory, Grade 1 enrolments would increase six years later in 1986. But many weren't prepared. School boards hadn't systematically scaled down elementary teaching staffs during the 1970s, but population growth gradually had filled up the classrooms, and by the time large numbers of echo kids arrived at school in the late 1980s, some elementary schools were short of teachers and classrooms.

For the rest of the 1980s and into the 1990s, the echo continued to push elementary school enrolment up. By the early 1990s, portable classrooms were appearing in schoolyards across the country. Many parents don't like portables. They are paying their share of taxes and they don't think their kids should have second-class facilities. School trustees got an earful and, as elected officials, they had to listen. Then they did what came naturally – they decided to build new elementary schools and expand existing ones.

Was that decision demographically sound? The echo began in 1980. The peak of this cohort born in 1990 will turn nine in 1999, after which elementary school enrolments can be expected to fall again. Immigration, even at the abnormally high levels of the 1990s, can't offset the inevitable drop in enrolment, except in certain parts of urban Canada where large numbers of immigrants congregate. The impact of declining enrolments will be felt at about the same time that some of the new schools open. As a result, many new elementary schools will be underused in the new millennium. By building new elementary schools in the 1990s, we built more waste into the school system, adding to Canada's excessive education costs.

The situation, however, will vary from community to community. If a school district is drawing new residents away from somewhere else, its school population could rise while overall enrolments fall. That's what the Carleton Board of Education in suburban Ottawa is counting on. It opened one new elementary school in 1996, another in 1998, and has approved two more for 1999. These schools are in areas that are slated for growth in the Ottawa-Carleton region's official plan. But the federal government is shrinking, not growing, and the echo is over, in Ottawa as in the rest of Canada. The new schools will fill up only if Ottawa's other industries prosper sufficiently to create large numbers of new jobs and draw migrants to Ottawa from other parts of Canada and abroad.

The millennium bust

In 1997, the board's plans ran into opposition from a citizens' group that argued the board was basing its argument in favour of the new schools on 1995 population projections that had not materialized. Parents opposed moving children from existing schools to fill up new ones. "A majority of parents have made it clear to the Carleton Board of Education that they would rather have their children going to local neighbourhood schools in portables than shuffled around to fill up an unneeded new school," Lorna Simard, of Orleans, Ontario, wrote to a local paper.

These parents appear to have a firmer grasp of demographic reality than the local school board. It makes no sense to be building elementary schools at the end of the 1990s, because demand is almost certain to fall. In the 1970s, our school systems kept the same amount of money in the elementary schools after the number of pupils had declined. In the 1980s, the same happened in high schools. Now we are in danger of doing the same thing again when elementary demand drops, as the echo graduates into junior high. If we want to ensure that Canada's education system remains more expensive than those of other countries, all we have to do is maintain the policy of refusing to trim school budgets when enrolments drop.

What about the high schools? The decline in enrolment caused by the graduation of the boom started in high schools in 1976 and continued until the mid-1990s when the echo children arrived. The peak of the echo was 1990. These kids will be 16 in 2006. That means we will have rising high school enrolments until 2006, after which enrolments will decline again.

To accommodate demographic change and avoid squandering money, our school boards need to practise flexibility. Any new elementary schools built as the millennium approaches should be easily convertible to high schools. And some of the high schools that were mothballed in the 1980s or switched to other uses should be switched back to high schools in the late 1990s.

School boards need to understand how demographics affect the mix of their school population, and teachers should understand the impact on them too. The demand for elementary school teachers will peak in about 1999 and then start to decline. Training to be an elementary school teacher is therefore a riskier career choice at the millennium than it would have been in the past. But someone who builds flexibility into his training, gradually moving from elementary school teaching to high school teaching, can grow with the echo children and enjoy the prospect of a longer teaching career. Not every elementary teacher should learn to be a high school teacher, but one in five should move up with the echo kids. School boards need policies to encourage that transition. This simply means saying to employees, "Five years from now we won't be needing as many Grade 3 teachers, but we will need more Grade 8 teachers. Will those interested come forward?" That's how an enlightened employer can use the predictability of demographics to make unavoidable change fulfilling and challenging for its workforce, rather than hurtful and stressful.

THE FUTURE OF PUBLIC SCHOOLS

Given the demands of an aging population and the desire of governments to restrain spending, it is hard to justify building new schools at the millennium. Most school classrooms are empty 17 hours out of 24 and 150 days of the year. Instead of enriching the system with ever more expenditures, why not extract the full potential from the existing system? We could be using schools 12 months a year and 10 hours a day. For example, if classes were held from 7 a.m. to noon and from 1 p.m. to 6 p.m., we could educate twice as many people in the same physical plant. We could get even more benefit out of the existing school buildings if they stayed in operation during the summer. The reason two-month summer vacations were built into the school system was to make the whole family available to harvest crops. But most young people now live in cities where their labour is not in great demand. Our school year, therefore, is organized to serve the needs of an agrarian economy that doesn't exist. Of course, kids should have an extended holiday. But they don't all have to take it in July and August.

The idea of using schools all year makes so much sense that it was gaining ground quickly as the millennium approached. In the

United States, 2,681 schools were operating year-round by 1998, up from only 411 in 1985. By 1998, Canada had 31 year-round schools, some private and some in public systems in British Columbia, Alberta, and Ontario.

In the late 1990s and beyond, the baby-busters will replace the boomers as producers of children. Because the busters are a 44% smaller cohort, the birth rate is falling. An ever smaller percentage of taxpayers will have children in public schools. Most taxpayers will be more concerned with maintaining a health care system that they increasingly depend upon than an education system that their families are no longer using. As good citizens, they will want to continue to support public schools as an essential part of the social infrastructure. But they will be increasingly intolerant of waste and less likely to vote for school trustees who decide to build new schools while keeping existing ones closed at times when they could be used.

POSTSECONDARY EDUCATION

At the end of the 1970s, something remarkable happened in Canada. Government agencies issued reports saying it was time to prepare for an inevitable decline in college and university enrolments. This prediction seemed to be based on sound reasoning. Enrolment had dropped in elementary schools in the early 1970s and in high schools in the late 1970s, so it was logical to assume that colleges and universities would be next. That these predictions were issued was in itself significant, because it was one of the first times demographic analysis was used in the Canadian public sector for strategic planning. Obviously, these agencies had learned something from seeing first elementary schools and then high schools react too late to inevitable declines in demand for their services.

Unfortunately, these predictions were off the mark. What the strategists forgot was that university enrolments are not predictable in the same way that elementary and high school enrolments are. University is not compulsory and, while 19 to 24 is the traditional university age, in an aging population increasing numbers of older students choose to acquire higher education, perhaps after spending some time in the workforce. But governments, responding to predictions of decline based on a simplistic use of demographics, cut postsecondary funding during the 1980s only to watch enrolments fail to decline as predicted.

The predictions based solely on the 19-to-24 age group ignored an important demographic factor: people over 24. In the 1980s these people were part of the large front end of the boom, and their presence in the labour force had created a bottleneck (see Chapter 4). Some of them decided to go back to school rather than continue to pursue non-existent job opportunities, while others decided to quit dead-end jobs and get trained for more promising careers. An economic recession and technological change further diminished job opportunities and increased the allure of postsecondary education.

The peak of university-bound boomers occurred in 1979, after which the numbers of 19-year-old new entrants declined. While this was happening, a new influx of people 25 and older was arriving. The result was that, by the mid-1990s, almost one-half of all postsecondary students, including graduate and part-time students, were 25 and over, up from one-third 20 years before. With an aging population, it was no surprise to see an aging of both college and university campuses. The average age of students has been rising, and so has that of teaching staff. The large number of teachers hired during the 1960s and early 1970s to teach the boomers who were flooding the colleges and universities are still in place, leaving few opportunities for younger scholars to obtain academic positions. In 1995, according to a Statistics Canada study, 61% of the faculty members at nine universities were born before 1945, and another 36% were born between 1945 and 1960. Only 3% were born after 1960.

In the late 1990s, demographics finally caught up to the colleges and universities in the form of falling enrolments. The aging of the boomers and improved economic conditions helped reduce the number of part-time and older students. Meanwhile, the 19-year-olds were coming from the smaller bust generation. At the same time, some young people were shying away from university, either because they couldn't afford the fees or because they doubted that a degree would help much on the job market. As a result, some universities found themselves in the unaccustomed position of having to lower entry marks and advertise for students. At the millennium, however, universities won't have to work as hard to attract students. With or without advertising, enrolments will rise because the large echo generation will be arriving on campus.

If we had had flexibility in our education system and good planning based on demographics, we would have taken money out of the high schools in the 1980s and transferred it to the universities and elementary schools. In the mid-1990s, when university enrolment was slipping and high school enrolment rising, we could have transferred some of it back from the postsecondary system to the increasingly crowded elementary and high schools.

This wasn't done, and once again we are left with an expensive education system. But it's not too late to learn from past mistakes and use the power of demographics to manage the education system more effectively. The echo generation is on the verge of entering colleges and universities. And we know that the millennium busters, the children of the busters, will be a much smaller cohort. The conclusion is inescapable. After the turn of the century, Canada's elementary and then high schools will need fewer resources while the postsecondary institutions will need more. Now is the time to start planning that transfer of resources.

THE NEW UNIVERSITIES AND COLLEGES

A society newly awake to the realization that its resources are limited will soon conclude that it can't afford the current postsecondary system. We are still shutting down most of our colleges and universities for three months every year. This is unreasonable. Universities and colleges should be used 12 hours a day for 12 months a year. Of course, this does not mean that every individual professor and student should be using them 12 months a year. In a three-semester system, everybody could get one semester off, but it doesn't have to be the summer.

As well, universities and colleges are going to have to adapt their teaching methods to their clientele. Just as a teacher approaches a 15-year-old differently than a 5-year-old, so a 29-year-old requires a different approach than a 19-year-old. The older student is more experienced, articulate, and self-confident and will do better at classroom participation than the younger student. The latter is more likely to excel at tests, where rote memory is an advantage. This means that instructors who continue to use only exams as a basis of evaluation are penalizing their older students, while instructors who don't use exams at all are taking away some of the advantage of their younger students. The older student is more likely to have workforce experience and may well still be in the workforce. She realizes time is valuable and doesn't want it wasted. She gets annoyed if classes are cancelled or if she comes to a class for which the teacher is not fully prepared. It's not as easy to push around a 29-year-old consumer as a 19-year-old who has never worked for a living and doesn't mind – or may even enjoy – having time wasted in school. The older consumer will complain if her expectations are not met. Student evaluations of staff performance are more meaningful, and more important, when the student population is older.

The older student wants his workforce experience reflected in his education. He is less interested in theory and more interested in application. Courses that are purely theoretical, unless they lead into other courses that have application, are likely to be less appreciated. An aging population creates more demand for practical courses, of the kind offered by colleges, than for theoretical courses that are the specialty of universities. That explains the results of an Angus Reid survey in 1998 that asked 1,000 Ontario adults what type of education they thought would be the most valuable in the workforce in ten years. The largest group, 35%, chose a college diploma in a technical occupation, while 24% chose apprenticeship in a skilled trade, and 18% a university science degree.

The growing appeal of technical colleges does not necessarily mean that universities are going to lose a lot of their business. In fact, with growing numbers of echo kids graduating from high school, all postsecondary institutions will prosper in the first decade of the new millennium. At the same time, however, the aging of the boomers will produce more mature students who want both an intellectual challenge and an applied approach. Because of these trends, a need exists for greater flexibility within the postsecondary system and perhaps for more integration between colleges and universities.

CONTINUING EDUCATION

Education is only one of several factors that determine a country's economic success and international competitiveness. If it were the only one, Canada and the United States would be much poorer countries. Both countries get mediocre results on international rankings of students' mathematics and science abilities yet both possess strong economies and high standards of living. The United States has a knack for innovation, which is why its software and biotechnology, today's growth industries, are world leaders.

"People don't learn only at school," economist Robert Samuelson wrote in the *Washington Post*. "What counts – for the economy at least – is what people do at work." One of the things people increasingly do at work is learn. A knowledge-based economy requires people who know how to learn and who keep learning throughout their careers. This is a major opportunity for Canada's universities and colleges. These institutions will be an integral part of the new economic system because many people are going to need retraining and re-educating during their working lives (see Chapter 4).

To meet the changing needs of their clientele, postsecondary institutions will have to become more responsive and flexible. Courses that have usually been offered only over a semester of 13 weeks can be compressed into 13 days for a different clientele. In this way, workers can come off the job and in three weeks get the latest thinking in industrial relations, international economics, computer-assisted design, or whatever other area of knowledge they need.

In the future, the need for education of people already in the workforce will grow at an even faster rate than the growth of traditional university education for 19- to 24-year-olds, although the arrival of the echo generation on campus will swell the ranks of the latter group. Rather than sit back and wait for customers, colleges and universities should build their businesses aggressively. If the demand for continuing education is coming from the workplace, it makes good sense to take courses to the source of the demand and present them in the workplace or close to it.

Universities such as McGill, Dalhousie, and Toronto have the good fortune to be located close to the centres of large cities and close, therefore, to the workplaces of managers and other workers requiring retraining and skills upgrading. To their credit, some universities with suburban campuses, such as York and Simon Fraser, have established downtown branches. Just as Oxford and Cambridge were built far from the hurly-burly of London, these Canadian campuses were originally cloistered away from the workaday world, in part so that scholars could think and do research in an atmosphere of serenity. Now these universities are facing sharp cutbacks in government support at the same time as demand from potential customers already in the workforce is increasing. They can no longer afford to be ivory towers.

People can learn on campus or in the workplace and they can also learn at home or in cyberspace. For example, the University of Waterloo offers a degree program in Management of Technology designed for scientists and engineers who need to improve their skills in evaluating new technologies and integrating them into their companies. Students need never come near the campus – the courses are delivered using the Internet and phone link-ups as well as through printed materials and audio and video tapes.

Continuing education for the pleasure and enlightenment of the individual is already a growth industry and, as the retired and early-retired population grows, will get bigger still in the years to come. The bookstore chain Chapters understands this, which is why it offers its customers in-store courses on such subjects as gardening and astronomy. Elderhostel, a non-profit international organization that provides short-term educational programs for seniors and pre-seniors, is increasingly popular. Elderhostel participants study on university campuses or at such sites as marine biology stations. Originally, the program was aimed at an over-60 market but, in response to demand, the age of eligibility has been dropped to 55 in the United States. In Canada, it is open to anyone who is retired or about to retire. These mature students may not care whether they get a degree, a diploma, or even a credit. But they can afford the time and money to go on an archeological dig or a museum tour. They will pay for the chance to work all day looking for dinosaur bones.

This kind of education can become an important source of funding for institutions experiencing declines in government support. The 60-year-old who has a good time on a dinosaur dig with an expert from the department of archeology or who benefits from a college course on home renovation may be favourably disposed when she makes out her will. Corporations depending on colleges and universities to help with upgrading their employees' skills should also want to ensure that postsecondary institutions remain financially healthy.

The popularity of Montreal's Robert Adams testifies to the thirst of middle-aged and older Canadians for intellectual stimulation. Adams is a retired English teacher who taught for 25 years at a junior college. In 1994, he began a series of one-hour lectures on novels. It's the oldest form of teaching – just one person at a lectern with no visuals or special effects. But Adams is such a talented lecturer, and his evangelical fervour for great literature so compelling, that tickets to what he calls his "book reviews" sell out quickly.

A great many teachers will be joining the ranks of the retired in the first decade of the new millennium. In British Columbia, for example, the average age of public school teachers in 1998 was 44 and the average age of faculty members at the University of British Columbia was 50. As Adams has shown, just because a teacher has retired doesn't mean he has lost his ability to absorb and impart knowledge. That is a skill that will be in increasing demand in the years ahead.

THE FUTURE OF EDUCATION

Our education system has some learning to do. It needs to learn to use demographics rather than forever being surprised by inevitable demographic change. By using demographics intelligently and being flexible, the education system could make the most of the resources it has, spend less on unnecessary buildings while using the ones it has more efficiently, and have the teachers it needs when and where they are needed. This would be an important step towards bolstering the public system at a time when it needs support.

Rightly or wrongly, the perception that public education is mediocre has become widespread. Partly, this is because small families have become the norm. Most boomer parents have only one or two kids. They want the very best for these children, and they know that the prospects will be grim for anyone entering the workforce of the future without a good education (see Chapter 4). Some of these people are making financial sacrifices to withdraw their children from the public system and send them to private schools. They are not rich, but they can afford private-school tuition for one child. As Mary Percival Maxwell, a Queen's University sociologist, told *Maclean's*, "The newest wave of parents are people with all their eggs in one basket and they can't afford to drop it."

Parents of school-age children at the millennium not only have few children, they themselves are slightly older and, for that reason, are both more assertive and more quality-conscious than previous generations of parents of young children. This demographic development underlies the growing demands by parents to have more say over what happens in the schools. They are also demanding that teachers and principals be more accountable for the performance of students. The movement to restore standardized testing reflects the desire for accountability. In some U.S. states, results of state-wide tests are published, putting pressure on underachieving schools to improve. Another U.S. innovation, which has been adopted by Alberta, is the charter school. These schools are run by groups of parents with public funding. To qualify, a group must meet broad curriculum guidelines while offering a program that is distinct from that of the regular public schools. Usually, this involves a back-to-basics approach, with a concentration on core subjects and standardized testing.

Critics of charter schools worry that they will fragment the public system. Supporters reply that these schools are open to all and that, by introducing competition into the public system, they make the whole system more responsive to demands for high standards. In 1998, several of the 11 Alberta charter schools were experiencing growing pains, including mismanagement, power struggles among founding parents, and conflicts with local school boards that were supposed to oversee them. Their problems are likely to be compounded over the next decade once most of the boomers' children have finished with the school system. Just as the demand for a national daycare program ran out of steam once the echo generation no longer needed daycare, so will pressure to start new and better schools diminish simply because there will be fewer parents to demand them.

But supporters of public education in Canada would be wrong to dismiss the charter schools and their supporters as irrelevant. That they exist at all reflects the growing disquiet many parents feel about declining educational standards. In the next decade, these same boomer parents may decide that their children need private colleges and universities.

Canadians have every right to demand more of their education system. Why should Korean students do so much better at science or students from Singapore so much better at mathematics than their Canadian counterparts? Canadian kids are as bright as any others. What both they, and the Canadian education system, need more than anything else is higher expectations. A country that can build a first-class health care system can also build a first-class education system. We just need to be smarter and try harder.

Chapter 9

Health Care at the Crossroads

ealth care in Canada is at a crossroads. Since medicare was
introduced in the 1960s, Canadians have been justly proud of
a health care system that provided an excellent level of care to
all citizens, regardless of financial means. But, largely for demographic
reasons, the health care system as it is currently structured will not be
able to continue offering excellent care at an affordable cost much
longer. The choice is a stark one – either we perform major reconstruc-
tive surgery on the publicly financed system or accept the inevitability
of a larger private sector in which people are allowed to buy any medical services they can afford whenever they want them.

Opinion polls reveal that most Canadians strongly support
medicare. At the same time, the public is growing increasingly restive
over funding cutbacks that are reducing the comprehensiveness and
accessibility of the health care system. The only way to maintain uni-
versality is through reforms that are bound to meet resistance from
those who feel they have a stake in health care as it is currently organized. It will take public pressure and courageous government action
to override this resistance and achieve the necessary change. Will it
happen? That is one of the most crucial public policy questions facing
Canadians at the millennium.

THE DEMOGRAPHICS OF HEALTH CARE
We use the health care system all through our lives, starting before we
are born. But once out of the hospital nursery, children don't cost the

system very much. Nor do people in their teens and 20s. The cost of health care rises gradually over a person's 30s and 40s. It is higher for women than men because of reproduction, but by their mid-50s, men are using the system more than women. Then, in the 60s and beyond, the cost of health care soars for both sexes.

Canada's 9.9 million boomers began turning 50 in 1997. Well before that important demographic milestone, the rising cost of health care was already a major public policy issue. Every provincial government tried hard during the 1990s to keep a lid on costs. And they appear to have succeeded. For years, Canada's spending on health care was the second highest after the United States among leading industrialized countries. Recently, however, the 9.6% of Gross Domestic Product (GDP) Canada spent on health care put us in fourth place on the list of big spenders, behind the United States, Germany, and France.

But this success was achieved through crude cost-cutting measures that weakened health care in Canada. Patients were left for days on stretchers in hospital corridors, others waited hours for attention in emergency wards, and still others waited weeks or even months for surgeries and diagnostic procedures. Many nurses were laid off or reduced to part-time status. The result was understaffed hospitals with the remaining nurses overworked and demoralized. Meanwhile, in the opinion of experts on health care economics, major cities still had a costly surplus of primary care physicians while rural areas remained woefully short.

Taking an axe to hospital budgets, de-insuring services, and subjecting patients to unreasonable delays is not health care reform. Neither provincial nor federal governments offered a vision of what an affordable but still excellent universal system would look like. What they appeared to want – and what they got – was the same system in a damaged condition. If government had wanted to increase support for two-tier health care, this was the way to go about it.

When examined more closely, the cost-cutting of the 1990s was not as successful as it seemed. True, Canada was now fourth instead of second among the major economies in health spending. But the biggest spender, the United States, is an anomaly because it is the only industrialized country without national health insurance and as a result squanders billions of dollars on administrative costs in the private sector. The two countries that passed Canada in spending, Germany and France, have older populations that require more medical attention and so could be expected to spend more. Canada's system, therefore, is still extremely costly by international standards even as the service it offers is in decline. This is the case at a time when the Canadian population is still comparatively young – in 1998, the peak of the boom was a robust 38 years old. By the second decade of the new century, when the front edge of the boom enters its senior years, our health care system will be confronted with sharply increased demand.

How much will demand for health care services increase? Reliance on doctors turns upward in a person's 40s and continues to increase gradually. Those in their late 70s need doctors twice as often as their lifetime average and those in their late 80s need them 2 $1/2$ times as often. Reliance on hospitals increases sharply in the mid-50s. By their late 70s, people use hospitals five times more than their lifetime average rate of use. Those who survive until their late 80s use hospitals 12 times more than their lifetime average.

These data explain why provincial governments decided the 1990s were a good time to close hospitals. Only the 7.5 million Canadians – one-quarter of the population – born before the boom were then at the stage of above-average need for hospitals. The same governments that accepted accolades for restraining the growth of their health care budgets will be safely out of the line of fire when voters start asking why hospitals were closed just before 9.9 million boomers would start to need them.

The reason demand for health care services rises with age is obvious – as people get older they are more likely to get sick. Heart disease, cancer, diabetes, arthritis, hip fractures, Alzheimer's disease, and kidney failure are some of the maladies whose incidence increases with age. Advances in public health and medical science have improved the health of Canadians, including older ones. The decline in smoking has also been a boon although, for a majority of Canadians, the benefits of not smoking are offset by a sedentary lifestyle. A study released in 1998 by the Canadian Fitness and Lifestyle Research Council stated that the 63% of the population classified as inactive are at serious risk of colon cancer, osteoporosis, and depression as well as heart disease and adult-onset diabetes. Failure to exercise, said Nick Busing, president of the College of Family Physicians of Canada, is as lethal to health as smoking a pack of cigarettes a day.

The full impacts of aging and sloth on the health status of Canadians will not be seen until well into the next century when the boomers are in the years when utilization of health services is highest. The aging of the boomers is the most critical demographic issue facing the health care system at the millennium. An older population is more demanding and more knowledgeable about the products and services it needs and is less willing to tolerate poor service. Moreover, older people have more disposable income than younger people, and they are willing to pay to get what they want, when they want it. The boomers have grown accustomed to a retail environment in which quality products and services are demanded and delivered faster than ever before. They expect their photos to be processed, not in a day, but in an hour. And because they have persuaded themselves that they are too busy to cook dinner, supermarkets are now cooking it for them (see Chapter 5).

What happens when large numbers of these consumers in a hurry need diagnostic procedures or elective surgeries? Will they be prepared to tolerate long delays? It is unlikely that they will. In all probability, the boomers will be at least as demanding when it comes to health care as they are when they buy any other product or service. If the public system can't give them what they want, they will demand the right to buy it for themselves. These demands will be difficult to resist, not because the boomers are more deserving than the cohorts currently most in need of medical services but because they are more numerous. At the millennium, fewer than 1% of Canadians were waiting for surgery. In 2020, if medicare is unreformed, a much higher percentage will be waiting and they won't wait quietly.

In summary, Canada has a good health care system that is not adapting quickly enough to the changing needs of its population. Unfortunately, much of the debate over health care reform has been unhelpful. Critics of the Canadian system, including the U.S. health care industry and a few Canadian ultraconservatives, exaggerate its deficiencies. These critics seem unwilling, as a matter of principle, to accept the fact that the Canadian public system is not only more equitable but also more efficient than the U.S. private system. On the other hand, defenders of Canadian medicare overstate its virtues, gloss over its deterioration, and argue that all it needs is more money. But this argument ignores the success of other industrialized countries that are able to deliver equally good care for less money.

Why is the Canadian system overpriced? One reason, says George Pink, associate professor of health administration at the University of Toronto, is that it is filled with "perverse incentives" that encourage doctors to maximize visits, procedures, tests, and referrals. "Everybody has the incentive to do volume. And nobody has the incentive to do only what's necessary or what's right." The way to correct this situation is to adopt an integrated health care system under medicare. This would involve significant changes for both patients and health care providers, but Pink and other experts contend it would be better for all. If, on the other hand, we wish to maintain medicare as it is currently organized, we had better get used to a much expanded second tier. Let's examine both alternatives.

THE TWO-TIER SYSTEM

Two-tier health care is often discussed as if it were an option to be considered rather than something that already exists. Yet Canada has many private clinics offering such services as eye surgery, cosmetic surgery, and in-vitro fertilization. In addition, many Canadians have private insurance coverage for such things as prescription drugs, private hospital rooms, and eyeglasses. About $24 billion was spent by the private sector in 1997, almost a third of the total health care bill of $77 billion.

The failure of medicare to cover drugs is increasingly unjustifiable at the millennium, so much so that it calls into question Canada's right to claim it has universal health insurance. "Drug therapy is the therapy of choice for a lot of conditions now, and yet [provincial health insurance plans] don't pay for it," says Pink. In fact, one of the justifications for closing hospitals is that pharmaceutical breakthroughs are keeping more people out of hospital. Yet medicare pays for hospitalization but not drugs although hospitalization is usually more expensive. In fact, drug coverage in Canada is a replica of health insurance as a whole in the United States. It is based, not on need, but on age, income level, and who one's employer happens to be. This regime leaves out an increasing number of working Canadians who are neither poor enough nor old enough to qualify for provincial drug coverage and whose employer doesn't provide it. Just as in the United States, illness can be a financial burden for such people.

The exclusion of drugs from the universal system combined with their growing importance means that the privately funded portion of health spending will continue to swell. Also fuelling growth in

The eyes have had it

the private sector will be advances in medical science, including procedures that government insurance will rightly exclude. No one would claim that the public system should pay, for example, for laser wrinkle removal for everyone who wants it. Similarly, laser surgery to allow people with vision defects to shed their eyeglasses is a growth industry (see Chapters 3 and 4) that is not covered by medicare because it is not essential.

But what of medically necessary surgery? Even with one of the most expensive health care systems in the world, Canada finds itself increasingly unable to provide it in a timely fashion to everyone who needs it. Entrepreneurial doctors like Brian Day would like to change that by offering medical services in private, for-profit clinics to anyone who can afford to pay. Day, an orthopaedic surgeon, is president of Cambie Surgeries Corp., which runs the Cambie Surgery Centre in Vancouver. It offers various kinds of surgery, including orthopaedic, urological, cosmetic, and dental. Day opened the centre in 1996 because his operating hours at a local hospital were reduced from seventeen a week to seven as a result of budget cutbacks.

It is legal to operate private clinics in Canada but, under the Canada Health Act, doctors working in them must not bill Canadian patients directly for services covered by medicare. The only Canadians the Cambie clinic can treat for such services are Workmen's Compensation Board cases, some patients covered by private disability insurance, and a few that Day operates on for free. On the other hand, covered services can be offered to foreigners who pay out of their own pockets or from their own insurance policies. Day and his colleagues have operated on patients from the United States, Cyprus, Australia, New Zealand, Germany, Japan, Taiwan, Hong Kong, Britain, Russia, and Mexico. These patients get immediate service, while Day's own patients, because they are Canadian, must endure long waits to be operated on in a public hospital.

Dogs and cats can get quick surgical attention in Canada, Day observes. Why, he wants to know, can foreigners and animals get the operations they need while Canadians have to wait? Proponents of private medicine argue that this situation is not only absurd, it is fiscally irresponsible. An expanded private tier would inject badly needed funds into the system, including the dollars of Canadians who now go to the United States to buy services they are denied in Canada. It would also be an incentive to top doctors to stay in Canada where they could be part of a lucrative industry.

If there were more private facilities, and if hospitals could do for-profit work on foreigners, then more such patients could be attracted to Canada. Just as the cheap Canadian dollar makes Canada attractive to location scouts from Hollywood, it would also make us competitive in the health industry. "We can charge half the price of any surgical procedure in the United States and still make a profit," said Day. Yet Day can't expand to take advantage of this business opportunity because he is convinced the provincial government would not allow it. If what the Cambie clinic is doing on a small scale were happening on a large scale, British Columbians would start asking why foreigners could get hip joint replacements in British Columbia right away while residents of the province had to wait a year. "It would be politically unacceptable," Day says.

Day knows that Canadians will have nothing to do with the American model. But what, he asks, is so bad about the models of industrialized countries other than Canada or the United States where universal public systems co-exist with private for-profit systems? In Sweden, the wait for surgery in the public system declined after private health care was allowed. Not only does a private sector relieve some of the demand on the public sector, the competition forces the public sector to improve its performance. That's why Day thinks expansion of the private tier into essential services is the best medicine for Canadian medicare.

Day knows the opposition to two-tier health care is strong, but he believes change is inevitable for demographic reasons. "Baby boomers like me are going to demand it," he says. "We don't accept that there should be a one-year wait for elective surgery."

Day makes a strong case in favour of two-tier but a powerful case also exists against it, essentially the same as the case against two-tier fire protection. If health care, like fire protection, is an essential service, it should be dispensed according to need, not according to ability to pay. If there were a private tier, many of the best professionals would gravitate to it, eroding the public system. The best way to ensure that Canada maintains a good public health care system is to give the rich and powerful a good reason to support it. Having their lives depend on it is a good reason. But as demographic pressures intensify, we can't cling to the status quo if we want our health care system to stay healthy.

THE INTEGRATED HEALTH SYSTEM

Anyone who has visited the Canadian Prairies knows what a silo looks like. A cylindrical tower for storing wheat, a silo is entirely self-contained. It is not connected to any other silo. Health care bureaucrats and experts in health care administration talk a lot about silos, by which they mean the self-contained budgets of the various parts of the system, including hospitals, doctors, and provincial drug plans. The lack of integration among these programs, the inability to move funds from one program to another, is the biggest barrier to reform.

Here's an example. A new drug for schizophrenia can help keep people out of hospital. It is much cheaper to dispense the drug than to admit these patients to hospital, and so dispensing it would save the system as a whole a great deal of money. It would seem a simple matter to take an amount of money out of the hospital budget to pay for the drugs so that the hospitals can save a greater amount of money, which they could use for other purposes. But it isn't a simple matter at all. In fact, it can't be done because the drug and hospital budgets are self-contained silos within the ministries of health, and money can't be switched from one to the other.

Another example is a recently invented pump that can be implanted near the spinal cords of patients who suffer from extreme spasticity. These patients currently cost the health system large amounts of money because they are frequently hospitalized. Morever, they are unable to work. The pump releases a medication into their body slowly and steadily so that the spasticity is controlled. The device allows them to lead a happier life, to return to work, and to stay out of hospital. But it costs about $7,000, which is too much for the neurosurgical departments of hospitals to pay. None of the other health care budgets have money for it either. The result? Society spends more to look after these patients in a less satisfactory way than it would spend to look after them in a much better way.

There are many such stories, and they are the reason Canada's health care system is wasteful. "The silos are perverse and they are pervasive," says George Pink. "Canadians like to think we've got the best system in the world. We've got the best system in terms of equity and access. But we've got a very static system when you compare it to other countries."

The way to save medicare is to demolish the silos and replace them with integrated systems. The number of people covered by each system would vary depending on the location, but Pink thinks 100,000 would be the norm. Each system would have one budget to cover everything, including doctors and other health care workers, hospitals, and prescription drugs, which finally would be covered under medicare. Under the current structure, says Pink, "we are restricted in what we do by where we get the money from. Hospitals have to spend money on hospital care, public health has to spend money on public health." An integrated system has no budget for surgery, no budget for home care, no budget for anything except curing the sick among its 100,000 customers and keeping the others healthy. Tossing all the money into one pot means that how much of it any one player in the system gets becomes irrelevant. All that matters is whether an expenditure advances the goal of improving the health of 100,000 people.

Where does one find a model for such a system? Within, of all places, the much-maligned health care system of the United States. Not the widely criticized for-profit health maintenance organizations (HMOs) that often deny patients necessary treatments in pursuit of maximum profit. But in about 30 non-profit integrated systems that operate with great success and high levels of patient satisfaction. Britain is in the process of adopting a form of integrated health care on a national level.

Integrated health care does away with the fee-for-service system of paying doctors. Instead they are paid for being part of a team of caregivers responsible for the health of a group of people; whether the doctor sees a particular individual 20 times in a year or only once has no impact on the doctor's income. The amount of money the team has for each patient depends on age, gender, and health status. This system, known as rostering or capitation, gives doctors an incentive to keep patients healthy, through such means as counselling on fitness and nutrition, and a disincentive to encourage unnecessary visits or to perform unnecessary procedures.

Some people fear such a system would mean they could be stuck with a doctor they didn't like but that isn't so. First of all, the vast majority of Canadians stay with their doctor anyway, so switching is not a major problem. And a patient would be able to leave one system for another if he wanted to with the money allotted for that patient also being transferred.

This kind of system can save money and improve health at the same time. One reason is that there is more emphasis on evaluation of quality and outcomes. Providers have an incentive to find out what works and what doesn't work. If you're a doctor, you don't order an unnecessary test, because it comes out of your group's budget. On the other hand, you do whatever is necessary to keep your patient healthy because if she gets really sick that costs more than the test you should have ordered.

Information technology is a key part of integrated health care in the United States and could be an even more powerful tool if the system were adopted in Canada. With electronic patient records, a patient's history could be instantly accessible no matter where he showed up in the system. This would reduce duplication of tests and the amount of time people waste repeating their history. "In a one-payer system like Canada's, this should be a piece of cake. Wal-Mart has been doing this for 20 years but we haven't been able to do it in our health care system," Pink says.

What of the fear, based on the poor reputation of U.S. HMOs, that a health care organization using capitation would deliver bad care or would reject expensive patients such as those who are HIV-positive? Not to worry. Integrated health care is a way of restructuring medicare to make it work better, not a plot to get rid of it. A province could pass a law saying that if an HIV-positive person showed up, the integrated health system has to take him. And it could increase the capitation rate for such patients enough to create an economic incentive to put them on the roster. Finally, health ministries would set up independent peer organizations to monitor the performance of all integrated health systems. Bad ones could be closed down.

This is one area where demographic trends and the need for governments to restrain spending point to the same conclusion. Not only can we no longer afford the fee-for-service system, it is inappropriate for a society with an aging population. Fee-for-service rewards doctors who maximize the number of patients they see and penalizes those who take the time to explain and discuss health problems with their patients. Yet the latter approach is exactly what a more mature, knowledgeable, and demanding consumer of health care needs and expects. A patient in her 50s, who may well be older than her doctor, is not going to tolerate patronizing, authoritarian, assembly-line medicine.

If fee-for-service is inappropriate for the middle-aged, it is even more remote from the needs of the elderly. Fee-for-service discriminates against doctors who specialize in geriatrics, according to Michael Gordon, vice-president of medical services at Baycrest Centre for Geriatric Care in Toronto. "As geriatricians, we get paid the same as a general internist for a consultation – about $100," Gordon said in an interview in the *Toronto Star*. "But a geriatric consultation can take an hour and a half whereas a general medicine consultation may take 45 minutes. We put in two or three years after our internal medicine training and often our incomes go down. In care for the aged, fee-for-service is counterproductive."

Of all the diseases that increase with age, diabetes most vividly illustrates the need to change our health care system in response to the demographic shift. Because of the aging of the boomers, North America is on the verge of an epidemic of adult-onset diabetes, an incurable disease caused by the body's failure to control sugar levels in the blood. Adult-onset diabetes afflicts mainly overweight people over 45, a category whose ranks are swelling. Even before most of the boomers had reached their prime diabetes years, one out of every seven dollars spent on health care in North America was being spent on someone with diabetes. One reason the bill is so high is that diabetes can lead to severe complications such as heart and vascular disease, blindness, kidney disease, and nerve damage that can result in loss of a limb.

Fortunately, there is a way of reducing the chances of such complications occurring, while at the same time maximizing the health and well-being of people with diabetes and minimizing the costs to the health care system. This approach is called disease management, which simply means managing chronic disease to avoid serious episodes of ill health and complications that would lead to hospitalization. This is the kind of health care that an integrated health care system has every reason to provide, and it is no accident that the largest integrated system in the United States, Group Health Cooperative of Puget Sound, based in Seattle, is a leader in diabetes management.

A medical practice that is appropriate to a mature population involves a partnership between patient and physician aimed at maintaining good health through a healthy lifestyle. It also requires the contributions of other specialists, including pharmacists, nutritionists, physiotherapists, nurses, and home care specialists. An integrated health system facilitates such coordinated delivery of health care because it puts the patients where they should be – at the centre of attention.

The Canadian health care system as it is currently structured has a bias towards acute care – that is, the patient gets help when disease causes a serious episode of ill health. The system doesn't focus enough on preventive medicine to avoid such episodes. A diabetic needs training in how to manage the daily routine of monitoring and controlling blood sugar. The health care team charged with his case should also provide nutritional counselling and should do follow-up to ensure he is managing his disease properly. These kinds of activities are not well-rewarded by the fee structure of medicare, and the silos make it difficult to free up funds for them. Yet studies conducted by the Centers for Disease Control in the United States demonstrate that compliance with a comprehensive program of patient education supported by a patient follow-up program reduced hospitalizations for diabetes and related complications by 50%. Potential savings if such a program were implemented on a large scale would be in the hundreds of millions of dollars.

Canada cannot afford not to practise medicine in this way. What is stopping us? Ontario's Health Services Restructuring Commission favours integrated health care, but Pink says most health bureaucrats do not want to dismantle the silos. "They have control over them and they love it. By making one huge silo and dividing it up around the province into integrated health systems, you are almost doing away with two-thirds of the Ministry of Health – you are decentralizing it to the local level, where people really know what the health care needs are."

In addition, the Ontario Medical Association reacted unfavourably when the commission proposed an integrated system. And many doctors want to keep fee-for-service. One problem, from the doctors' point of view, is that integrated care tends to make less use of doctors and more use of nurse practitioners and other health workers without medical degrees. Some primary care doctors now working in major cities might have to relocate to smaller cities if an integrated system replaced the current one.

Yet integrated health care offers advantages to both bureaucrats and doctors. The provincial health ministries, as the payers, would play a crucial role because they would determine the funding rate and would assess outcome, satisfaction, and access. They would also have the satisfaction of supervising a health care system designed for the 21st century instead of one designed for the 1960s.

And it is in the best interests of the medical profession to alleviate the disarray of the Canadian system and ensure maximum benefit is obtained from the large amount of money being spent on it. The

U.S. example is instructive because it shows that when doctors resist necessary reform they can wind up with something worse. The United States does not have national health insurance because doctors, through the American Medical Association, and insurance companies have resisted all attempts to introduce it. Yet the insurance companies had to find some way to restrain costs. And now many American doctors complain about for-profit HMOs that, in the name of cost control, interfere with doctors' ability to practise medicine in the best interests of their patients.

Canada, fortunately, long ago won the battle for national health insurance. But now we have to modernize it to meet the needs of a changing population. Doctors would flourish within such a system because it would be led by primary care providers, not by accountants. Would integrated health care be the end of agitation to expand the private tier? Probably not. But, by improving the health status of Canadians while reducing waste, it would free up resources to achieve more within the public system. Canadians will have little use for private health care when public health care is working as it should.

HOSPITAL OR HOME?

Since the first edition of *Boom, Bust & Echo* was published, home care has moved onto the Canadian political agenda. That is because provincial governments are working hard to reduce our reliance on hospitals, which are the most expensive part of the health care system. Patients either are not being admitted to hospital or are being released much earlier than before. As a result, care that used to take place within hospitals is being shifted to the home.

Because of the demographic shift, home care is a growth industry in North America. In Nova Scotia, for example, the home care budget grew from $19 million to $70 million between 1992 and 1997. In Ontario, home care was $1.2 billion of the province's $18 billion health care budget by 1998, and that was expected to grow rapidly as funding was shifted from hospitals to the home.

The argument for home care is part medical and part financial.

Health care delivery has undergone dramatic changes in recent years. New diagnostic technologies, new drugs, new surgical methods, and new ideas about treatment have all contributed to shorter hospital stays for many patients. This has made it possible to use hospital beds more efficiently and has facilitated the closing of thousands of beds. Yet reducing reliance on hospitals does not necessarily lead to lowered health status; research shows no correlation between hospitalization and good health. In fact, a patient is at greater risk of acquiring infections in hospital than at home. Moreover, many people simply prefer being in the familiar environment of their own homes, and if they feel better chances are their health will improve more quickly.

As for the financial side of the argument, one reason our health care system has been so expensive was that we had a large number of hospital beds. Some doctors are more likely than others to put patients into hospital, and the more hospital beds available, the more patients will be admitted to fill them. Two Ottawa doctors, Jacques Lemelin and Bill Hogg, who work at Ottawa Civic Hospital,

Health care in a hurry

are heading up a program to have doctors and nurses care for patients in a "home-hospital" once they no longer need the labour-intensive care the actual hospital provides. A home-hospital treats people whose condition is not acute enough to require their presence in a traditional hospital but who are too sick for conventional home care programs. In the Ottawa proposal, the cost would be $190 a day compared to $350 in a traditional hospital. This could produce annual savings in Ottawa of $28 million. The concept of home-hospitals – otherwise known as virtual hospitals, hospitals without walls, or extra-mural hospitals – dates back to the 1950s. Examples exist in several other countries, including Britain, France, and Australia. The Canadian province in which the concept is most advanced is New Brunswick, whose entire population is covered by the Extra-Mural Program.

Clearly, home care will be a more and more important part of the health care system in the coming years but, as of 1998, many issues remained unresolved. The federal government had stated its commitment to home care but had not committed any funds to it. In contrast to the rest of the health care system, there were no national or provincial standards. As a result, service was uneven. Patients told of hurried visits by nurses, sometimes a new face each visit, who didn't have time to dispense the necessary care. Grace Taylor, herself a nurse, tried unsuccessfully for several days to get a visiting nurse to examine an incision from major surgery. When a nurse finally took time to look at it, Taylor told the *Toronto Star* in 1998, the incision was found to be infected.

As this incident reveals, the main problem with home care is that there is not enough of it. A Statistics Canada study released in 1998 showed that about half the people needing help with such basics as eating, getting dressed, and moving about the house were getting no formal home care. In most cases, family members are assuming these caregiving responsibilities. This was already starting to take its toll on relatives of the sick and elderly. A study published by Statistics Canada in 1997 showed that more than one in eight Canadians were looking after someone with chronic health problems and that these caregivers were suffering deterioration in their own health as a result of stress and lack of sleep. Another survey, published in 1997 by the Heart and Stroke Foundation, found 58% of boomers expected to be the primary caregiver if a parent had a stroke. An increasing number will find themselves in this situation because two-thirds of strokes occur in people over 65, and the risk doubles in every decade after age 60.

Just as obvious as the fact that home care will grow is the certainty that governments will not pick up all of the cost. Many patients, or their adult children, are already paying for nursing care out of their own pockets. Some take time off work to care for family members who would previously have been in hospital. In this way, the cost of care is partially shifted to employees and employers, eroding their productivity and competitiveness. David Naylor of the Institute for Clinical Evaluative Sciences at the University of Toronto has called this cost-shifting "indirect and unfair hidden sickness taxes." In fact, some of the reduction in the percentage of the Canadian GDP being spent on health care may be illusory. Some expenditures have been shifted so that they are no longer included when health care costs are counted, but they are nonetheless real. If the shift of health care from hospital to home is excessive, these costs will become unbearable for many people.

It remains open to doubt whether closing large numbers of hospitals is the right thing to do just when increasing numbers of Canadians are about to start needing them. If we close too many hospitals now, we may find we are going to have to reopen them ten years from now. If they have been taken out of service in the interim, that may prove to be extremely costly or impractical. Health care planners seem especially eager to close hospitals in outlying areas whose populations are currently too small to support them. This is a questionable policy given the different demographics of rural and urban Canada (see Chapter 7). Most parts of rural Canada are older than urban Canada. Moreover, many urban people choose to move back to the country in their 50s and 60s. This phenomenon has already been seen in European countries that have older populations than Canada. Over the next two decades, as the whole boom turns 50, we will witness a significant exodus from big-city Canada to small-town Canada. The participants in this exodus are going to need the same hospitals that provincial governments closed in the 1990s.

Governments should view small-town hospitals not as a burden on the health care budget but as a powerful tool for the economic development of rural regions. In the years to come, the reassuring presence of a good local hospital will act as a magnet for relatively prosperous new retirees, whose arrival will create new demand for goods and services. These people will bring new wealth with them rather than drawing their incomes from the local economy in competition with the original residents. It is already happening in the Okanagan and other parts of the B.C. interior, where people from Vancouver and other major cities have settled after deciding to trade their city homes for some small-town tranquillity. This is one scenario where increased population really does lead to increased prosperity – something that many parts of Canada haven't seen much of in recent times. A region that loses its local hospital may be losing its best chance for economic rebirth (see Chapter 2).

DRUG USE IN AN AGING SOCIETY

Taste in drugs, as in so much else, changes with age. The average drug user sniffs glue at the age of 12, smokes pot at the age of 20, shoots crack or sniffs cocaine at the age of 30, and takes a Valium at 40. Note that all but the last of these drugs are illegal. An older person is much less likely to engage in reckless experimentation than a younger one. Partly that's because a young person who persists in heavy illegal drug use has a reduced chance of ever becoming an older person. Also, an older person is more aware of mortality and more concerned about health than a younger one. Consequently, in an aging population, illegal drug use declines.

Because the boomers are the largest cohort, their drugs of choice are the ones that make the news. When the boomers were teenagers, glue sniffing was big. In the late 1960s and through the 1970s, pot smoking was rampant, and the campaign to legalize marijuana attained the status of a political movement. Why did this political movement run out of steam? Because the boomers passed through their pot-smoking years. As the echo generation moved into its pot-smoking years, interest in legalizing pot revived at the millennium. A legal drug, tobacco, was also attracting new customers as the echo generation began to experiment with smoking. The tobacco industry cannot survive unless it persuades children and teenagers to try its product, because few adults take up the habit that is the leading cause of death in Canada. Eighty per cent of smokers are addicted by the age of 18, and 90% are hooked by 21.

It is not necessarily a boon that a large segment of society is switching from illegal to legal drugs. The legal ones can also be dangerous to health. In 1995, the *Canadian Medical Association Journal* published a study that found that the doctors who wrote the most prescriptions also had the highest death rates among their patients. This study found that some doctors, in trying to maximize the number of patients they could process per day, did not take the time necessary to find out what was wrong with these patients. That kind of medical practice results in overmedicated and inappropriately medicated patients. It increases the risk of adverse reactions, and it is costly.

Our society is highly dependent on chemicals. With an aging population, we need to devote increased attention to the misuse of drugs, both legal and illegal. The managers of both public and private drug benefit plans along with the medical community should develop prescribing guidelines to ensure that misuse does not occur. And law enforcement agencies will need increased forensic accounting capabilities to examine hospital records and doctors' records for evidence of the abusive use of legal drugs.

HEALTH CARE IN THE FUTURE

For the time being, Canada does not have a health care crisis because it still has a relatively young population. The crunch won't really come for another 20 years, when the boomers are in their late 50s and 60s. That gives us time to learn how to allocate our resources wisely and ensure the maintenance of a first-class medicare system.

During the 1990s, the fastest-growing segment of the population was the over-80s, mostly poor older women born before and during World War I. They are a relatively large group and have put pressure on the supply of chronic care facilities. But that problem will dissipate over the next decade as the oldest seniors depart and the current young senior group moves into the senior senior category. These people are wealthier and thus better able to finance their own care, and because they were born in the 1930s, they are fewer in number than the current batch of senior seniors.

Boomers have a tendency, annoying to post-boomers and pre-boomers alike, to assume that whatever phase they are going through must be of universal interest. Nothing can cure them of this and, given their dominant position in the mass media, there isn't much the rest of society can do about it. That is why the aging Mick Jagger gets his picture on page one every time he rouses himself to take the Rolling Stones on tour yet again. That is why the impotence cure Viagra (see Chapter 3) overnight became one of the most famous drugs in history and why so many other articles are published about health issues related to aging. Prostate problems are big news. Menopause, which affects the entire female population, will be even bigger.

The menopause debate will be interesting, because it highlights a conflict between two values dear to many members of the boomer generation. One is the high status given to things "natural," whether it was dispensing with bras in the 1960s or eating unadulterated food and wearing clothes made from natural rather than synthetic fibres in the 1970s and 1980s. The less one tried to improve on nature the better. The other value is the one that has made the cosmetics industry, along with cosmetic surgery and cosmetic dentistry, into a booming business; it says that just because a person is no longer young doesn't mean she can't look good and feel good. In the case of menopause, this value clash is represented by the controversy over estrogen.

After menopause, which usually occurs by the early 50s, women stop producing the hormone estrogen. Taking estrogen, in the form of pills, patches, or creams, is a way to offset the physical impacts that occur naturally as a result of this change. Estrogen relieves the hot flashes, vaginal dryness, and night sweats that occur as the ovaries reduce their estrogen production. More important, research indicates that it reduces the risk of heart disease, adult-onset diabetes, and osteoporosis (thinning of the bones), which can result in severe fractures. Estrogen also improves a woman's sex life by rejuvenating the vaginal tissues and reducing dryness. And there is evidence that it improves memory. Against these significant benefits are a number of drawbacks, including increased risk of breast cancer, the possibility of weight gain, and the expense and nuisance of having to take drugs for many years.

Many doctors are in favour of estrogen, saying that the benefits far outweigh the risks. That explains why, well before the first female boomer had turned 50, estrogen was already the best-selling prescription drug in the United States. But some doctors, along with writers such as Germaine Greer, argue that it's wrong to interfere with nature's course and turn a normal event in a woman's life into a condition requiring long-term drug therapy. With the front end of the boom entering its menopause years, this debate will be with us for many years to come.

The advance of medical science holds out great promise that today's huge middle-aged population cohort will march through its senior years in healthy and vigorous style. As discussed in Chapter 3, the pharmaceutical industry is working feverishly to produce better treatments for such age-related ailments as elevated cholesterol, arthritis, diabetes, and osteoporosis. Other technologies will also help counteract the ravages of time. For example, mechanical pumps are under development that can revive damaged heart cells and may eliminate the need for heart transplants.

In 1997, the United States's first boomer president, Bill Clinton, announced he would be fitted for hearing aids. Hearing loss often accompanies the aging process, and yet an estimated one-third of those who need hearing aids don't have them, either out of embarrassment or because the devices don't work well. A new generation of lightweight digital hearing aids will change that. These gadgets can be programmed for the individual and can adjust automatically to changing sound levels. And, unlike conventional hearing aids, they can be used with cell phones.

While high technology can advance health and well- being, an old-fashioned form of medical practice – the doctor's house call – is an increasingly important part of our health care future. John Sloan, a Vancouver family doctor whose patients' average age is in the high 80s, found he was doing so much of his work in his clients' homes that he shut down his office. House calls are the best way to deliver high-quality care to older patients. The doctor who visits at home can check on his patients' living conditions, ensure that any other home care they are receiving is effective, go into their medicine cabinets and get rid of dated drugs, and give a boost to their morale simply by letting them know that someone cares enough to come and see them. In some cases, a paramedic, working under the direction of a doctor and trained in geriatric care, could make these visits. If we want people to remain independent as long as possible, and if we are serious about reducing reliance on hospitals at the same time as our population is aging, then this old-fashioned kind of medical practice has to be the wave of the future.

Finally, as our health care system evolves, Canadians will have to wake up to the close link between health and the economy. In 1996, 18% of Canadians, some 5.3 million people, were living below the poverty line. That is not a prescription for a healthy society. A mountain of evidence exists to prove that unemployment and poverty are the prime causes of poor health, yet this fact is rarely discussed in the context of our health care system. Canada's high international ranking in such population health indicators as life expectancy is often misleadingly cited as proof of the excellence of our health care system. But the healthiest Canadians never go near the health care system. They are healthy because they have well-paid jobs, happy lives, are well-nourished, don't smoke, and get plenty of exercise.

If the health care system were the key to health, universal medicare would have produced equal health status for all Canadians, but it hasn't come even close. "Studies in all parts of Canada consistently show that people at each step on the income scale are healthier than those on the step below," John Millar, the British Columbia health officer, wrote in a 1995 report. In Vancouver and Victoria, for example, twice as many infant deaths occurred in low-income neighbourhoods as in wealthy districts.

What this means is that we can't expect our health care system to deliver miracles, no matter how well we reform it or how much money we spend on it. An effective way to keep health costs down is to make sure Canadians are working in well-paid jobs and have sufficient incomes, especially into their retirement years. Given the demands on our health care budget that an aging population will make, sensible economic development and social policies are more urgently needed than ever before.

Chapter 10

What's a Family?

D emographics are an invisible force that can affect even our most intimate relationships in surprising ways. For example, it would never occur to a 25-year-old who is popular with the opposite sex that if born 10 years earlier, he or she might not have been quite so popular. But in romance as in so much else, being born in the right year is an advantage. In some cases, what seems like a new behavioural trend – "cocooning," for instance – is in fact the inevitable result of a demographic shift. Let's take a closer look at how demographics can affect family life and other relationships among people.

BABIES

In the early 1980s, a senior official in the Ontario Ministry of Health with some knowledge of demographics had a plan. He knew that births had declined through the 1960s and 1970s. He knew that the fertility rate was way down and that the chances of modern women reverting to having three or four children each were remote. Therefore, he reasoned, Ontario's hospitals should be developing a strategy for closing maternity wards during the 1980s, since births would surely continue to decline. At the same time, in preparation for the aging of society, these facilities should be transformed into geriatric wards.

As Alexander Pope wisely said, "A little learning is a dangerous thing." It was true that the fertility rate was down, and it was also true that society was aging. But there was more need for maternity wards than for geriatric wards at the start of the 1980s because the birth rate would inevitably go up, and seniors, just as inevitably, would remain very much a minority in Canadian society.

The birth rate did go up because the huge number of women born during the 1950s and 1960s moved into their childbearing years. Even if women have relatively few kids, as these boomer women did, a lot of people having one or two kids each at the same time means a lot of business for maternity wards. That's what happened during the 1980s as the echo arrived. Hospitals had to give up any ideas of closing maternity wards, just as schools had to contend with a sudden rise in kindergarten enrolment, followed of course by rising elementary school enrolment. As for the seniors, the growth in their numbers slowed during the 1980s for the simple reason that not many people were born during World War I. Demographics are easy to understand, but without careful analysis, the timing of appropriate policies can be way off.

At the millennium, some of the younger boomers are still producing babies, but annual births began declining in 1991. By 1995 it was clear that Canadian women were no longer delivering a large cohort of offspring, and therefore that the echo was at an end and the Millennium Bust underway (see Chapter 1). This development surprised some who thought that because the birth rate rose during the 1980s, it would continue to rise during the 1990s. Instead, births declined because the most proficient baby producers – women in their 20s – had declined in number.

The 1980s, after a 20-year decline in births, was exactly the wrong time to consider closing some maternity wards. The right time would have been in 1995, after 15 years of high births. The health care resources saved by reducing the size of maternity wards should have been shifted to heart disease, arthritis, and diabetes, all of which are on the increase because of the aging of the boomer generation.

People are waiting longer to get married than they used to and career-minded women are delaying childbirth longer than they used to. As a result, 29% of first-time mothers in 1995 were in their 30s, a higher percentage than in the past. More than 58% of first-time mothers were women in their 20s, a smaller majority than previously but still a majority. Childbirth can be delayed only so long before a

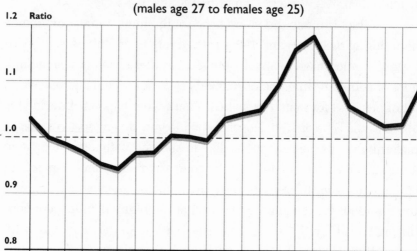

FIGURE 10: GENDER RATIO AT MARRIAGE
(males age 27 to females age 25)

Source: Calculations by David K. Foot based on Statistics Canada, *Revised Intercensal Population and Family Estimates, July 1, 1971-1991*, catalogue 91-537 occasional (July 1994), and on unpublished estimates from Statistics Canada.

woman runs into the limitations imposed by biology. A 28-year-old is still about five times as likely to have a baby as a 38-year-old. In 1998, the peak of the boom was 38 and that explains why births have declined. Some older boomers would like to get pregnant but are having trouble. That accounts for the significant improvements in recent years in techniques to treat infertility. This scientific effort is driven purely by demographics. But it is already running out of steam because an increasing number of boomers are too old to have babies, with or without pharmaceutical help.

MEN AND WOMEN

When they marry for the first time, men usually marry women about two years younger than they are. And women, obviously, tend to marry men about two years older. This simple demographic fact has important social implications. For women of marriageable age it means that, in the 1990s, they have more choice among potential partners than men do. The balance of power in male-female relationships has shifted their way (see Figure 10).

The number of people born in each year kept climbing until 1959, the peak of the boom. After 1960, the boom declined into the baby bust, which lasted until the late 1970s. When birth numbers are rising, there will inevitably be more 26-year-old females than 28-year-old males. That puts the 28-year-old male in the driver's seat, because he has a greater choice of females of the right age to choose from. That's what happened in the first phase of the boom. But if numbers are dropping from year to year, then 28-year-old males will outnumber 26-year-old females. This started to occur by the mid-1980s, when the peak of the boom reached its mid-20s, the age when permanent relationships are generally established. It's definitely the situation for young people contemplating partnerships at the millennium. There aren't enough 27-year-old women for all the 29-year-old men who are looking for partners. The women can pick and choose.

The average age of those embarking on first marriages declined during the 1950s, 1960s, and 1970s, and then climbed back up in the 1980s and 1990s. By 1996, newlyweds were 29 and 27. The gap of about two years has remained fairly stable since the end of World War II. This gender gap can have a big impact on social mores. Take the case of a front-end male boomer, born in 1950 and reaching 29 in 1979. Fewer men were born in 1950 than women in 1952. This meant that in the potential marriage relationship, men were in short supply relative to women. This may explain the growth in cohabitation as the huge boomer generation moved into its adult years over the late 1960s and 1970s. The shortage of male partners may have contributed to a decision by more women to get on with their lives by looking for ways to fulfilment other than marriage and a family.

There were other reasons for the changes in personal morality that marked the 1960s and 1970s, including the arrival of the birth-control pill, the relaxation of the divorce law, and the movement of women into the labour force. These were events of far-reaching significance for family life. Women were now free to have multiple partners, to postpone or reject motherhood, and to pursue careers. And as they pursued those careers, they gradually evened the balance of power between men and women still further. A woman whose earning power is as great as a man's can do without one if she prefers; or if she does choose to have a partner, she can leave him if she becomes dissatisfied.

This new fact of life has contributed to a decline in the popularity of marriage in Canada. So has the reality that many people, having lived through their own parents' divorces, have a negative opinion about marriage. Many others, whatever their attitude to marriage, tend to avoid or postpone it during rough economic times. For all these reasons, the marriage rate in Canada has been dropping steadily since 1990, and those who are getting married aren't doing very well at it. Based on 1996 divorce rates, 37% of marriages can be expected to fail.

The change in social mores is so profound that many Canadians are abandoning the concept of marriage. Over the last two decades, the number of persons living common law has increased spectacularly, from 700,000 in 1981 to 2 million in 1995. Almost one in three new babies in Canada is born to unmarried parents.

Evidence of the huge advance made towards equality of the sexes is that some men now admit without embarrassment to being "househusbands." This is the result of the simultaneous arrival of the echo and the movement of women into high-paying jobs. If the arrival of small children requires one partner to stay at home and the wife is earning the larger salary, then it makes obvious economic sense for her to stay in her job. And of course, in many cases there is no choice in the matter: he has lost his job and she has kept hers.

At the same time that some men are claiming househusband status, many women are reclaiming that of housewife. Demographics are the reason. During the late 1980s and early 1990s, the peak of the boom was passing through its family formation years, the late 20s and early 30s. Families with children under five are often easier to manage when one partner stays home. This demographic event coincided in most of Canada with a severe recession. Jobs were scarce, and that was another good reason to take a temporary break from work. As their children grow up, many of these temporary housewives and househusbands re-enter the workforce.

The redefinition of the family in Canadian society also includes the movement to formalize and legitimize marriages of same-sex couples. Demographics again play an important role. People in their 20s are more likely than older people to engage in temporary relationships and don't concern themselves with such boring matters as health plans and pension benefits. But at the millennium, even the youngest boomers are well into their 30s. They are ready for a more permanent relationship and are becoming concerned about their future and their children's future. As part of a large cohort, boomers are not shy about asserting their rights. That's why in the 1990s, same-sex couples in permanent relationships began demanding the same legal and economic benefits that society confers on traditional marriages, including the right to adopt children. Some women choose to introduce children into existing lesbian relationships. In other cases, gays and lesbians who entered heterosexual marriages in their 20s have abandoned those marriages in their 30s and 40s, replacing them with openly homosexual alliances. Because children are involved in some of these situations, the issues of custody and adoption have become extremely important.

All these complex changes in the structure of the family add up to a social experiment of major proportions. The results so far are mixed. That men and women are better able to free themselves from unhappy relationships is all to the good. It is also good that women now have equal opportunity to fulfil their talents in whatever way they choose. On the other hand, the breakdown of the traditional family has brought with it a huge increase in the number of single-parent families. And the evidence is mounting that children in such families are at a disadvantage. Studies show that they are more likely than the children of two-parent families to be undernourished, to get pregnant as teenagers, and to drop out of high school, and they are less likely to go on to postsecondary education.

A new development in family life in the 1990s was an increase in the number of adult Canadians living alone. The number of people in this situation grew by 11% between 1991 and 1995, twice as fast as the rate of population growth. This group includes older women, many of them widows, as well as younger ones. In fact, younger women living alone were helping to fuel a construction boom in downtown condos. Single women "have become a large and significant buying force," development consultant Barry Lyons told the *Toronto Star* in 1997.

But despite all the change that is taking place, it is too soon to write off the traditional family. For one thing, the ideal of a lifetime marriage that produces children is still popular. And the age gap favouring females probably also favours the traditional family. Marcia Guttentag and Paul Secord of the University of Houston studied several societies where men compete for a smaller number of women. They found that in such societies, the traditional marriage flourishes. The average age of first marriage drops, marriage and birth rates climb, and females quit the workforce to become full-time homemakers. This demographic trend in favour of traditionalism will be operating in Canada until the echo generation reaches marriageable age, starting around 2005.

Probably the most that can be said for the age gap favouring females, however, is that it may have restrained the pace of change in the 1990s. While it is premature to write off the traditional family, it would be wrong to put too much stock in the alleged revival of "family values" during the 1980s and 1990s, because that phenomenon was transitory. When do you have family values? When you have families. In the 1990s, the boomers were in their 30s and 40s, with houses and mortgages and children to fret over. Family values didn't matter to them much as 20-year-olds in the 1970s, any more than they interested 20-year-olds during the Roaring Twenties.

As the echo generation leaves home in ever larger numbers in the new millennium, it will seem society is once again neglecting family values and rediscovering sex, drugs, and new music. Social observers will herald the arrival of yet another value shift, but the real reason will be the demographic shift. Sex, drugs, and alternative music were alive and well throughout the 1990s, but the baby-bust generation that enjoyed them was 56% as big as the boom, and so the rest of society paid less attention to its preferences.

COCOONING

Faith Popcorn, the American marketing guru, succeeded in putting a new word into the language: cocooning. The notion of cocooning struck so strong a chord when Popcorn invented it that *le cocooning* was adopted by French-speakers as well. Cocooning means cosying up at home. Whereas in the 1970s people were dancing and drinking all night in discos, Popcorn's research revealed that in the 1980s – stressed out by overwork, noise, crime, and sundry other ills of modern life – the same people preferred to snuggle up in their living rooms, shades drawn tight, in front of their television sets and VCRs. Of this, Popcorn had ample proof: VCR sales were skyrocketing, as were sales of take-out food and microwave popcorn. And along with rising VCR sales, Popcorn noted one other result of cocooning: births in the United States in 1990 were the highest since the baby-boom year of 1960.

Popcorn confused cause and effect. In her book *The Popcorn*

Suburban cocoons

Report, she suggested that people first decided to stay home and then, to give themselves something to do, decided to have children. But the reality was exactly the reverse. The huge boom generation, in both Canada and the United States, moved into its childrearing years and, inevitably, started spending more time at home. Call it cocooning or what you will – it was normal, predictable behaviour.

In this as in so much else, the boom was no different from any previous generation. Children are great consumers of their parents' time, energy, and money. Couples raising children have less time, less energy, and less money to go out on the town than they had when they were childless. So they settle for ordering take-out and renting a video instead of dinner in a restaurant followed by the theatre or a movie. But they still love going out (see Chapter 6), and now that the kids are old enough to stay home without a babysitter, they are leaving the cocoon more often, although they don't stay out as late at age 41 as they did at age 21. Cocooning seemed to be a popular new lifestyle only because so many boomer parents were passing through the same phase of their lives at the same time. The next cohort entering the cocoon is the baby-bust generation. As that happens, it will seem as if cocooning has gone out of style – and that will be true, not because of a value shift but because there are half as many busters as boomers.

THE OLDEST PROFESSION

Much confusion surrounds the subject of prostitution because Canadian newspapers, inexplicably, insist on subjecting their readers to a regular stream of articles discussing the pros and cons of "legalizing prostitution" as if this ancient profession actually were illegal in Canada. In fact, no law forbids prostitution although, like many other occupations, its conduct is subject to strict regulations.

The effect of these regulations is to prohibit prostitutes from soliciting clients in the street, from working for someone else, and from carrying on business in a permanent location. Of course, the regulations are often disobeyed, with the result that illegal prostitution flourishes in our major cities. But many other prostitutes operate as independents, and they are engaged in a lawful business. The courts do not interpret their advertising – through word of mouth or in explicit newspaper ads – as soliciting. They do not work for pimps. They do not operate out of a single place of business, which would be an illegal bawdy house, but instead meet clients in locations not primarily used for paid sex.

What are the implications of demographics for these law-abiding prostitutes, as well as for their colleagues operating outside the law? Most prostitutes are women or men in their late teens and 20s; most of their customers are men aged between 30 and 50. This means that changes in the age structure of society can have a major impact on both the supply of prostitutes and the demand for their services. During the 1990s, prostitutes have been drawn from a smaller cohort, the baby bust, while their customers have come from a large one, the boom. In other words, the impact of demographics has been both to limit the supply of prostitutes and expand the demand for them. The demographic situation therefore has been favourable to sellers of sexual services.

But this situation is changing at the millennium as the leading edge of the echo enters young adulthood, thereby increasing the potential supply of prostitutes. This development can be expected to drive down prices, making it harder for those already in the business to earn a decent living. Should the lower prices eventually slow down the entry of new suppliers to the marketplace that would be to the good because prostitution is not a desirable occupation. It can be dangerous and degrading even for independent, law-abiding professionals. As for street prostitutes, they suffer appalling working conditions. Most of them become drug addicts and, because of exploitation by pimps, are able to retain only a small fraction of their earnings.

There is evidence that prostitution increases with unemployment and therefore the best way to reduce the appeal of prostitution is to build an economy that offers challenging, well-paid employment to young people. Meanwhile, since attempts to enforce the regulations against illegal prostitution have proven extremely ineffective, municipal governments and police forces in recent years have been looking for ways to protect residential neighbourhoods from the sex trade while making life less dangerous for prostitutes. Some reform is badly needed. In view of the demographic trend favouring the growth of prostitution, making it tempting to many echo teenagers, that need is more urgent than ever.

THE SANDWICH GENERATION

Life expectancy at birth for Canadian men is 75.7; for women, it's 81.5. At the millennium, the parents of the boomers are approaching those ages. Some of these parents are already in declining health and needing extra attention from their offspring. At the same time, boomers are engaged in the often difficult task of guiding their teenagers through the transition from childhood to adulthood. They also have increasing responsibilities at work. These people are the meat in a generational sandwich.

This phenomenon isn't new, but a number of factors are at work that make sandwiching a bigger problem for more people than ever before. Many women are working in senior, stressful, time-con-

The generational sandwich

suming jobs. That's important because women are the ones who most often take on the job of caregiving. Many of these same women had children later in life than was the norm in past generations. Meanwhile, people are living longer. All these elements increase the chances of someone being responsible for both children and parents at the same time. In some cases, however, the dual responsibilities occur sequentially rather than simultaneously. The teenagers grow up and move out of the house but the middle-aged caregiver has barely any time to savour the state of not being responsible for another person's welfare because that's when her parent falls seriously ill.

Because life expectancy is lower for men, chances are that a woman will be present to take care of a male partner who has a disabling health problem. But if a widow falls ill, there's no partner around to look after her needs. At that point, the responsibility falls on the children, who are in their late 40s and 50s. A 1994 Statistics Canada study found that twice as many women as men were both working full-time and caring for an elderly relative. Because women are more likely to be sandwiched than males, sandwiching is an important reason why more women haven't risen to senior positions in their careers. The woman who becomes a senior vice-president at the age of 51 may not go on to become president, because she chooses to devote more time and emotional energy to caring for a dying parent.

Here's how one family has responded to the needs of a mother in declining health. Of the three sons, the youngest still lives close to his mother, while the two older ones, who have been more successful financially in their careers, live in distant cities. The two wealthier brothers have paid for a house for their mother to live in and pay two-thirds of the cost of owning and running the house. But all three brothers share ownership of the house, the youngest paying his share by spending time caring for the mother. The mother pays the youngest son's share of the costs as rent. This arrangement works to everyone's satisfaction because all three sons are doing their part, none feels taken advantage of, and the mother is well looked after.

In the world of mobility we live in, this is an example of the kind of innovation that will be needed as families cope with the decline and death of parents. The boomers, because there are so many of them, grew up in a world of sibling rivalry. But to help their parents complete life's journey in peace and dignity, they will have to learn to exercise sibling cooperation instead. In the past, there were two options for an older person unable to care for herself without assistance – moving in with a relative or moving to a nursing home. At the millennium a third option – assisted independence – was gaining ground. In a U.S. survey, more than 80% of seniors said they wanted to stay in their own homes as long as possible. Yet many of these people need assistance from children or other relatives which is why absenteeism by caregivers costs employers an estimated $29 billion a year in the United States. The home care industry can be expected to continue its rapid growth in the decades ahead because relatives will not be able to give all the care that will be required (see Chapter 9).

The inevitable decline in health of one's parents has other implications as well. It increases a person's awareness of mortality, which often leads to an increased interest in spirituality. This often coincides with the presence of teenage children whose parents would like to acquaint them with their spiritual heritage. It also results in greater health awareness, which is why 45-year-olds tend to drive more safely, smoke and drink less, and pay more attention to what they eat than 25-year-olds. These trends are likely to continue as the rest of the boomers enter their 40s during the first years of the new century.

Chapter 11

An Older, Wiser Canada

D emographics are so fundamental a phenomenon, operating at so deep a level in human society, that most of us are not aware of them, just as we are not aware of an underground stream flowing silently beneath a big city street. Yet demographics are too useful a tool for explaining the world to remain underground. The preceding chapters have shown how they can throw light on the future of such things as school enrolments, real estate investments, and public taste in cars. Demographics also have a lot to say about such big issues as Canadian constitutional negotiations and international flows of goods and people. Demographics help us understand what was at stake when anglophone Canada sat down at the negotiating table with Quebec, just as they enable us to anticipate Canada's future place in a world of expanding global trade. Let's conclude this survey of the impact of demographics on Canada's future by looking at some of those big issues.

DEMOGRAPHICS AND THE CONSTITUTION

Canada is composed of three distinct societies, each with a different fertility rate. These societies are anglophone Canada, francophone Canada, and aboriginal Canada. (Within anglophone Canada, there is some variation from province to province. In 1996, Newfoundland had the lowest fertility rate, 1.3, while Saskatchewan and Manitoba, at 1.9, had the highest.) The dramatic demographic differences among anglophone, francophone, and aboriginal Canada help explain why both the Meech Lake and Charlottetown constitutional negotiations ended in failure.

In the 1920s, the fertility rate in Canada was around 3.5 children per family. This national rate included an average of 4.5 children for each Quebec family and 3 children for each family in Canada outside Quebec. Quebec's relatively high fertility, reflecting its Roman Catholic heritage, continued throughout the 1920s, 1930s, and 1940s. During this period it didn't matter whether Quebec took in as many immigrants as other parts of the country. Higher fertility allowed Quebeckers to maintain or even increase their relative share of the Canadian population.

The Quiet Revolution of the 1950s and 1960s included a demographic revolution, as Quebec women increasingly ignored the Catholic prohibition on birth control. As a result, fertility started to fall. By 1959, the fertility rate in Quebec was the same as in the rest of the country, and since then it has often been lower. Quebec's fertility reached a low of 1.4 children per family in 1986, well below the replacement rate of 2.1 and at that time one of the lowest fertility rates in the world. Since then Quebec's fertility has recovered a bit. Its rate in 1996 was 1.6, which was higher than that of three Atlantic provinces and British Columbia and the same as the rate for Canada as a whole.

At the millennium, therefore, Quebec's fertility is low but not abnormally low – in fact, it is significantly higher than the European average of 1.4. Quebec is merely exhibiting the reproductive behaviour that has become the norm in all modern industrialized societies. Nor is it remarkable that women in a predominantly Catholic society would decide to have few babies. Such Catholic countries as Spain, Portugal, and Italy also have low fertility: Italy and Spain, at 1.2 children per family, have the lowest in the world.

The recent upward movement in Quebec's fertility rate wasn't enough to prevent the province's population from dropping below 25% of the Canadian population in 1994 for the first time since Confederation. This happened not only because of continuing low fertility but also because more people leave Quebec every year than move to it. Quebeckers also have somewhat lower life expectancy, adding further to the downward pressure on the population.

Quebec started as one of two founding nations of Canada, with 43% of the total population. Now it finds itself as one among ten provinces with a shrinking share of the total population. For Canada as a whole, the proportion of the population whose mother tongue is French slipped from 29% in 1951 to 23.5% in 1996. Justifiably, Quebec fears these trends will lead to a loss of power and political influence within Canada. It is not surprising that a cultural minority in such a situation would reach out to the majority for some assurances or guarantees. Nor is it surprising that some members of that minority would push for sovereignty in the belief that it would enhance their power and protect their culture.

This demographic crisis helps explain the Quebec position over the past 20 years of constitutional negotiations and two referendums on sovereignty. The dip in the population below 25% was disturbing to the collective psyche of Quebeckers; that is why Quebec fought during the Charlottetown negotiations for a guarantee of 25% of the seats in the federal Parliament. Quebec's demographic crisis provides much of the impetus for the sovereignty movement, but it may also be a reason why the sovereignty movement has lost two referendums. The supporters of sovereignty are drawn almost exclusively from old-stock French Canadians and, because of their low fertility, there haven't been enough of them to win a majority for their cause. Should continuing political and economic uncertainty cause an exodus of non-francophone Quebeckers, that could be enough to tip the balance in favour of secession in a future referendum, assuming that the separatists can maintain the loyalty of a large majority of francophones.

The Charlottetown constitutional process, in addition to being about the francophone-anglophone divide, was also about the relations between the native and non-native populations. While Canada as a whole has a below-replacement fertility rate, the rate for native Canadians, although it has been in steady decline, is still well above the replacement level. As a result, 35% of the aboriginal population was under 15 in 1996 compared with 20% in the total population. The youngest part of Canada is Nunavut, the eastern Arctic territory where almost 40% of the mainly Inuit population is under 15. As a whole, the aboriginal population is ten years younger on average than the general population. Quebec's demographics stand in stark contrast to native Canada's: in 1995, it surpassed British Columbia as Canada's oldest province, with only 19% of Quebeckers under 15.

The major need of any nation with a youthful population is education and jobs for its young people. If these are not available, the inevitable results include migration (in the case of native Canadians, away from their own communities to Toronto, Winnipeg, Saskatoon, and other cities), rebellion, suicide, crime, and family breakdown, among other social pathologies. This is the context in which aboriginal leaders, understandably, are seeking greater control over land and resources in order to rebuild their communities.

The demographic divide among Canada's three distinct societies helps explain why it has been so difficult to reach agreement on a new constitutional framework for Canada. We Canadians tend to be overly self-critical in castigating ourselves for our seemingly endless constitutional bickering. But in fact, compared with many other countries facing similar situations, we have generally managed our differences peacefully, even in the absence of a fundamental agreement.

Other demographically divided societies have not fared so well. In the Pacific nation of Fiji, the fertility rate of the East Indian community is higher than that of the native Polynesians. This demographic disparity resulted in an electoral victory by a party representing the Indians, followed by a military coup by the Polynesian-dominated military. In the Middle East, the fertility rate of the Arabs in the occupied territories, at 5.4, is much higher than that of Israel, which has a fertility rate of 2.9. Clearly, demographic differences are not the only reason for the ongoing resistance to Israeli military rule. But 15-year-olds are more likely to throw rocks than 50-year-olds. And when a whole generation of young people has nothing to do, resentment against an unacceptable political situation turns readily into violence.

This does not necessarily mean that, in its attempts to solve its problems, Canada won't face an escalation of the sort of violence that erupted in some native communities during the 1990s. But our chances of living in harmony will be enhanced if we have a better grasp of the demographics and hence the needs of Canada's three distinct societies. Once the opposing sides in constitutional negotiations understand these crucial demographic realities, they will understand one another's positions better. And that enhanced understanding will improve our chances of coming to agreement.

DEMOGRAPHICS, TECHNOLOGY, AND EMPLOYMENT

A fundamental link has always existed between demographics, technology, and employment. In a society with a lot of young workers, labour is in abundant supply and is thus cheap. Moreover, young people are still borrowing – for an education, a car, or a house. A young person who has just struck out on his own has to spend all of his income getting established in life. If he has a job, it's an entry-level job at a relatively low salary. He has no money left over for investments. In a predominantly young country, because only a small section of the population has any savings, capital is priced high because it is in short supply. Consequently, real interest rates, which are the return on capital, are high. That is why young countries have abundant labour and scarce financial capital.

That was the situation in Canada during the two decades, from the mid-1960s to the mid-1980s, when the huge boom generation was moving onto the labour market and becoming borrowers. In those economic conditions, a new technological advance has to be either extremely good or absolutely necessary for competitive reasons before a company will adopt it. In a labour-rich, capital-scarce country, there is no great incentive to borrow money in order to acquire new technology. Borrowing is further inhibited by the high interest rates that are the norm in a capital-scarce country. As a result, from 1965 to 1985 Canada trailed such older countries as Japan and Germany in adopting new technologies. It wasn't because we were Luddites, but because we were younger and had more labour and less financial capital than those countries did. What we needed to do during those years was not to install robots in our factories but to find jobs for our young people. And that is precisely what Canada did.

This was a good strategy if what we wanted was to preserve social harmony. But it was not a strategy that would increase productivity. When the workforce receives a huge influx of young people, lacking both experience and the latest machinery, labour productivity falls. On the other hand, these young workers gain valuable experience, which contributes to future productivity. And social harmony is enhanced when they are able to get established in the workforce.

In an aging society, the growth of the workforce slows down. Meanwhile, because more people are older, they have more money to invest, and the supply of capital increases. Because of demographic change, wages ultimately rise while interest rates come down. Capital therefore becomes cheaper, and there is more incentive to use it to invest in new technology as an alternative to increasingly expensive labour. This demographic phenomenon was at the root of Japan's transformation into an economic superpower. Japan, which had a birth dearth following its defeat in World War II just when North America was starting its baby boom, had no alternative but to be an early postwar adopter of technology. When you put lots of new machines in place and you have a slow-growing workforce to use them, productivity soars. In the automobile and consumer electronics industries it specialized in, Japan became the most efficient producer in the world over the 1960s and 1970s. As a result, it could produce cars more cheaply than the Big Three in North America. The early Japanese cars weren't always the best or most reliable, but they were the right price and the right size for a young North American population. Japan's achievement eventually forced American automakers to automate in order to compete. Strange as it seems, Detroit got robots in the 1980s because Japanese women didn't have babies in the late 1940s.

In Canada, we should have seen a similar pattern towards the end of the 1980s, when the last of the boomers became adults and the new entrants to the labour market were coming from the smaller baby-bust generation. And in fact, Canada did experience a decline in youth unemployment during the 1980s because we had fewer young people to be unemployed. At the same time wages for entry-level positions increased. But a severe recession in the first part of the 1990s drastically reduced the availability of jobs for everyone, especially the young and inexperienced. Moreover, the presence of the entire boom in the labour force at the same time meant that labour continued in abundant supply, depressing wages. To make matters worse, the federal government sharply increased immigration levels to 250,000 per year, by far the highest per-capita levels in the world, further increasing the supply of labour and adding to the downward pressure on wages. Other forces keeping a lid on wages included the globalization of the economy, which meant Canadian workers were now competing with workers in low-wage countries. Free trade prompted some Canadian companies to relocate their manufacturing operations to low-wage areas outside of Canada. Global competition also led Canadian companies to trim

Expert tutoring

their workforces as part of a desperate search for higher productivity.

Nevertheless, there remained in Canada in the mid-1990s an underlying demographic trend towards higher wages for entry-level workers. Without this trend, wages for young people would have been even lower than they were. But at the millennium this trend has run its course. During the next decade, the echo will enter the job market, once again putting downward pressure on wages and upward pressure on the unemployment rate.

The North American Free Trade Agreement is an experiment in creating a trading bloc of countries with different demographic profiles. Mexico is much younger than Canada or the United States. For Mexico to embrace technology in the 1990s would have been misguided, just as it would have been wrong for Canada to do so in the 1970s. The Mexicans' need is not to save labour but to create jobs for their many young new entrants to the job market. But as Mexico's trading partner we have to accept that, because the supply of Mexican labour is so large, the wages Mexican workers can command will be lower than would be acceptable in Canada. This is not a malevolent policy imposed by advocates of free trade but rather an inevitable result of the different demographic profiles of the partner countries.

DEMOGRAPHICS AND MIGRATION

To uproot oneself and attempt to build a new life in a new location is a difficult and challenging undertaking. If you are going to migrate, the best time to do it is in your 20s. At that stage in your life, you have finished your education but haven't yet launched your career. You are old enough to cope with the arduous process of moving to a new country but still adaptable enough to integrate into a new culture and, perhaps, to master a new language. You have the latest skills but only entry-level salary expectations. And you have a long lifetime ahead of you to reap the benefits of the move.

These facts explain why countries with a high percentage of people in their 20s are the major sources of migrants. Even if such a country is doing well economically, it may not be able to provide enough jobs for all of its young people. Some of those who can't get good jobs will leave in search of economic opportunities elsewhere. One of the places at the top of their list will be Canada, which, with the United States and Australia, has been one of the three major immigrant-receiving countries since the end of World War II. These three, along with Israel and New Zealand, are the only countries that officially want immigrants. They are the only countries that operate immigration programs through which they set numerical targets and apply selection criteria.

A demographic perspective reveals that the changing character of immigration to Canada is determined more by the demographics of the source countries than by immigration policies made in Canada. Until our immigration regulations were revised in 1962, non-whites were systematically excluded from coming to Canada as immigrants. Not surprisingly, therefore, during the 1950s the countries of northern Europe – Britain, Germany, Scandinavia – were our major source of immigrants. But that would have been the case for demographic reasons even in the absence of a "white Canada" policy. Northern Europe, today the region with the oldest population in the world, in those years had plenty of people in their 20s who believed they could improve their economic circumstances by departing a Europe devastated by war for Canada, the United States, or Australia.

The second-oldest region of the world is southern Europe: Greece, Spain, Italy, and Portugal. But in the 1960s and 1970s, those countries had plenty of people in their 20s. That's why so many of Canada's immigrants during those decades came from the countries of southern Europe.

The next-oldest region of the world is southeast Asia, which began sending people to other parts of the world, including Canada, in the 1970s and 1980s, decades when it had a surplus of people in their 20s. Asia remained our major source of newcomers throughout the 1980s and into the 1990s. But much of Asia got its fertility rates under control during the 1960s, which is why the stream of newcomers from that region will probably slow down during the millennium period.

Latin America took longer to reduce its fertility rates. That is why it is the next region of the world with a surplus of people in their prime migrating years. Over the next decade, an increasing number of Canada's immigrants will come from Latin America.

What of the more distant future? A phenomenal 44% of the population of Africa is under 15 – almost half the population. These people will reach their prime mobility years shortly after the turn of the century. At that time, all the Western industrialized countries, including Canada, will experience huge migration pressures from Africa.

What should Canada's policy be in the face of immigration pressures from Latin America, Africa, or anywhere else? To maintain a sensible immigration program that balances our own needs with humanitarian goals. There was no demographic basis for the high immigration levels of the early 1990s. As was pointed out earlier, Canada's population would have been increasing even without any immigration, because Canada then had one of the highest birth rates among industrialized countries. It was this high birth rate that created the echo generation. At the millennium, the birth rate is in decline as the boomers age past their childbearing years. But this does not mean, as advocates of high immigration levels sometimes claim, that Canada is in imminent danger of depopulation.

Nor does it mean, as these same advocates sometimes suggest, that Canada should increase its existing immigration intake, already the highest per capita in the world, in order to avoid a labour short-age. Even during the 1990s, when the new entrants to the workforce were coming from the small bust generation, Canada did not have a labour shortage, the proof being a stubbornly high unemployment rate. At the millennium, the larger echo generation is about to enter the labour market, and it will provide an ample supply of new work-ers. There is no connection between the reproductive behaviour of Canadians at a given point in time and labour market conditions at that same point in time. It would therefore be senseless to raise immi-gration levels now in response to a hypothetical labour shortage that may or may not occur at some time in the distant future.

Just how likely is it that Canada will find itself short of people? No one can predict what will happen to fertility in the future. The fertility rate fluctuates, and even a small increase can have noticeable impacts on future population size. If fertility were to rise to 1.9, for example, the number of immigrants needed to maintain the existing level of population would be half that required when fertility was 1.7.

A federal investigation of Canada's demographic future, the Demographic Review, proved that no demographic case exists for high immigration levels. In its report, issued in 1989, it made a projection of what would happen to Canada's population if we had no population growth from immigration. Assuming a fertility rate of 1.7 and net migration (immigration minus emigration) of 0, Canada's population would stop growing in 2011 and then begin a long, lingering decline that would continue until the last Canadian, unable to find a mate anywhere from Victoria to St. John's, died of loneliness in 2786. This sequence of events, of course, is purely theoretical. No modern society has ever vanished because of the failure of its people to reproduce, although it has been suggested that such civilizations as the Roman and Aztec empires declined in power as their fertility declined.

The point is that even if below-replacement fertility continues in Canada, we need only a relatively small amount of immigration to maintain a substantial population. This simple point requires emphasis because misinformation is widespread. For example, a 1995 article in the *Toronto Star* stated: "As in the rest of Canada, Quebec's low reproduction rate requires massive infusions of immigration if the population is not to decline." Exaggerated claims like this create confusion in the public mind over the important policy issue of immigration levels. The fact is that even with net immigration of only 80,000 a year (about half the level during the 1990s), our population, according to the Demographic Review, would continue growing until 2026 and then decline almost imperceptibly until it stabilized at 18 million eight centuries in the future. In other words, with immigration at levels well below "massive," Canada's population would not decline at all until after 2026, and the decline during the rest of the 21st century would be minimal. As for the prospect of Canada arriving at a stable population in the distant future, that is not cause for alarm. Many

European countries already have stable populations, and Europe remains prosperous. An absence of population growth results in increased productivity, less unemployment, and reduced pressure on both urban and rural environments.

Immigration policy should not be based on an imaginary demographic crisis. Many people would like to move to Canada to work or to join their families or because they are fleeing persecution. But we should manage the policy so that both immigrants and hosts benefit from it. That requires taking demographics into account when we set both immigration levels and selection criteria. During the latter part of the 1990s, more by accident than by design, immigration policy was temporarily in line with demographic realities, because immigrants in their 20s were coming at a time when the number of Canadians in that age group had declined. But as the echo generation enters the labour market in the first decade of the next century, Canada will need to consider curtailing immigration. It does not make sense to bring in a flood of 20-year-old immigrants to compete for scarce jobs just when large numbers of Canadian-born 20-year-olds are also entering the labour market. Doing so would be unfair both to immigrants and to resident Canadians.

Just as they influence immigration, demographics also influence emigration. People tend to return to their roots when they retire. Many Atlantic Canadians who moved to central and western Canada in search of jobs will return home when they retire. And so will many Germans, Italians, and other immigrants who came to Canada during the 1950s and 1960s. Emigration from Canada to western Europe will probably exceed immigration for the foreseeable future. We don't know how many people moved from Canada to Italy in 1997, but it was probably more than the 527 Italians who became landed immigrants in Canada in that year. Economics has little to do with the flow of people between two countries such as Italy and Canada that have similar per-capita incomes. Demographics are the decisive factor: Italy has few people of migrating age, while Canada has many Italian-born people of retirement age ready to return home.

DEMOGRAPHICS AND TRADE

Since young people eat a lot, a country with many young people will have a high demand for food. People in their 20s and 30s are setting up new households, and they need furniture and appliances and cars. That's why a country with many people in their 20s and 30s experiences intensified demand for manufactured goods. People in their 40s and 50s don't eat as much as people in their teens and 20s, and they have already bought most of the major manufactured goods they need. They need travel, financial, and health care services. Countries with a high percentage of middle-aged people have reduced demand for agricultural and manufactured products and increased demand for services.

Canada has already lived through these transformations. First we increased our agricultural productivity. Then we developed a strong manufacturing sector. Finally, over the late 1980s and 1990s, our service sector experienced rapid growth. That is why we have seen a proliferation of small companies in Canada. A small company can't produce automobiles, but it can provide financial planning or travel services.

In international trade, older countries have an advantage. They know the marketplaces of younger countries because they have already experienced the same demographics in their own domestic market. Ikea had had plenty of experience supplying household furnishings to young Swedes assembling their first homes before it arrived in North America to exploit a huge new market of young boomers.

Canada is now in a position to benefit from growing demand for manufactured goods in southeast Asia and especially Latin America, parts of the world that are younger than we are. That doesn't mean our companies can't continue to sell manufactured goods in North America, or that a Canadian company such as Magna can't continue to do well in the auto parts business in Europe. But the big growth in demand is more likely to come outside of our traditional European and North American markets. Our exporters need to be aware of the demographic basis for this opportunity and become more aggressive in exploiting these new markets.

In recent years, Canadians have become more knowledgeable about Canadian demographics, but few are aware of the important differences among countries, including some of our major trading partners. Many people assume that the Canadian and U.S. pattern – a small percentage of seniors, a preponderance of people in their 30s and 40s, a smaller number in their 20s, and a bigger group of teenagers – is the norm. But this population structure is the unique result of a postwar baby boom followed by declining fertility in the 1960s. Other parts of the world had different experiences.

In Italy, for example, which did not have a postwar baby boom, 17% of the population were seniors in the late 1990s, compared with only 12% of Canadians. And because Italy had no boom, it also had no echo, so that only 15% of its population is under 15 compared to 20% of Canada's.

Canada is a young country compared to Italy but it is old compared to many others. Mexico, one of our partners in the North American Free Trade Agreement, has a mere 4% of its population older than 65 while 36% are under 15. As discussed above, these countries present different opportunities to Canadian exporters. Obviously, a consulting company with expertise in the design and management of maternity wards would find a more receptive market in Mexico than in Italy. And a company with products or services that appeal to seniors would be well-advised to concentrate on western Europe and Japan, the two oldest regions in the world.

Canada is in a unique position entering the new millennium of global trade. Demographically, it is one of the most favoured countries in the world, with a relatively low share of juniors and seniors and a high share of the population of working age. The big boomer generation is in its most productive years. These demographic circumstances give Canada a golden opportunity to market to the world over the next decade if it can learn to exploit its age structure. Being between the younger marketplaces of Africa, Asia, and South America and the older marketplace of Europe, Canada is in an excellent position to understand the needs of all countries, whether it be schools for the young, houses and cars for young adults, communications and management services in the workplace, or retraining programs for older workers and pharmaceuticals for seniors.

Demographics also influence money movements. A young country needs to borrow and an older one needs to lend. That's why the lending countries are older ones such as Germany, the United Kingdom, and Japan. People in their 40s and 50s are savers and investors, and those age groups are where the largest chunk of Japan's population has been over the past two decades. But as they reach retirement age, people start to cash in their chips because they need the money to live on. That means Japan is being forced to draw on its assets to support the retirement and health care needs of an older population. After the millennium, when demographics have turned Canada and the United States into nations of savers rather than spenders, Canada and the United States will begin to take Japan's and Germany's places as lenders to the world.

PENSIONS

When Canada chose a retirement age of 70 in the 1920s, life expectancy was 61. Almost nobody lived long enough to collect a pension. At the millennium, pension eligibility is 65 and life expectancy is almost 79, so the average Canadian can expect to collect a pension for about 14 years. Life expectancy will probably rise in the years to come as medical advances lead to increased longevity. The result will be greater pressure on both public and private pension programs. That's why pension reform has taken centre stage as a key public policy issue in recent years. In 1997, the federal government decided to increase premiums for the Canada Pension Plan by 73% over a period of six years and cut benefits by about 1.6%. Only the pensions of those who were 65 by the end of 1997 escaped being cut. Was this the fairest and soundest way to reform the Canada Pension Plan, given what we know of Canada's demographic situation?

Because the Canada and Quebec pension plans were created in 1966, those receiving unreduced pensions will have contributed for at most 31 years and some for a much shorter period. The rest of the population will contribute for 45 years to get a reduced pension. This contribution period is 50% longer than that of those who turned 65 in 1997 and twice as long as the contribution period of those who were 74 in that year. Under this so-called reform, the Canada Pension Plan is a much better deal for those who are currently in the senior category than those who will be there in the future.

The pension problem was caused by leaving the retirement age at 65 while life expectancy kept rising. In the past, when work was so physically demanding that most people were worn out by their 50s and dead not long after, a retirement age of 65 was too high. In an era when most people are still healthy and vigorous at 65 with many active years ahead of them, it is too low. The United States recognized this in 1983 when it raised eligibility for pensions by an average of one month a year, starting in 2003. The change is being phased in over 24 years, by which time pension eligibility will begin at age 67.

If the federal government had raised the retirement age by two or three years, it would not have had to raise premiums or cut benefits. At the least, some small gradual increase in the age of pension eligibility could have been used to moderate the increase in premiums. That should have been done because the premiums, which are paid by both employers and employees, are a tax that discourages employment. So not only are the young workers of the millennium era being told to work longer to get less pension than today's seniors, they are paying a higher tax for the privilege – a tax that, by its very existence, increases their chances of joining the ranks of the unemployed.

The 1997 alterations to the Canada Pension Plan did nothing to reform the pension system in any meaningful way that recognizes the profound demographic changes that have taken place since it was launched. They were, however, a most unfortunate step towards creating intergenerational conflict in Canada.

Raising premiums is a simple-minded approach to pension reform. Better and fairer options are available. Gradually raising the retirement age is one. Flexible workplace policies, as discussed in Chapter 4, are another. Why shouldn't an older worker be able to work part-time while still making pension contributions? This would maintain revenues to the pension fund while creating employment for young workers. Pension reform thus would become a way to attack youth unemployment. All these options should be considered as part of a process of integrating workplace policy, tax policy, and pension policy. Canada needs a whole new approach to retirement, and the sooner we begin the less painful the process of change will be.

THE GREY INTERLUDE

What sort of future will population aging bring? Writer Nicholas Kristof offered a gloomy view in the *New York Times* in 1996, envisioning a world of conflict between a minority of working young and a majority of retired "greedy geezers." Perhaps the botched reform of the Canada Pension Plan in 1997 will some day be seen as the opening shot by future geezers, led by Finance Minister Paul Martin, in a Canadian war between the generations. In his book *The Future of Capitalism*, U.S. economist Lester Thurow described an ominous incident of the same kind in Kalkaska, a Michigan town with a large retired population. Elderly voters there used the school budget to pay for non-educational purposes such as snow ploughing and then refused to vote more money for the schools, forcing them to close early. When placed in perspective, the behaviour of the Kalkaska voters does not look like an isolated incident. "For all the talk of educating children to secure the nation's future," writes Kristof, "for all the knowledge that children are the sector of the population most likely to live in poverty, the U.S. government spends nine times as much on each elderly person as on each child."

In the pessimistic view, the greedy geezers won't be in good enough health to get much enjoyment from the political power they wield so selfishly. While herpes was the disease of the moment in the 1970s when the boomers were young, in the pessimistic view dementia and depression will take centre stage as those same boomers age, prompting many of them to call it quits early. "Suicide is disproportionately common among the elderly, as people face loneliness, infirmity, and a mental slide into oblivion," Kristof observes.

Fortunately, there is solid evidence that the greyer world of the future may turn out to be not quite so grim after all. Perhaps not surprisingly, long-term improvements in economic status, public health, medical care, education, and working conditions are bearing fruit at the end of the century in a healthier generation of older people. The National Long Term Care Surveys, a study by the U.S. federal government that surveys 20,000 seniors, finds a smaller percentage every year who can't take care of themselves or go for a walk. Those surveyed are a sample of the entire senior population, regardless of income.

Not only has disability dropped every year since the survey began in 1984, so has the percentage of people with such chronic diseases as high blood pressure (down from 46% in 1982 to 40% in 1989) and arthritis (from 71% to 63%). Such health improvements in the elderly have important economic implications. Kenneth Manton, a demographer at Duke University, calculated that declining disability rates between 1982 and 1995 saved Medicare, the U.S. public health insurance system for seniors, $200 billion. If the 1982 disability rates had held steady, there would have been 300,000 more disabled people aged 65 to 74 instead of 121,000 fewer, as actually occurred. Manton finds that people either are not developing disabling diseases or are getting them at older ages. The diseases with the largest declines were arthritis, high blood pressure, and heart disease.

Another study, by Eileen Crimmins, of the University of Southern California, lends support to the view that it's time to raise the retirement age. For 11 years, she has asked 12,000 people aged 50 to 69 whether their health was affecting their ability to work. As the years go by, fewer and fewer people say they are too sick to work. In 1982, 27% of men aged 67 to 69 said they couldn't work but by 1992, only 20% said so.

So it seems that older people are staying healthier longer than they used to. Moreover, North American society is not dominated by old people at the millennium; indeed, it never will be, to the extent that some writers claim. The first boomers won't turn 65 until 2012. By then, the era of grey power will be underway: from 2012 to 2031, all the boomers who are still alive will be seniors. But it's not true that Canada at the millennium is the most rapidly aging society in the world. Japan has a much more rapidly aging population than Canada, because its fertility rate dropped in the 1940s and ours did not begin to fall until the 1960s. The Europeans are also older than we are and will be for the foreseeable future. Canada starts the aging process from a much younger base than Japan and Europe. In 1998, Canada had only 12% of its population over 65 whereas Sweden, one of the oldest countries, had 17% over 65. In 2020, Canada will be where Sweden is today. When all the surviving boomers are over 65, Canada's elderly as a percentage of its population will be about 22%, a level that will match, not exceed, the rest of the developed world.

Children and old people depend on people of working age to support them. If a country has a lot of working-age people relative to those under 15 and over 65, it has a favourable dependency ratio. Canada, with small senior and junior populations relative to many other countries, has one of the most favourable ratios – more than two workers per dependant – of any country in the world. By comparison, the continent of Africa as a whole, with about one worker per dependant – has the least favourable ratio of any region. In fact, even in 2025, when all the boomers are in their 60s and 70s, Canada will have a more favourable ratio of workers to retired people than many other countries. Austria, for example, will by then have 61 people of retirement age for every 100 working-age adults while Canada will have only 40.

The reality of Canada's demographic situation at the millennium, therefore, is a far cry from the gloomy portrait painted by newspaper articles that exaggerate the implications of increased longevity and lower birth rates. People are going to keep having babies because they want babies. If they didn't, Canadian women unable to achieve pregnancy would not be combing the world for children to adopt and paying large amounts of money to fertility clinics. Meanwhile, when the last boomer turns 65, many early boomers will be dead. This isn't cause for celebration, but it is the major reason why Canada is never going to turn into a country of the aged. The bust, a smaller group, will replace the boom to become Canada's young seniors when the larger echo will just be leaving its productive middle years. And the echo, because it is larger than the bust, will produce a bumper crop of kids. And so it goes – Canadian society will continue to rejuvenate itself as the decades unroll.

Canada can cope, and even prosper, during the grey interlude of boomer retirement if we plan for it and make the necessary changes. How do older countries cope with an older population profile? They let younger countries do the low-wage, labour-intensive jobs while they develop a highly skilled, technology-based workforce at home. The best technology enables them to add value to the products they produce. In short, they compensate for the increase in the retired population by doing everything possible to enhance the productivity of the working population.

They also make changes to their taxation and pension policies. Because there will be relatively fewer taxpayers, government will have to move gradually from taxation of labour income to taxation of capital income. At the millennium, large numbers of boomers are in their prime earning years and entering their saving and investing years. In such a society, a tax system based on income and sales taxes makes sense. It won't make as much sense in a future in which more income, of necessity, will be generated by technology and capital. A country with an aging population has to consider increased taxes on interest, dividends, capital gains, and corporate profits. It also has to consider taxes on things that currently are not taxed, including foreign exchange transactions and, in Canada's case, wealth. There is plenty of room for reform without imposing any undue hardship on the wealthiest Canadians. A study by American economist Edward Wolff in 1995 found that personal wealth was taxed at a much lower rate in Canada than in such staunchly capitalist societies as Switzerland and the United States. Among 22 countries, Canada ranked 21st in percentage of tax revenues derived from wealth taxes.

For the next two to three decades, the boomers will be workers, taxpayers, and increasingly savers. Because more Canadians will be savers, more money will be available for capital investment to make our industry more technologically advanced, more competitive, and more productive. Meanwhile, other countries will offer growing markets for the goods and services that these industries produce. And Canada will become less dependent on foreign lenders.

Fears are often expressed about how Canada will cope once the large boom generation reaches its retirement years. Before panic sets in, it should be remembered that even the oldest boomers won't reach 65 until 2012. It should also be remembered that the Canadian workforce by then will have been reinforced by the large echo generation. The combination of the echo and the baby bust is larger than the baby boom, so there is little reason to fear a shortage of working-age Canadians during the grey interlude of boomer retirement. Who knows, we might even get the Canadian unemployment rate down. If we are truly successful in finding employment for all Canadians who are eager to work, the ultimate proof of that success would be labour shortages. Should those occur, jobs can be filled by young workers who wish to immigrate to Canada from countries that have a surplus of young workers. But there should be no illusions about the ability of immigration to make a grey Canada less grey: an immigration policy based on the family, as Canada's is, can never rejuvenate a society.

Some of the changes wrought by the demographic phenomenon of population aging pose difficulties to society while others are beneficial. For example, an older society requires fewer goods, which hurts those in the business of manufacturing and selling goods. But an aging society requires many more services, and that means new business opportunities for other entrepreneurs. An aging population is more knowledgeable and experienced, but it is also more prone to health problems. In the final analysis, what is the balance between these pros and cons? Is the demographic shift good or bad? The answer is that it is neither. It is simply a fact of life, and the better we understand it, the better we can prepare for the changes before they occur and adjust to them once they have taken place.

One important benefit of having an aging population is that older people traditionally have shown themselves to be more generous than younger ones. They give more, both of their money and of their time. Older people are also more knowledgeable, because they've been around long enough to learn something. So while Canadians aren't about to become a nation of greybeards, they are about to become an older, wiser, and perhaps more caring people.

If we prepare for the grey interlude to come, we can both enjoy the benefits and manage the inevitable challenges. Demographics enable us to do that because they give us the power to see the future. All we have to do is use it.

Demographic Forecasting

This appendix describes the technical framework of demographic forecasting, the science that provides the foundation for the conclusions in this book. Although demographic forecasting is based on mathematical concepts, one does not need to be a mathematician to understand demographics. With a little effort, anyone can grasp the basics of demographics and appreciate its implications.

Applying demographic forecasts, as presented in Appendix II, is the next step. It is easy to develop a forecast for an individual product or activity using a calculator or a spreadsheet on a home computer.

AVAILABILITY AND USE

Demographic forecasts, or population projections as demographers prefer to call them, are available from many sources. Statistics Canada, the national data gathering agency, not only collects all the data that are needed to produce demographic forecasts but also produces such forecasts for the nation, provinces, and territories. These demographic data and forecasts are used for many purposes. Besides the numerous uses outlined in this book, they also play an important role in influencing the monetary transfers between governments in the Canadian federation. Private consulting firms use these Statistics Canada projections or, alternatively, develop and sell their own population forecasts based on their own variation of the Statistics Canada approach.

Many regional and municipal governments also produce demographic forecasts to assist them in land use and transportation planning. Population projections can reveal their future requirements for roads, schools, sewers, and parks. Not surprisingly, these forecasts can become political footballs, as each local authority attempts to attract federal or provincial funds to pay for infrastructure. You can usually get copies of forecasts for your own use from the relevant agencies, for a modest fee to cover the cost of reproduction. A good general rule to remember when using them is that they are much more likely to overstate population growth than to understate it. A small but expanding list of consulting companies and consultants also provide regional demographic data and forecasts. Once again, these must be viewed with a critical eye. But they tend to be more conservative on population growth unless they have been produced for developers trying to obtain zoning changes for commercial or residential construction.

An understanding of population growth and aging illuminates both the past and the future. Although the past can be measured with considerable accuracy, the future is inherently uncertain, so different agencies and consultants can come up with different forecasts. They cannot all be correct, but some will prove more accurate than others.

The ideas of the analyst who is producing the demographic forecast are called assumptions – for example, assumptions about future immigration policy. No one can be certain what political party will be in power in the next 20 years or even the next five, nor can anyone know what policy regarding immigration levels will be in effect in the future. To account for this inherent uncertainty about the future, demographers have adopted the alternative scenario approach. Since different assumptions about immigration will automatically lead to different population projections, demographic forecasts have to account for different scenarios. Different forecasts will have different numbers, but all are produced from a common understanding of the determinants of population growth.

This common foundation is called a population projection model. In practical terms, this model is a set of mathematical instructions programmed into a computer that calculates the numerical implications of the various ideas or assumptions provided by the analyst.

This is where informed judgment is crucial. Only a few assumptions are needed to produce a population forecast; anyone with access to a population projection model can produce one. What makes one population forecast better than another is the quality of judgment that has been brought to the task.

This is why demography is a social science. Demographic forecasts are scientific in the sense that the results are reproducible: the same assumptions always lead to the same results. However, their use involves judgment about human behaviour – fertility, mortality, and migration – which varies over time. That is why the future can never be predicted with certainty.

That is also why demographers prefer to call their forecasts "projections" – they project the consequences of informed judgments. Population forecasts are not predictions. The population projection model is not a crystal ball that sees the future. It enables the user to see a variety of futures depending on the assumptions that are put into the model. The projection that has, in the analyst's judgment, the most likelihood of coming to pass may be labelled the most likely or base-case scenario. This is often mislabelled the forecast by those who desire a prediction. It is this confusion that often gives demographers, economists, and anyone else who uses a model to peer into the future a dubious reputation.

Strategic planning needs alternative scenarios to be strategic, so alternative demographic forecasts can be an important component of strategic plans. Of crucial importance is whether the alternatives lead to different action plans. Fortunately, in many cases alternative population forecasts do not require dramatically different action plans. Generally they are not different enough. So for many purposes, it really does not make a big difference which population forecast is used. But it is crucial to use a population forecast in any strategic plan.

In the end, even an uninformed forecast may turn out to be an accurate prediction of reality, but this can never be known until the future has passed. Meanwhile, population forecasts can provide a powerful way to understand and anticipate the inherently uncertain future.

POPULATION PROJECTIONS

What are the essential ingredients of a population forecast or projection? Another way of asking the same question is, What makes a population change in size? Clearly, births increase a population while deaths decrease it. In-migrants increase a population and out-migrants decrease a population. Therefore, population change is defined as births minus deaths plus in-migrants minus out-migrants. This is the first foundation of all population forecasting.

What is true for the whole population is also true for any subgroup in the population, with one notable exception. Births can be added only at age zero, so in all other age groups births are not part of the formula. The number of 50-year-old males in Canada today is the number of 49-year-old males last year, minus the deaths of those in their 50th year, plus the number of any new immigrants, minus any emigrants who would have been 50 by the end of the year. This calculation is based on the unassailable fact that every year a surviving individual gets one year older. This is the second foundation of all population forecasting.

Note that the same calculation underlies all population projections whether for a nation, a province, a region, or a town. The only difference between these applications is the definition of a migrant. For a national projection, migrants include both immigrants and emigrants. For a provincial projection, they include those who arrive in the province from another country or another province and those who leave the province. For a region, those moving between regions within a province are also included as migrants. For a town, all people moving in and out of the town are considered migrants. This makes population forecasts for smaller areas somewhat less accurate because, with more elements to consider, there is more uncertainty. But the basic foundations remain the same.

The same principles that determined the past can be used to forecast the future. So the population next year is the population this year plus the expected number of births, minus the expected number of deaths, plus the expected number of in-migrants, less the expected number of out-migrants over the next year. The key to making this calculation successfully is finding the expected numbers to put in the forecast.

Where do the expectations for births, deaths, and migrants come from? Births depend on fertility in a population, which reflects a myriad of factors that determine human behaviour and procreation. Obviously health status is important for both the mother and the child if both are to survive childbirth. Beyond that, the decision to have or not to have children depends on the availability, use, and effectiveness of various birth-control techniques and the economic status of the family into which a child would be born. Finally, the likelihood of giving birth depends on the age of the mother. Younger and older women are less likely to give birth than those in their high fertility ages of the 20s and early 30s.

Since a society is a collection of individuals, collective fertility is determined by the same considerations as individual fertility, including the age distribution of women in the population. Societies with proportionately more women in the prime childbearing ages will produce comparatively more births.

To take this into consideration, demographers focus on a society's fertility rate (children per woman) rather than the birth rate (births per thousand people). The fertility rate measures the average number of children a woman will have over her lifetime if she follows the current fertility behaviour of all women. The number differs by where she lives, and it changes over time. It is a useful number that is indicative of the average family size. Since two children are necessary to replace the two parents, replacement fertility is a number around two.

The fertility rate in Canada was more than 3 in the 1920s and under 3 in the 1930s before it began to rise in the 1940s. At the peak of the postwar baby boom in 1959, fertility peaked at almost 4 children per woman. By the late 1960s, it had fallen to well below replacement. At the millennium, it is around 1.6 children per woman.

What of the future? Will fertility remain below replacement, will it decline even further, or will it rebound to replacement or even higher, as it did after World War II? No one can be sure. But the demographic forecaster can explore all possibilities using alternative fertility rates of, for example, 1.2, 1.6, 2.1, and 2.5 to generate four alternative scenarios. The forecaster might label the 1.6 fertility scenario the most likely or base-case scenario given current information.

A similar approach is followed with respect to deaths. Once again, the number of deaths in a population reflects a host of factors, prime among which are the psychological, physical, and economic status of the individual in the population at large. Because older people are more likely to die than younger people, an older population is likely to have comparatively higher numbers of deaths and thus a higher death rate than a younger population. To take this into account, demographers focus on the average life expectancy (years per person) rather than the death rate (deaths per thousand people) as an indicator of longevity. It measures the average length of life for an individual of any age if that individual could live out the remainder of his or her life under current mortality conditions. Average life expectancy varies over jurisdictions and over time because mortality conditions are different. The most frequently used number is life expectancy at birth, which also means the average age of death. In most societies, women live longer than men, with the result that the average is higher for females than for males. Life expectancy at birth in Canada has been rising since the 1930s, when it was about 60 for men and 62 for women. By 1996, it had reached 75.7 for men and 81.5 for women.

Will this trend continue? Many believe it will, especially given continuing progress by medical science in combatting disease. But it is not certain, as the recent decline in life expectancy in the former Soviet bloc and the emergence of a new disease (HIV/AIDS) have indicated. Once again, the demographic forecaster can explore alternative assumptions. The most likely or base-case scenario would probably be a continuation of past trends. An optimistic scenario, perhaps based on a major breakthrough in medical research, would show acceleration of past trends, while a pessimistic alternative, perhaps based on recent experience with the impacts of rising crime and poverty in the former Soviet bloc, might forecast a reversal of past trends.

For a nation, the relevant migrants for demographic forecasting are people coming from other countries (immigrants) and people going to other countries (emigrants). Canada's annual immigration over the 20th century has been volatile, ranging from a high of 400,870 in 1913 to a low of 7,576 in 1942. More than 100,000 people came to Canada in every year between 1903 and 1914, while fewer than 30,000 people came to Canada in every year between 1931 and 1945. In the postwar period, the largest number of immigrants was 282,164 in 1957; the smallest was 71,689 in 1961. These numbers probably provide reasonable bounds for any realistic immigration assumption. The average for the postwar period is about 150,000 persons a year. Levels in the early 1990s exceeded 200,000 persons a year.

Federal legislation requires that Canada's future immigration levels be announced in October of the preceding year. These levels must be determined in consultation with the provincial governments, taking economic and demographic considerations into account. The interpretation of these "considerations" is variable even within the mandate of one government, and can be even more so if governments change. As a result, it is almost impossible to predict what the chosen level of immigration will be from one year to the next, let alone from one decade to the next.

Once again, the demographer can explore the implications of different immigration levels for population forecasts. Perhaps the postwar average (150,000 persons a year), current levels (200,000), and even the occasionally mentioned figure of 1% of the population (300,000 a year) might be considered. The middle of these three would probably be designated the most likely or base-case scenario.

The final component for a national population forecast is expected emigration. Births, deaths, and immigration can be measured through administrative registration requirements, but no direct measure of emigration exists because exit permits are not required for people leaving Canada. Estimates of emigration can be compiled from statistics that count Canadians entering other countries such as the United States, and these can be checked every five years using census counts. But it is an imprecise measure.

Most recent estimates place emigration at about 50,000 people a year. In its population projections, Statistics Canada uses an assumption that generates a forecast of rising emigration over time, starting at around 47,000 people a year. Some evidence exists that emigration is related to previous levels of immigration and, perhaps, to the state of the economy, but it is doubtful that a more precise assumption is available, given the current state of the research. Once again the demographic forecaster can choose alternative emigration levels or rates to develop alternative population scenarios.

For provincial and regional demographic forecasts, further migration assumptions are necessary to account for migration between provinces (interprovincial migration) and migration within provinces (intraprovincial migration). This is a data-intensive task. Because Canada has ten provinces and two territories, there are 132 bilateral flows to consider in the Statistics Canada provincial and territorial population projections alone. For intraprovincial migration, the data requirements can be much larger still, since there are many levels of local agglomeration (regions, counties, municipalities, cities, townships) and many jurisdictions that people can move between. In these cases, it is common to consider each unit in isolation and just look at the in-migrant and out-migrant flows combined, without considering the different sources and destinations. Although this approach requires far less data and analysis, it comes with a cost. Unlike international migrants, whose arrival changes a nation's population size, people moving within a country leave the total size unchanged and influence only the distribution of the population.

In this internal movement of people there must always be both winners and losers among the various regions. When all regions are not explicitly considered together in a population forecast, it is easy to lose sight of this basic consistency requirement. Localities wishing to show future population growth may overestimate in-migration and underestimate out-migration. Without the winners-and-losers requirement explicitly built into the population forecasts, there is no way to determine whether all the individual locality assumptions when taken as a whole are consistent. Migration assumptions that deviate substantially from past averages should, therefore, be treated with caution.

RESULTS

Statistics Canada periodically publishes *Population Projections for Canada, Provinces and Territories* (as catalogue 91-520 occasional). The December 1994 issue of this publication, which covers the period 1993 to 2016, notes that the population projections are based on a combination of component assumptions, encompassing:

- three fertility assumptions: the total fertility rate remaining constant at 1.7 children a woman or gradually changing to 1.5 or 1.9 children a woman by 2016;
- three mortality assumptions: the 1991 life expectancy at birth of 74.6 years for males and 80.9 for females, reaching 77.0 and 83.0, 78.5 and 84.0, or 81.0 and 86.0 years respectively by 2016;
- three immigration assumptions: the annual number of immigrants in 1993 of 250,000 persons remaining constant or changing to 150,000 or 330,000 by 2016;
- one emigration assumption: the 1988–93 annual average age- and sex-specific rates remaining constant over the projection period (which results in emigration levels of from 46,800 to a maximum of about 59,000 persons by 2016);
- three interprovincial migration assumptions: central, which is most favourable for Ontario, Quebec, Manitoba, and Saskatchewan; west, which is most favourable for British Columbia, Alberta, Yukon, Northwest Territories, and the Atlantic provinces; or medium, which is an average of the central and west scenarios.

Additional assumptions for non-permanent residents and for returning Canadians are also used. This set of assumptions yields a total of 27 possible national projections, with a combination of three fertility, three mortality, and three immigration assumptions, and 81 possible provincial-territorial projections with the three additional interprovincial migration assumptions. In order to keep the analysis and report within manageable limits, only four were selected for inclusion in the publication to provide plausible maximum, medium, and minimum population growth levels for each province or territory and for Canada as a whole. All projections commence in 1993.

The low-growth alternative combines the low fertility, low life expectancy, and low immigration assumptions with the central inter-provincial migration assumption. Population growth averages 0.8% a year over the projection horizon, resulting in a total Canadian population of 31.4 million in 2001 and 34.2 million in 2016.

The medium-growth alternative combines the medium fertility, medium life expectancy, and medium immigration assumptions with the medium interprovincial assumption. Population growth averages 1.1% a year over the projection horizon, resulting in a total Canadian population of 31.9 million in 2001 and 37.1 million in 2016.

The high-growth alternative combines the high fertility, high life expectancy, and high immigration assumptions. Population growth averages 1.4% a year over the projection horizon, resulting in a total Canadian population of 32.4 million in 2001 and 39.9 million in 2016. In addition, the high-growth alternative is available under both the west and central interprovincial migration assumptions.

In all population projections, the baby boom shows up as aged 35 to 54 years in 2001 and aged 50 to 69 years in 2016. By 2001, its relative size will have shrunk somewhat, to about 31.4% of the Canadian population. By 2016, the baby boom's share of the population will be declining faster, depending on the growth of the population, from 27.6% in the low-growth alternative to 26.3% and 25.3% in the medium-growth and high-growth alternatives, respectively. Births stopped augmenting the boom in 1966, and by the turn of the century immigrants will be in the younger age groups. Moreover, the boomers' influence on Canadian society will diminish in the future as increasing numbers of them die. Nonetheless, even in 2016 they will remain over a quarter of the population under the more likely scenarios.

Which of these scenarios should the informed user of demographic forecasts use? By implication, Statistics Canada suggests the medium-growth alternative. However, since the production of these population projections, immigration levels have been reduced from 250,000 a year to about 200,000 a year. Over a decade, this difference amounts to half a million people. This substantial difference is concentrated in certain age groups, so using projections based on the medium-growth alternative will probably overestimate growth. On the other hand, immigration levels at the millennium are well above the postwar average and the low-growth assumption of 150,000 a year, so use of the low-growth alternative will probably underestimate future growth, especially in the 21st century. The strategic planner could use both; the pragmatic user might use an average of these two publicly available forecasts (see Figure 4). The alternative is to purchase a custom forecast either from Statistics Canada or from any other provider in either the public or the private sector.

Product and Activity Forecasting

Appendix I explained how demographic forecasts are created. This appendix shows you how to use one or more alternative demographic forecasts to assess the future of a particular product, service, or activity.

The procedures outlined here are equally applicable to both the private and public sectors. They can be applied to both goods and services, to both appliance sales and health care delivery. They can be applied to products sold in the marketplace, such as binoculars, and to activities for which no market exists, such as birdwatching. They can guide business plans and public policies. Every application can be viewed as an activity that involves a product. Playing tennis requires both a court and a racquet. Even walking requires walking shoes. This is why this appendix is titled "Product and Activity Forecasting."

Once again the procedures, while mathematical in nature, are not difficult to understand. Numerical examples are provided on which to base your calculations, as well as tips on the presentation of results. But before investigating these procedures it is useful to ask a few questions. These questions can help in getting the best use out of the forecasts.

DEVELOPING USEFUL FORECASTS

First, what is your catchment area? Are you primarily concerned with the town, the region, the province, the country, or even the world? It might be useful to carry out a series of forecasts based on an ever-expanding market area. If they all suggest a similar conclusion, then you can proceed with confidence. If the conclusions differ, as they might for Alberta and New Brunswick or for Canada and Japan, this would suggest the need to consider a different marketing strategy in each area or, perhaps, to abandon a particularly unattractive market for the products under consideration.

Second, what is your vision? What do you expect to learn from the forecasts? Chapter 5 outlined the base-case scenarios against which your product and activity forecasts can be compared. The North American marketplace is dominated by the boomers and, to an increasing extent, by their children, the echo generation. The boomers are in their 30s, 40s, and early 50s at the millennium while their children are teenagers and preteens. These facts suggest that the most rapidly growing markets of the following decade are going to be for products and services used by, and activities participated in by, those in their 40s and 50s. At the same time the declining teenage and early 20s market of the previous decade should produce moderate growth over the next decade, at least in Halifax, Ontario, and western Canada, where the echo is apparent.

Another growth market is seniors. The older seniors born before World War I and during the 1920s will provide a rapidly growing market for a limited range of appropriate goods, services, and activities. On the other hand, the younger seniors who will turn 65 during the late 1990s are a smaller group as a result of the birth dearth that occurred in the 1930s.

A third question is about alternative scenarios: How many should you use? More often than not, population forecasts will indicate qualitatively similar conclusions because of the dominance of one trend: the aging of the boomers. Obviously, population forecasts with faster growth will generate more rapid growth forecasts for products and activities than population forecasts with slower growth. Very often growth is essential to business success, and alternative forecasts can give the planner the information necessary to estimate the likelihood of success. Suppose it is discovered that the success of a particular venture depends on market growth that will occur only in the event of a fertility rate of 2.3 children per woman or an immigration intake of about 350,000 persons a year; the viability of such a venture will be drawn into question by alternative demographic forecasts. If a drop in fertility to 1.2 children per woman, the current rate in some European countries, would bankrupt a product line, that information may be an important advance warning of the need to diversify.

The next question concerns the level of detail required. How much information about age, gender, components of growth, and number of years is needed? An important tip is to make sure that the key population assumptions are clearly specified on every page of projection output. It is easy to mix alternatives up when the amount of detail skyrockets. For most purposes, five-year age groups will suffice. It is usually desirable to break these down by gender if there is reason to believe that men and women purchase or participate differently in the product or activity under consideration. In some applications, such as daycare and school enrolment projections, single years of age data will be necessary. As for projection horizon, it is a good idea to produce a forecast for at least 20 years into the future and perhaps for a subsequent 30 years in quinquennial (five-year) intervals. These data may not be necessary for most purposes, but they will allow you to explore and understand the longer-term trends at work. For example, with births falling and deaths rising in an aging population, constant levels of immigration inevitably imply a slower-growing Canadian marketplace. As a result, even a product that has consistently outperformed the market may experience slower growth in the years ahead.

What do you really want to find out from the forecasts? Do not hesitate to request a components-of-growth table with each population forecast, which summarizes births, deaths, in-migrants, and out-migrants in each year. This can often be a useful diagnostic tool that can refine your understanding of the numbers and can sometimes lead to refining the assumptions. It is a good idea to obtain birth, death, and migration rates and any other convenient indicators over the forecast horizon. Growth rates for age groupings can be particularly useful in product and activity forecasting. You may even wish to keep track of certain generations (see Chapter 1) and their shares in the population over the forecast. These are all relatively easy programming add-ons that can be done by the forecast provider or by the user once the forecast has been completed.

How will the data be presented? Remember that pictorial representations of data have a greater impact than tabular representations, especially in an aging population, where increasing numbers of users are suffering from deteriorating eyesight. Always make sure that printers are producing clear copy in large print. Colour also adds to a document's impact. All these requirements should be considered before embarking on a forecasting project and signing a contract.

Probably the most important question is "How can I make population forecasts work for me?" Customization is the essential ingredient of product and activity forecasting. But do not forget to give thought to the questions outlined above as you work through the following procedure.

CUSTOMER FORECASTING

Population forecasts are the first component of product and activity forecasts. The second component is who makes use of the product or activity in question. This could apply equally well to toothpaste, beer, automobiles, cocaine, insurance, symphonies, or hospital beds. Although this section focusses on product forecasting, the procedure would be the same if the focus were on a service such as dry cleaning or an activity such as theatre-going. Moreover, the procedure is not limited to privately produced products sold in the marketplace. It can also be applied to services supplied by the public sector.

Who are your customers, demographically? Some organizations, such as hospitals, have excellent records of their customers. Good marketing departments usually have a solid understanding of a company's customers, developed either from customer files and direct contacts or from market surveys. Beer companies have a pretty good idea of who consumes their products. Trade associations frequently assemble information on an industry's or sector's customer base and make it available to all members. The Canadian Direct Marketing Association has information on how its members can reach their clients for different products. And Statistics Canada often collects information on sectors of the economy and their customers. From these data it is possible to find out, for example, who reads books and magazines. Finally, you may have only a rough idea of your customer from fragmentary files, direct contacts, or anecdotal evidence. Even this can be used if no better data are available.

One useful and often overlooked source for demographic information on customers is Statistics Canada's Family Expenditure Survey. This survey has been conducted periodically since the early 1960s at approximately three-year intervals. It shows expenditures on more than 400 individual items in the consumer budget that can be classified by the age of the head of the household. This source can be especially useful to small and medium-sized firms that do not have marketing departments with research capabilities.

In short, there are many different potential sources for demographic information on the customers of your products or product lines. As many as possible should be consulted because – compared with the population forecast, which is based on census information – all product information is based on a much smaller sample. It is simply not possible to consult every possible consumer on the likelihood of their purchasing your product. So customer information must be estimated from sample surveys and other sources, and estimates need to be checked as often as possible.

Usually there are noticeable variations in the likelihood that a customer will purchase a product over his or her life cycle. Young people eat lots of food, whereas older people tend to eat less. Young people play sports, while older people tend to seek out less active pursuits. Young criminals are more likely to commit a break-and-enter, while older criminals are more likely to be involved in fraud. Expenditures on video rentals decline with age, while spending on prescribed medicine increases. Sometimes the age profile differs noticeably by gender. Women, for example, are less likely to hunt and fish than men but more likely to attend the opera or ballet.

The likelihood that an individual in any age category purchases a product (or participates in an activity) can be measured in one of two ways. Surveys can ask respondents whether they have purchased or intend to purchase a certain item. The proportion responding in the affirmative in each age group then provides a measure of the likelihood of purchase. Alternatively, the number of customers can be measured by selling tickets, memberships, or products, and the ratio of the total customers to the population in each age group gives a measure of the likelihood of purchase by any individual customer. Usually it is only possible to do this for the population at large. Other methods must be used to break it down by age group.

If you know the likelihood that any individual will purchase your product and you know the number of individuals in the population, you can count your customers by multiplying one by the other. The same calculation can be done in each age group as well. In this way, you can build up a demographic profile of your customers or customer base. Note that this separates the task into two parts: human behaviour, represented by the likelihoods or probabilities of purchase, and numbers of potential customers, represented by the population. This separation is the foundation of product and activity forecasting.

An example can illustrate the calculations. Figure 11 represents the customer base of an unidentified product. Many real-world data are presented in this way, but the use of an unidentified product enables us to focus on the calculations without speculating on the accuracy of the data. This is a product that is not used by children, so the data commence with 12-year-olds. These data may have been obtained from a customer database, an industry survey, or a representative sample compiled by a marketing department or market research firm commissioned to construct a profile of a company's or industry's customers. The customers are allocated into various age categories (column 1), which may or may not be equal in size and probably have no relationship to any of the generations outlined in Chapter 1. In this example, the various age groupings cover 6 to 15 years, and maybe 35 years for seniors; the boom, which was aged 25 to 44 in 1991 when the data for this example was taken, is spread out over three age categories. The estimated or actual number of consumers in each age category is shown in column 2. This is followed by a percentage distribution over the age groups (column 3). This column may be referred to as the market share column, and these numbers often form the basis for the marketing strategy.

There are two limitations to the numbers in columns 2 and 3. First, they inevitably reflect the size of the chosen age categories, which are usually arbitrary and chosen for convenience. It would be surprising if there were not more consumers in the 15-year 40-to-54 category than in the 6-year 12-to-17 category or the 10-year 30-to-39 category. The second limitation of these data is that they inevitably reflect the age structure of the population. They may indicate more about the age distribution of consumers in the marketplace than anything about the market penetration of the product, even though they represent the product's customers. Note that, by definition, market shares must add up to 100%, and no product has a 100% market share.

To understand product market penetration, it is necessary to combine the customer data with data on the overall marketplace – that is, with demographic data. If these customer data are nationwide, the relevant demographic data are Canadian population data from the 1991 census. These can be broken into age groups and presented opposite the customer data (column 4) and also presented in share or distribution format (column 5). Note that the total population of 23.434 million is the population 12 years and older, and that the shares are relevant to this total. Thus, for example, the 65-plus group is 13.7% of this population, whereas it was 11.4% of the total Canadian population in 1991.

Seldom does the share distribution of the marketplace (column 5) match the share distribution of the customer base (column 3). This is good news for demographic forecasting of products, because it implies that product market penetration differs by age. If this is true, then the changing age distribution in the marketplace will have an impact on the fortunes of the product. The more the distributions differ, the more important demographic analysis is.

FIGURE 11: SAMPLE CUSTOMER BASE

Age Group (1)	Customers ('000) (2)	Distribution (3)	Population ('000) (4)	Distribution (5)	Rate (%) (6)=(2)÷(4)
12-17	215	5.1	2283.6	9.7	9.4
18-29	780	18.7	5415.7	23.1	14.4
30-39	982	23.5	4942.6	21.1	19.9
40-54	1331	31.9	5152.7	22.0	25.8
55-64	486	11.6	2428.6	10.4	20.0
65+	385	9.2	3211.0	13.7	12.0
TOTAL	4179	100.0	23434.2	100.0	17.8

Population data (column 4) are for 1991. Source: Statistics Canada, *Revised Intercensal Population and Family Estimates, July 1, 1971-1991,* catalogue 91-537 occasional (July 1994). Remaining calculations by David K. Foot.

Reviewing these data yields some interesting puzzles. There were more actual customers in the 40-to-54 age category, yet there were more people or potential customers in the 18-to-29 category. The average number of customers in any age group is highest in the 30-to-39 category (at 98.2 in each year), even though there were more customers in the 40-to-54 category. The challenge is to make sense out of these numbers.

With 4.2 million customers in a target population of 23.4 million, the average market penetration of this product is 17.8%. The same calculation can be carried out for each of the age categories (column 6). These numbers reveal that above-average market penetration occurs in the middle ages (30 to 64) and below-market penetration occurs for the younger and older members of the population. Consequently, the higher number of customers in the middle ages reflects both the higher number of boomers in these ages and a higher likelihood that they will purchase the product.

It is the age-specific penetration rates (or, in other applications, participation rates) in column 6 that are particularly important for product forecasting with demographics. They provide the likelihoods that each member in any age category will be an actual customer. They capture the purchasing behaviour of the population. They may be broken down by gender or other demographic descriptors, but these are not considered in this example to keep the calculations as simple as possible.

These market penetration data are often a closely guarded corporate secret. Sometimes, for confidentiality or other reasons, the only data that are released to the public are the percentage distribution of customers (column 3) and the overall market penetration rate (17.8% in this example). However, this information is sufficient to calculate market penetration by age (column 6). Note that if the customer distribution (column 3) is divided by the relevant population distribution (column 5) for each age category and then multiplied by the overall market penetration rate (17.8%) the result is the market penetration by age (column 6). For example, if 23.1% of the population (aged 18 to 29) accounts for only 18.7% of the customers, then there must be below-average market penetration in this group.

Now look at the figure from right to left. Note that the penetration (or participation) rate (column 6) multiplied by the population (column 4) produces the number of customers (column 2). This calculation is the basis of demographic product forecasting. Different population numbers will produce a new column of customer numbers. This is where the results of demographic forecasting enter the calculation. Note that this calculation effectively holds customer behaviour in each of the age categories (column 6) constant. This is exactly what is needed if the impact of demographics on product performance is to be isolated. Moreover, it provides a solid first estimate of the customer base of the future. As has been noted elsewhere in this book, this calculation alone can explain at least two-thirds of the future.

Population forecasts enable this calculation to be done for every year into the future, which produces a projected stream of future customers. Alternative demographic forecasts will produce alternative customer streams. The faster growing the population, the faster growing will be the customer base, although because of the subtle influence of age structure there will not be a one-to-one connection. This simple multiplication can be done by hand or by using a calculator or a computer spreadsheet package. Anyone can become proficient in demographics-based product forecasting.

Applying these participation rates to Statistics Canada population projections for the years 2001 and 2011 results in customer forecasts that indicate a product that experiences market growth of 17% over the 1990s (1991–2001) followed by slower growth of 10% over the subsequent decade (2001–2011). These figures correspond to average annual growth of 1.6% and 0.9% a year, respectively.

How can these forecasts be evaluated? First, they can be compared with total population growth over the forecast period. The easiest way to do this is to calculate the overall market penetration rate in each year. If this is rising, then the product is performing better than the market; if it is falling, the product is not keeping up with market growth. In this example, market penetration rises to 18.3% in 2001 because the boomers are moving through their maximum penetration ages. It then remains unchanged in 2011 as the boomer children start entering the high penetration ages and compensate for the boomer departures into the lower-penetration older ages. However, the distribution of customers has changed dramatically. In 1991, 53% were 40 and over; by 2011, 64% will be 40 and over.

These forecasts can also be placed in a historical context. Of course they can be compared with recent history for the product. But probably a fairer comparison is to re-estimate the past under the same procedures. This is called backcasting. It helps answer the following question: If current age-specific penetration rates had applied in the past, what would have happened to customer growth and to the overall market penetration rate? Applying this procedure to the 1971 and 1981 population data reveals a product whose customer base just kept up with population growth in the market, resulting in overall market penetration rates of 17.2% and 17.3% respectively. This means that for this product line, it was more difficult to raise market share in the 1970s than it was in the 1980s or 1990s. The aging of the boomers will result in an increase of one percentage point in overall market penetration between 1981 and 2001. This may not seem like a large increase, but many companies fight over numbers like this and such an increase can make all the difference to the bottom line. Of course, it is predictable that the management of this product line will probably receive good bonuses for these good results – results that have almost nothing to do with their performance.

SALES FORECASTING

Often the number of customers does not tell the whole story of a product's performance. That a person is a customer is useful information but it tells little about the strength of his loyalty. A golf course, for example, is interested not only in the size of its membership but also in the number of times each member plays over the season.

This type of information can also be incorporated into product projections. Here the focus moves from market penetration rates to the average customer purchases (or use) over a year. This could refer to the average number of tubes of toothpaste or the number of rounds of golf. Now the numbers of customers in Figure 11 (column 2) are replaced by product sales by weight, volume, or some other physical measure in each age category. Then, as before, these total sales figures (column 2) are divided by population (column 4) to obtain sales per capita in each age category (column 6). Where company data do not permit total sales to be broken down by age of customer, there may be other sources that can be used to accomplish the task. Often industry averages can provide one means of disaggregating company sales by age category. Another potential source is Statistics Canada's Family Expenditure Survey, which shows average expenditures by Canadian families on over 400 consumer items including food, clothing, household, transportation and recreation, personal care, and health care product lines. These expenditures can be categorized by the age of the head of the household. Although this may not be a perfect indicator for sales by weight or volume for any particular product, it can provide a useful approximation on which to base a product forecast.

It is also easy to extend the procedure to accommodate revenue from sales. Revenues reflect not only the number of customers and their loyalty in terms of volume of sales, but also the price of the product. Moreover, it is revenues that directly affect profits. In this application, customers or sales are now replaced by revenues in each age category (column 2), and the same procedure is followed to obtain average per-capita revenues (that is, customer expenditures) in each age category for the product. Once again, if relevant company data are not available, other sources can be used to provide an estimated age distribution of revenues. The Family Expenditure Survey is a particularly attractive source because it refers directly to average family expenditures in dollars. Its major limitation is that it may not be available in the desired year, especially if the year is recent.

The procedure is the same in sales forecasting as in customer forecasting. The task is separated into two components: the population forecasts component described in Appendix I, and the human behaviour component represented by per-capita sales information described in this appendix. Multiplication of these two components in each age category then produces a sales forecast for each year over the forecast period. Alternative population forecasts will generate alternative sales forecasts, which can be especially useful for use in strategic plans. Growth rates can be calculated and product viability assessed. It is even possible to examine the numerical implications of product price changes and of age-targeted marketing strategies by modifying the per-capita sales figures and recalculating the results.

STABILITY

Human behaviour is remarkably stable over the life cycle, at least when it comes to market purchases and participation in many activities. We go to school, leave home, rent apartments, start families, buy homes, and make intensive use of hospitals at similar ages.

Of course, we do not all get our first pet at 28, our first house at 34, and our bifocals at 48. Nonetheless, enough people do experience these events around these ages that the likelihood of the average person experiencing them is both high and stable over time. In fact, the likelihood or probability of doing all kinds of things often varies quite predictably over the life cycle. It is this stability in human behaviour that makes demographic forecasting such a powerful tool.

Increasing longevity may mean that each generation is health-ier at each age than its predecessor. But this may only mean that on average the tennis racquet gets put on the shelf four or five years later in life over a generation of perhaps 25 years. Even these changes occur very slowly and predictably. Of course no one wants to be average; we all want to be individuals. But each of us is average over a broad range of human behaviour. That we like to emphasize the things we do that are not average, such as going to the symphony at 17 or rock climbing at 70, verifies the proposition. Our non-average behaviours make us individuals. But for the majority of product purchases in the market-place or other activities, we act much like the average.

This stability is not universal. Pollsters have demonstrated that our attitudes on a variety of issues often change, and our voting preferences have certainly been volatile in recent years. That is why many topics that interest sociologists and political scientists cannot be satisfactorily explained using demographic forecasting. But these are not the subjects of this book.

The introduction of new products into the marketplace cannot be anticipated by demographic forecasts. But once they are estab-lished in the marketplace, demographic forecasting can be a useful predictor of future trends.

But even in these cases the procedures outlined in this appen-dix can be used to examine the implications of changing human behaviour or new products. If a company believes that it has a suc-cessful new marketing program or a new product that can change behaviour in the market, or in a segment of the market such as the youth segment, the product forecaster can modify the market penetra-tion (or participation) rate to reflect the anticipated impacts and use the same procedure to trace out the implications for the future cus-tomer base or sales. Similarly, if a government believes that promotion of healthier lifestyles results in the population being more active, appropriate activity participation rates can be modified to reflect these anticipated changes and the implications traced out for the future. It is even possible to simulate the impacts of everyone in the population acting as if they were five or ten years younger by moving the entire participation profile back one age category. This is called sensitivity analysis. How sensitive are the numerical results to the introductions of new behaviours? The procedures outlined in this appendix provide a way to answer this question.

Such changes in practice usually occur slowly and so have little impact on product forecasts over the next five or ten years, which is where demographic forecasting has its greatest power. Moreover, the numerical implications of quite noticeable changes in behaviour are not nearly as dramatic as is often believed. In Canada, the aging of the baby-boom generation tends to dominate all product and activity forecasts based on the Canadian marketplace. It is this feature of the demographic profile that solidifies the stability of most product and activity forecasts in Canada.

Obviously, the further one looks into the future, the more uncertain the results. New behaviours and products have more time to get established, and there is more time for changes in the assumptions underlying the demographic forecasts. For this reason, long-term projections of more than, say, 20 years are not the focus of this book. But assuming that a 40-year-old today will behave like a 45-year-old of today in five years' time and like a 50-year-old of today in ten years' time is a solid foundation on which to build a vision of the medium term future.

Demographic forecasts provide an excellent foundation for planning over the next three to fifteen years. But they are not useful in explaining volatile movements in the stock market or the economy that are short-term in nature. And they are not crystal balls that permit us to gaze accurately over a lifetime of almost 80 years, although they may work better than many other crystal balls.

Index